ENTERTAIN

the EN

John Houseman

ERS *and*

TERTAINED

Essays on theater,

film

and television

SIMON AND SCHUSTER
NEW YORK

10   9   8   7   6   5   4   3   2   1

Library of Congress Cataloging in Publication Data

Houseman, John.
    Entertainers and the entertained.

    "The essays . . . have been previously published in periodical form"—
T.p. verso.
    Includes index.
    1. Performing arts—United States—History—20th century. I. Title.
PN2266.H68   1986   790.2'0973   86-3947
ISBN 0-671-62233-1

The essays in this book have been previously published in periodical form.
The author gratefully acknowledges permission to reprint material that
originally appeared in:

The Introduction by John Houseman to As Time Goes By, *copyright ©*
1979 by Howard Koch. Reprinted by permission of Harcourt Brace Jovan-
ovich, Inc.;

"Charlie's Chaplin," by John Houseman, in The Nation, *Vol. 199, No.*
10, October 12, 1964. Reprinted by permission of The Nation *(Maga-*
zine). The Nation Associates Inc.;

"Native Son on Stage," by John Houseman, from New Letters *maga-*
zine, Winter 1971, Volume 38, issue number 2, University of Missouri-
Kansas City;

"What Makes American Movies Tough," from the January 15, 1947 issue
of Vogue, *Vol. 109, No. 2. First published in* Vogue. *Reprinted by per-*
mission of Conde Nast Publications, Inc.;

Harper's *magazine. Reprinted by permission of Harper's Magazine Foun-*
dation, a division of the John D. and Catherine T. MacArthur Foundation;

USA Today, *review of* A Private View, *copyright 1985 USA*
TODAY. *Reprinted by permission;*

The New York Times, *copyright © 1964, 1969, 1976, 1981, 1984 by*
The New York Times Company. Reprinted by permission;

Also, The Chicago Tribune, The Los Angeles Times, *and* The
Washington Post.

Contents

Introduction

THE EVENTS REFERRED to in these pages occurred at various times between the thirties and eighties of this century. It was a time of violent, continuing change that saw the near-death and partial resurrection of the American theater, the rise and fall of Radio Drama, the apotheosis and gradual decline of Theatrical Film and the emergence of Television as the world's dominant medium of mass communication. It has been my good fortune to witness most of these events at close range and to play a personal part in some of them.

The pieces have appeared in diverse forms—as articles in newspapers and magazines and as speeches, reviews, publicity releases, and interviews on radio and television. Some of the narratives have undergone what Ray Chandler used to call "cannibalization" between their original text as magazine articles and the form in which they appeared in my memoirs. I have generally favored the former. And I have done my best to resist the strong temptation of hindsight.

BOOK ONE

THEATER U.S.A.

The Theater
of the Thirties

 The Good Old Days

> *In July of 1964, on the twenty-fifth anniversary of the disso-
> lution of the Federal Theatre, The New York Times asked
> me for a piece of reminiscence, which it printed under the
> somewhat ironic title of "The Good Old Days."*
>
> *The Federal Theatre was created in 1935 under President
> Roosevelt's New Deal, as one of the Arts Projects of the
> Works Progress Administration. It ended five years later—a
> few months before our entrance into World War II.*

THINGS HAVE CHANGED in the American theater. "Defi-
cit," "endowments" and "subsidy" are no longer dirty
words and it is not unusual, these days, to hear nostalgic
references and comparisons made to that short-lived but
important theatrical phenomenon of the thirties—the
Federal Theatre of the W.P.A., which was assassinated a
quarter of a century ago this summer.

Most of these analogies are false. There was no federal
subsidy for the arts in America—then or for the next

Previously published in *The New York Times,* July 16, 1964.

twenty-five years. The Federal Theatre projects of the Works Progress Administration were part of a desperate relief measure, conceived in a time of misery and despair. It came into existence at a time when the established "commercial" theater and its middle-class audiences had been grievously hit by the Depression. What "artistic" policy it had was based on the assumption that unemployed theater-workers got as hungry as anybody else, that they were eager to work and that millions of Americans might even enjoy the results of this work if it could be offered free or at prices they could afford to pay. At its peak the Federal Theatre had 15,500 theater workers on its payroll at an average wage of approximately twenty dollars a week. During the four years of its existence it played to an estimated total of fifteen million people the country over.

To those of us who were lucky enough to be a part of it, it offered a unique and exhilarating experience. Added to the satisfaction of our specific tasks was that very rare and special excitement that is generated when the theater is suddenly projected into the historical mainstream of its time.

The Federal Theatre's guiding personnel, headed by Hallie Flanagan, was drawn mostly from outside the "commercial" hierarchy, from among the dreamers and eggheads of the American theater. The New York Projects—in addition to its circus, vaudeville, marionette and other "free" attractions and the Dance Project which was a separate unit—consisted of five main theatrical units: the "Living Newspaper," the "Popular Price Theatre," the "Experimental Theatre," the abortive "Try-Out Theatre" and the "Negro Theatre." This last was under the joint direction of the great black actress Rose McLendon (who fell ill and died tragically in the first months of the project) and myself—chosen at her suggestion.

To house the Negro Unit, the largest and most explosive of New York's theatrical projects, the W.P.A. took over the old Lafayette Theatre on upper Seventh Avenue. Within a month there were over seven hundred people on the project, including the ten percent non-relief supervisory and "creative" personnel which the rules of the Arts Projects allowed us to hire. Our immediate assignment was not the production of masterpieces; we were instructed to find useful and, if possible, creative theatrical work for the hundreds of needy men and women on our payroll—and to find it quickly.

Since unemployment had long been chronic among Negro theater workers, ours had not only the largest but also the most eager and impatient group of personnel on any of the projects. With a surge of racial emulation driving them to efforts beyond the normal call of work-relief duty, the Lafayette was the first of the New York W.P.A. theaters to open.

Walk Together Chillun was a sincere but conventional play of Negro life written and directed by Frank Wilson (creator of *Porgy* in its original production). A month later, our shabby brocaded curtain rose on *Conjur' Man Dies,* a comic whodunit by a prominent Negro physician, full of the violence and the bitter jokes of Harlem's troubled streets.

Then, in April, came a night when the massed bands of Harlem's Elks, in light-blue and gold, marched with flying banners up Seventh Avenue behind a large sign reading: McBETH BY WILLIAM SHAKESPEARE. This was a critical production for the Negro Theatre Project. Through the long weeks of arduous rehearsal, this—our first classical production (grown to monstrous size, frequently postponed and directed by an unknown white youth of twenty)—had become the subject of passionate speculation and discord in Harlem, where many suspected it of being a deliberate and cruel hoax calculated to ridicule the Negro in the eyes of the white world. It was not till after the triumphal consecration of opening night and accolades from local and downtown reviewers that these doubts were finally dispelled.

What came to be known as the *Voodoo Macbeth* was an artistically desegregated production. It was Orson Welles's first American professional direction; his collaborators were Nat Karson (scenery and costumes), Virgil Thomson (music), Abe Feder (lights), Leonard de Paur (chorus), with magical rites under the supervision of Asadata Dafora Horton (now Minister of Culture for the Republic of Sierra Leone) and a cast that included such well-known black actors as Jack Carter, Edna Thomas, Canada Lee, Maurice Ellis and Evelyn Ellis together with sixty-five courtiers and soldiers in brilliant Napoleonic costumes, five cripples, twenty witch-folk and twenty-two voodoo dancers and drummers, all appearing in a jungle-girt castle "shot with such lights from both heaven and hell as no other stage has ever seen."

Macbeth ran for a year; it played in Harlem for four months, then moved downtown to Fifty-fourth Street, then westward through New England and the Midwest as far as the Dallas State Fair. Its successor at the Lafayette was *Turpentine,* a crude but energetic play of protest against conditions in Southern labor camps, which ran for three months with strong local and left-wing support. In the South it was condemned as a "malicious libel" and, later, cited unfavorably by Senator Russell of Georgia before the Senate Appropriations Committee.

By the summer of 1935 the Negro Theatre was firmly established. Feeling that its direction, both artistic and administrative, belonged in Negro hands, I obtained permission for Orson Welles and myself to transfer our producing activities downtown to what came to be designated as the Classical Theatre—also known as "Project 891."

These were the golden days of the Federal Theatre when, according to the country's leading drama critic, it was becoming the "chief producer of works of art in the

American theatre." In Maxine Elliott's Theatre on
Thirty-ninth Street—still elegant for all its yellowing
marble and frayed velvet—Orson Welles and I set about
organizing our own uninhibited version of a People's Theater. For our opening attraction we presented *Horse Eats
Hat,* a nineteenth-century French farce adapted by Edwin
Denby, the dance critic, who also played the front legs of
the offending horse. Among those who ran and flew across
the stage were Joseph Cotten, Arlene Francis, Sarah Burton, Paula Laurence, Hiram Sherman and Welles himself—in and out of scenery by Nat Karson, to music by
Paul Bowles orchestrated by Virgil Thomson.

Our reception was mixed. One critic found this "de-
mented piece of surrealism perilously close to being a genuine work of art." Others professed to be offended by such
extravagant frivolity on a Relief project. But we were still
running strong when we embarked on our next venture,
Christopher Marlowe's *Tragical History of Doctor Faustus.* In
her book, *Arena,* Mrs. Flanagan has described the rehearsals of *Faustus:* "It was," she wrote, "like going into the pit
of Hell—total darkness penetrated by stabs of light and
sheets of flame; trap doors opening and closing to reveal
bewildered stagehands or actors going up and down or
around in circles; explosions, properties disappearing in a
clap of thunder, and on stage—surrounded by Bil Baird's
puppets flapping and crawling around as the Seven
Deadly Sins—Orson, a thundering Faustus alternately
howling the mighty lines and interspersing them with
fierce adjurations to the invisible but omnipotent Feder at
his switchboard."

This "black magic" *Doctor Faustus,* which I have always
regarded as one of Welles's most brilliant theatrical creations, ran for five months to ninety percent of capacity at
a fifty-cent top. One night, halfway through our run,
Harry Hopkins, head of the Works Progress Administration, appeared in the theater unannounced. After the play
I led him through sulphurous fumes to what had been

New York's most lavish backstage suite, once occupied by Maxine Elliott but now shared by Welles, still loaded with nose-putty, sweating and panting from his descent into Hell, and Jack Carter, the Negro actor who had created the *Voodoo Macbeth* and who was now playing a sorrowful and tragic Mephistopheles. After the usual backstage amenities, Hopkins asked us all if we were having a good time on the Federal Theatre. We told him, in all sincerity, that we were.

❀*The Night
the Audience Walked*

Within a few months our relations with the W.P.A.'s Federal Theatre administration had sadly deteriorated. It had become clear, by the spring of 1937, that the halcyon days of our artistic association with the U.S. Government were past. Our conflict over the opening of The Cradle Will Rock *gave us the chance to go out with a bang—not a whimper.*

A version of this narrative was used as an introduction to the production of The Cradle *presented by* The Acting Company *in New York in 1983 and in London two years after that.*

AS OUR THIRD PRODUCTION for the Federal Theatre "Project 891," Orson Welles and I chose a new musical work unlike anything either of us had ever tried before. It was described by its author, Marc Blitzstein, as a Labor

Opera—"in a style that falls somewhere between realism, romance, satire, vaudeville, comic-strip, Gilbert and Sullivan, Brecht and agitprop." It was laid in a company town known as Steeltown, U.S.A., which might have been Youngstown or Bethlehem.

The spring of 1937 was a troubled time, filled with violent conflict between management (many of them members of the reactionary Liberty League) and organized labor (led by the newly formed C.I.O.). As one strike followed another with increasing violence, it gradually dawned upon the W.P.A. administration (which was about to go to Congress for a renewal of its appropriation) that, with *The Cradle Will Rock*, it had caught a tiger by the tail.

Neither Welles nor I were particularly political. In fact, among the more radical elements of the W.P.A. workers' organizations, ours was considered a reactionary management. Our choice of *The Cradle* had been purely theatrical, and throughout rehearsals we were totally absorbed in the quality of our production, for which more than twenty thousand tickets had been sold by early June—mostly in benefits to left-wing groups. On June 12th, while we were in our final rehearsals, with masses of scenery piled on the stage and an orchestra of twenty-six in the pit, an order was received by all W.P.A. directors that no new play, musical performance or art exhibit was to open until further notice. Welles and I assumed that the order was aimed specifically at us and *The Cradle* and countered with an announcement that, as artists, we had every intention of opening our show on June 17th—as scheduled and announced.

Three days before our premiere a dozen uniformed W.P.A. security guards invaded the Maxine Elliott Theatre. They occupied the box office and the front of the house; they also took over backstage and dressing rooms to make sure that no government property was used or re-

moved. This covered scenery, musical scores and costumes, including actors' underwear and our leading man's
toupee.

But there was one place in the building from which the
Cossacks (as we called them) were barred—the pink powder room that the great financier, J. P. Morgan, had deco-
rated years ago in raspberry-colored velour for his favorite
actress, Maxine Elliott, and which now became our headquarters in our campaign to save *The Cradle*.

The authorities had called all ticket-buyers and can-
celed reservations for the performance. We called them
back and urged them to show up that night in full force;
we gave them our personal assurance that *The Cradle*
would be performed as announced.

In fact, we were so busy asserting our integrity that we
hadn't given much thought to the problems of performance. Members of our orchestra had already been noti-
fied by their union that in order to perform under the
management of Houseman and Welles they must sign
new contracts at full union scale for rehearsal and performance. Since we didn't have five cents to our names, this
was out of the question. The next morning Actors' Equity,
in a special meeting of its board, reached a similar decision. Our actors were forbidden to appear for us on stage
unless they were given new contracts, which meant our
paying them for three weeks of rehearsal and two guaranteed weeks of performance. Again, this was out of the
question.

We felt betrayed and defeated. We could give a show
without scenery and costumes and, if need be, without an
orchestra—but not without actors.

On June 17th the temperature in New York was in the
upper eighties, edging on ninety. Midday found us in the
powder room, still blithely announcing the opening of *The
Cradle*. We summoned an agent— a small man in a black
felt hat who specialized in distressed theaters. It was midsummer and not one was open or available. After he left

we sat down to face the fact that we had neither scenery, nor costumes, nor orchestra, nor actors—nor a theater—for our scheduled world premiere of *The Cradle Will Rock*.

By midafternoon the press had begun to collect in our powder room. They were invited to wait while we held an emergency meeting in the ladies' toilet next door. Jean Rosenthal, then a technical apprentice just out of Yale (who later became America's most successful lighting designer), had been sent out with a five-dollar bill and instructions to acquire a piano. She called to say that she had got one (a battered upright) and what should she do with it? Now we told her to hire a truck, load the piano onto it, then call for further instructions. Once again we told the press that *The Cradle Will Rock* would be presented that night, with Marc Blitzstein performing it alone on a piano and singing all the parts. When they inquired where this interesting event would take place, we suggested they stay around and find out.

A little before six Jean Rosenthal was on the phone again to report success. After standing on various corners in the garment district, she had found a truck, bribed its driver and hoisted the piano aboard. Now what should she do? "Keep riding around," we said, "and call in every ten minutes for orders." An hour later, at seven o'clock, we were no nearer to giving a performance than we had been at noon.

By seven-twenty a crowd of several hundred credulous customers had gathered in the street outside the theater. Some of our actors—Will Geer, Hiram Sherman and Howard da Silva—went out on the sidewalk and sang songs from the show to keep them happy.

It was now seven-forty—twenty minutes before our announced curtain-time; our piano, with Jean Rosenthal on top of it, had been circling the block for close to two hours and the driver was threatening to quit. It was becoming apparent that, for all our big talk, for lack of a theater *The Cradle* would *not* rock that night.

At that moment the little man in the black hat reappeared suddenly with a large rusty key in his hand which, he assured us, would admit us to the Venice Theatre on Seventh Avenue at Fifty-ninth Street at the cost of one hundred dollars. The key was snatched from him and he was paid with money borrowed from members of the Press.

Within seconds, Abe Feder, our technical director, was in a cab, headed uptown. Jean Rosenthal, reporting for orders for the fourth time, was told to route her truck at full speed up Seventh Avenue. She got there first, and four firemen from the hook-and-ladder station next door helped her to break into the abandoned theater and hoist the piano up onto its deserted stage. Meantime, back at the Maxine Elliott, Orson and I went upstairs where our cast (including our black chorus of twenty-eight) was patiently sitting in the darkened theater awaiting orders. We told them we were moving uptown to the Venice Theatre, invited them all to accompany us as spectators but made it quite clear that we would not hold it against them if they didn't.

We went out onto Thirty-eighth Street, informed the assembled crowd of our move and invited them, too, to follow us uptown. Then, accompanied by Archibald MacLeish in a white linen suit and Lehman Engel, our musical director, who unaccountably on this sweltering summer night was wearing a heavy winter overcoat, we piled into a cab and headed north.

From the Maxine Elliott to the Venice is a distance of twenty-one city blocks. Our curtain-time had been changed to 9:00 P.M., and, since our adopted theater was three times larger than our own, everyone was urged to invite one or more friends. On the way uptown our audience trebled! They arrived by cab, by bus, by subway and on foot—twenty-five hundred of them, including Hallie Flanagan, director of the Federal Theatre. They found the doors of the theater wide open.

There were no ticket-takers that night, no ushers and no programs. But, by 8:50, there was not an empty seat in the house; standees were beginning to clog the back of the theater and the side-aisles. As they waited they became aware of a large, faded Italian flag draped over the upper-right stage-box, left there by the Italian stock company that used the theater for weekend performances. Mussolini's activities, first in Ethiopia and then in Spain, had not endeared him to left-wing audiences. Amid loud booing and cat-calls someone clambered up and tore the flag down. This gave the crowd a release; they laughed and applauded. Finally, at 9:01, like partners in an old-time vaudeville act, Orson and I made our entrance in front of a shabby curtain that depicted Mount Vesuvius smoking above the Bay of Naples.

We thanked our audience for making the long voyage uptown and related the history of *The Cradle Will Rock*. We were not subversives, we insisted, but artists fulfilling a commitment. We told them how the show would have looked and sounded and described all the wonders they would *not* be seeing. In conclusion—"We now have the honor to present, with the composer at the piano, *The Cradle Will Rock*."

As we left the stage the curtain rose on Marc Blitzstein, sitting pale and tense but calm at our eviscerated piano.

The Cradle Will Rock starts cold, without an overture. Behind us we heard Marc's voice, setting the scene:
"A Street Corner, Steeltown, U.S.A."
followed by a short vamp that sounded harsh and tinny on our untuned upright.

Then an amazing thing happened. Within a few seconds Marc became aware that he was not singing alone. It took our hand-held spotlight a few seconds to locate the source of that second voice; it came from a stage-right box in which a frail, red-haired girl in a bright green dress was standing glassy-eyed with fear, only half-audible at first but gathering strength with every note. Her name was

Olive Stanton; she had been cast almost by default and I knew that she and her mother were entirely dependent on the small weekly check she was receiving from the W.P.A.

Years later, after he had become famous, Hiram Sherman wrote to me that "if Olive had not risen on cue in that box I doubt if the rest of us would have had the nerve to stand up and carry on." But she did—and *they* did.

Our actors had been forbidden by their union to appear *on stage*. There was no ruling against their appearing *in the house*. And that's what they did! They acted all over that theater—in the aisles, in stage-boxes (upper and lower), in and out of the audience, between rows of seats, in the rear of the house so that the audience had to turn to see them. Improvising with amazing ingenuity—unrehearsed, undirected—they played each scene in a different and unexpected part of the house. A few were missing. Others took their parts while Marc at the piano set the scenes and played four parts himself. Lehman Engel, who had used that mysterious overcoat to smuggle the score out of the theater, sat in the third row of the orchestra, surrounded by our black chorus, conducting as best he could. It was a glorious evening and the cheering and applause lasted so long that the stagehands demanded an hour's overtime—which we gladly paid.

We made the front page of every newspaper in the city and ran for eleven performances to packed houses. Then the entire cast went back to Maxine Elliott's Theatre to conform with the W.P.A. regulations that limited their absence to twelve days. Two of us—Orson Welles and I—did *not* return. We had been fired for insubordination. Two weeks later we announced the formation of the Mercury Theatre. Eleven weeks after that, when we opened triumphantly with Welles's modern-dress *Julius Caesar,* a good part of our cast, some of our crew, most of our experience and a large part of our audience were directly inherited from the Federal Theatre of the W.P.A.

❧ Hallie Flanagan, 1890–1969

IN THE HISTORY of the American theater, Hallie Flanagan's place is honored and assured. She had two careers— one academic, the other national. As head of Vassar's Experimental Theatre in her early thirties, she became famous in college circles and beyond for the range, quality and originality of her productions. Those included the American premieres of T.S. Eliot's *Sweeney Agonistes,* her own *Can You Hear Their Voices?* and a number of what were then considered "radical" plays of social content. But when Harry Hopkins chose her to head the Federal Theatre of the New Deal's W.P.A. (they had been in college together at Grinnell in Iowa) she was quite unknown to the professional theatrical world.

From unknown she became anathema: a woman, an amateur, a fanatic armed with millions of the taxpayers' money, who on assuming office heretically announced that "while our aim is to put to work thousands of theater people, our more far-reaching purpose is to organize and support theatrical enterprises so excellent in quality, so low in cost and so vital to the communities involved that they will be able to continue after federal aid is withdrawn."

She never deviated from this objective and, if the Federal Theatre in its brief existence showed the energy and the quality that caused a New York critic to describe it as "the chief producer of works of art in the American theater," the credit is mostly Hallie's. The choice of personnel

Published as an obituary in *The New York Times,* August 3, 1969.

was hers; so was the imagination and the nerve. Accused alternately of being arty, elitist, subversive and reactionary, an impractical dreamer and an unscrupulous politician, this small, red-haired lady with the firm mouth and the ferocity of a roused tiger was receptive to almost any form of creative theatrical activity: The Living Newspaper, the Poets' Theatre, the Classical Theatre, the Experimental Theatre, the Negro, Dance and Children's theaters—these were only a few of the projects she organized and fostered the country over.

This courage and open-mindedness extended to her human relations in the troubled world of the Works Progress Administration. Faced with sit-downs and picketing within some of the groups she had so lovingly created, she informed a convention of the American Theatre Council that her Federal theater workers were striking "for what was once described as life, liberty and the pursuit of happiness," adding that "if we object to their method I feel that some word should come from this gathering as to a better one."

Her loyalty to her people was unwavering. When the ruckus broke out over Marc Blitzstein's *The Cradle Will Rock,* she neither reproached us nor tried to dissuade Orson Welles and myself from our defiance of the administration upon whose support the continuation of the W.P.A. Federal Theatre depended. When, two years later, her project was being assassinated by Congress, Hallie fought like a fiend to save it. Having failed, she did not waste her time in rancorous regrets. She wrote the definitive book on the Federal Theatre and returned with undiminished enthusiasm to her academic life—first at Vassar, then as Dean of Smith College.

It is for those frantic and fantastic years of the W.P.A. that we in the theater will remember her—the four years in which she and her collaborators turned a pathetic relief project into what remains, after thirty years, the most creative and dynamic approach that has yet been made to an American National Theater.

❖*Theater of the Left*

The revival of theatrical energy that took place during the Great Depression had a strong, inevitable left-wing bias— particularly in New York City. Besides the theatrical activities of the Communist Party, expressed directly through agit- prop groups and New Theatre *magazine, this radical influence was exerted through such organizations as Theatre Union, Theatre of Action and, indirectly, through members of the Group Theatre and certain units of the Federal Theatre of the Works Progress Administration.*

It took close to twenty years for books to appear on the sub- ject: I reviewed two of the first for the Book Section of The Washington Post.

To THE RISING tide of publications about the American theater of the thirties two new books have recently been added.* Both deal with the theater of the Left in New York City and concentrate on its activities before and during the Depression. Both make it clear that this was not an isolated phenomenon but an organic symptom of our national growth and artistic development; both trace its roots back into the early twenties and both suggest that its aftereffects are still with us.

* *The Political Stage: American Drama and Theatre of the Great Depression,* by Malcolm Goldstein, Oxford University Press. *Stage Left,* by Jay Wil- liams, Scribner's. Reviewed in *The Washington Post* Book World, 1974.

The Political Stage was written as an academic disserta-
tion. Its author was not around when it all happened and
his sources seem to be limited to printed material—books,
articles and the press of the period. His research extends
from the theater's first traces of social consciousness at the
turn of the century to the reactionary wave that hit us in
the years following the atom bomb. It is comprehensive
and, as far as I can tell, factually accurate. Until a more
inspired or comprehensive work comes along, it should
prove useful to anyone interested in the social and theatrical ferment of that turbulent time.

In reporting on this variegated activity (which by the
mid-thirties had brought together such disparate elements
as Sinclair Lewis, the American Communist Party, the
International Ladies Garment Workers Union, Mike
Todd, Bertolt Brecht and the United States Government),
Goldstein has organized his material with academic effi-
ciency. He has structured his narrative on the two slopes
of a great divide (which he places between the end of the
1934–35 and the start of the 1935–36 seasons) which coincides with the flowering of the New Deal and the Comin-
tern's strategic switch from aggressive class war to the
more expansive tactics of the Popular Front. On the
whole, this design is valid, though it applies most directly
to the brief but intense activity of the so-called Proletarian
Theatre—from the pure, early fervor of "agitprop" and
"conversion-drama" to the generalities of "a theatre that
naturally fights along with the masses for an extension of
democratic rights, for the right to organize trade unions,
against war and fascism—in brief, for a better and richer
life."

Inevitably this documentation includes copious quotations from the columns of the Communist press (how
tediously arbitrary much of it seems today!) and considerable space is devoted to tracing the effects of shifting Party
doctrine on the organization and product of the radical
theater. Unlike some of his predecessors, he does not exag-

gerate its influence on what was, in fact, an explosive release of collective emotional energy in which politics, in
my opinion, played only a minor part. Once again theater
people were making the best of their social and economic
circumstances; they used the cultural apparatus of the
American Communist Party for their own artistic purposes far more effectively than the Party ever succeeded in
using them.

By contrast, it is the principal and very different virtue
of Jay Williams's *Stage Left* that he manages to recreate
some of the special feeling of that period. In his preface he
warns us that "like everyone who ever worked in show
business," he is "romantic, sentimental and unreliable."
He stands convicted on all three counts; his book abounds
in inaccuracies and omissions. It is also rich with nostalgia
and vivid memories of that extraordinary time. And it
possesses what the other book totally lacks—a sense of
personal involvement in the excitement of those hungry
years and an understanding of the spirit that animated
those passionate young people for whom the Depression
was both a devastating catastrophe and a wonderfully lib-
erating experience—one which, by depriving them of all
security, drove them to express themselves more intensely
and more freely than they might have done under stable
and predictable conditions.

For a visit, through time, to a squalid, ill-smelling but
exhilarating world I recommend Williams's account of
communal life among members of the "Shock Troupe" of
the Workers' Laboratory Theatre in an abandoned apartment on Twenty-seventh Street, east of Second Avenue. If
the roster of its occupants reads rather like a page from
Red Channels, it also introduces us to a surprising collection
of men and women who later became famous in American
show business and elsewhere. The Left was clearly where
the action was to be found. For many—writers, designers,
directors, actors, musicians—a radical orientation of their

creative activity was the era's equivalent of today's foundation-grants and subsidies in the performing arts. Except that, on the whole, they were freer and they had rather more fun. And there was generally more love in the air.

❧ *Native Son*

Richard Wright's Native Son *opened in New York City early in 1941. It was the last Mercury production to be presented on Broadway by Orson Welles and myself. Some years ago* New Letters *(a publication of the University of Missouri at Kansas City) requested an article about that production for an issue devoted entirely to the late Richard Wright and his work.*

AMONG THE BOOKS we brought with us in the spring of 1940 to our retreat at Victorville, where Herman Mankiewicz and I had holed up to work on the script of *Citizen Kane,* was Richard Wright's *Native Son.* Mank and I read it and decided immediately that it would make a wonderful play. Having learned that Wright was in Mexico, I asked a visiting friend to call upon him and stake our claim. She found him by the side of a pool in Cuernavaca and learned that arrangements had already been made for Paul Green to dramatize Wright's novel. I was disappointed, but it was a reasonable choice: Green was the first white playwright to write sympathetically of Negro life in the South. (*In Abraham's Bosom,* starring Rose

Published in *New Letters* by the University of Missouri at Kansas City, Winter 1971.

McLendon, had won a Pulitzer Prize in 1927. More recently *Evenin' Sun Go Down* had been performed on the same *New Theatre* night as Odets's *Waiting for Lefty*.)

I had my own personal doubts as to Green's suitability for the task: *Native Son* was a violent, revolutionary work that did not accord with Green's sensitive but essentially Southern, rural attitude. His contract contained three "stipulations" which he described years later to the editor of *Black Drama*—"one being that I would have freedom to invent new characters and make editorial story changes where necessary, another being that I could make the Communist slant in the book comic when I felt like it." The third was that, though he would not be writing any of the dramatization, Wright would "come and be with me during my dramatizing work—this last being necessary for discussion purposes as I went along."

Having failed to obtain the rights of dramatization the next best thing for me was to try and secure the producing rights. With my record in the Negro Theatre this was not difficult and, in July, Paul Reynolds (Wright's agent) informed me that Dick was returning from Mexico and would go directly to North Carolina to work with Paul Green on the play script.

I was there when Wright arrived—a surprisingly mild-mannered, round-faced, brown-skinned young man with beautiful eyes. It was only later, when I came to know him better, that I began to sense the deep, almost morbid violence that lay skin-deep below the smooth surface. At our first meeting I was surprised—not altogether agreeably, having read his books—by the blandness with which he recounted the shameful story of his return to his native land. At Brownsville, at the border, a Texan customs inspector had pawed through his baggage, suspiciously examined and criticized his manuscripts and books ("Where's your Bible, boy?") and demanded to know where he got the money for travel and clothes. On the train that carried him across the South he had been denied access to the dining car, and the black waiter carrying his meal to the Jim Crow chair-car had been stopped as he passed through the train and threatened for serving a nigger on dining-car china with white man's linen and silver.

I spent a day with him and Green, listening to Paul's ideas for the play. I watched Dick Wright for his reactions; I saw nothing. But my own apprehensions rose sharply. Paul Green was a man who sincerely believed himself free of racial prejudice. Inviting Wright to live in his home during their collaboration was an act of some courage—even in an academic community like Chapel Hill. Throughout his stay, according to Dick, he could not have been more courteous, thoughtful and hospitable in his treatment of his black guest.

But having granted him social equality, he stopped there. From the first hour of their "discussions" it became clear that he was incapable or unwilling to extend this sense of equality into the professional or creative fields. Whether from his exalted position as a veteran playwright and Pulitzer Prize–winner or from some innate sense of intellectual and moral superiority (aggravated by Wright's Communist connections), Paul Green's attitude in the collaboration was generally insensitive, condescending and intransigent. No less disturbed than Wright by the injustices and cruelties of the racial situation in America, he was in total disagreement with him as to its true nature and solution. The basic and radical premise of Wright's novel—that only through an awful act of violence could a Negro like Bigger Thomas break through the massive and highly repressive structure by which he was surrounded ("the most I could say of Bigger was that he felt the *need* for a whole life and acted out that need; that was all,") was something that Green absolutely refused to accept—morally or artistically. Resenting what he called Dick's "existentialism," he attempted, till the day of the play's opening—through madness, reprieve, suicide, regeneration and other "purging" and sublimating devices—to evade and dilute the dramatic conclusion with which Wright had consciously and deliberately ended a book in which he wanted his readers to face the horrible truth "without the consolation of tears."

When I left them to their uneasy collaboration, Green estimated it would take him less than two months for a first draft. Until then there was nothing I could do but tamp down my apprehensions and start making arrangements for an early production, so as to profit from *Native Son*'s continued presence on the best-seller lists. Not more than five or six weeks later I got a call from Richard in North Carolina saying that Green's first draft had gone to the typist and that he would be returning to New York. I asked him to wait till I had a chance to read it, but he said there was nothing more he could do. He sounded so discouraged that I told him I would be down the next day, pick him up and drive him back to New York. My mother had come over from Paris to visit me. Knowing her passion for motoring, I invited her to drive with me through country she had never seen.

In Chapel Hill I met with Wright and Green. Richard said nothing, but on the way home I sensed enough to ask him with some impatience why, if he was so disturbed, he had not spoken up and provoked a confrontation. Wright, who had quit the Party but remained a disciplined Marxist, replied that under no circumstances would he risk a public disagreement with a man like Paul Green. There were too many people on both sides anxious to enjoy a dogfight between a successful black intellectual and a white Southern writer of progressive reputation—an avowed "friend" of the Negro people.

It was getting dark when we reached Washington, D.C. We had agreed to go on through to New York, but we were famished and we decided, now that we were out of the South, to stop for something to eat. We parked the car on an avenue facing the White House and the three of us went into a cafeteria on the corner which, at that hour, was almost empty. We had served ourselves and were about to sit down when the manager came up and informed us quietly but firmly that no colored were allowed. I asked him if that was the law. He said it was. I began to yell at him: in that case why had my friend been allowed to serve himself? He said that was a mistake and he was sorry. I asked where we were to eat the food we had paid for. He said he would gladly take back my friend's food and refund the money. I refused. My mother had begun to express her cosmopolitan views on racial equality when Wright, who had not said a word, started for the exit with his tray and we followed him. It was a warm night and the three of us sat on the curb and ate our supper while Dick explained to my mother that he was accustomed to this sort of thing, which would never change until the entire system was altered. We left our trays on the sidewalk when we were finished and as we got back into the car and headed north, we saw the man from the cafeteria picking them up.

Some days later a "first rough working draft" arrived from Chapel Hill—a hundred and forty pages long. Structurally it stayed fairly close to the book, which Wright had consciously written in dramatic scene form ("I wanted the reader to feel that Bigger's story was happening *now* like a play upon a stage or a movie on a screen."). But the "editorial changes"—the additions and modifications—exasperated me. Among the former was a wholly invented, Dostoyevskian police "reenactment" scene for which I saw no necessity in a script that was already overlong. Among other modifications was the blending of the dead girl's Communist boyfriend with the left-wing labor lawyer who finally undertakes Bigger's defense. Even more serious in my opinion was the changed moral attitude that pervaded the script, leading inevitably to a total betrayal of Wright's intention in the closing scene. This was the scene of which Wright had written:

At last I found how to end the book; I ended it just as I had begun it, showing Bigger living dangerously, taking his life in his hands, accepting what life had made of him. The lawyer, Max, was placed in Bigger's cell at the end to register the moral—or what I felt was the moral—horror of Negro life in the United States.

This final facing of the terrible truth of his life was distorted, in Green's version, by giving Bigger lyric visions in which he saw himself as "a black God, single and alone."

BIGGER

Ring the bells! Beat the gongs! Put my name on the hot wires of the world—the name of Bigger, Bigger—the man who walked with God—walked this earth like God—was God!

During the final fade-out a priest in a white surplice, "with a great book in his hand," intoned "I am the resurrection and the life."

I called Wright as soon as I had read it and told him of my indignation. He asked me to call Paul Green and explain how I felt and why. I tried, and it was like talking to a stone wall. Some weeks later a revised script arrived. It was down to reasonable length; the Dostoyevskian reenactment was gone and the lawyer, Boris Max (rechristened Paul), had been restored to life. But the basic flaw—the distortion of Wright's ending—remained.

I urged Wright to repudiate what I considered a deliberate betrayal of his work. I told him I had no intention of producing the play in its present form. Dick continued to be distressed but repeated that he preferred not to see it produced than to risk a public disagreement with Paul Green at this time. There was nothing more I could do. My option ran for three and a half months longer. I put the script away in a drawer, swallowed my disappointment and turned back to other work.

Then one morning, shortly before Thanksgiving, I awoke in my red velvet bed and raged at the thought that I owned one of the hottest theatrical properties in the world and was prevented from doing anything with it by a peculiar combination of Southern moral prejudice and black Marxist scruples. I called up Dick Wright and asked him to come over to Ninth Street for lunch. I assured him that I understood his scruples but that, as his producer and director, I refused to accept them. I had reexamined the book, and Green's dramatization of it was structurally sound: wherever it followed the novel it was usable; where it deviated, as in the absurd final scene, it was reparable by returning to Wright's own original text. Dick asked if we would let Green know what we were doing. I said no. I wanted Wright's help in the restoration, but it would be done entirely on my authority as producer and I would assume full responsibility for it.

Almost every morning, for the next three weeks, he came over from Brooklyn and we would work our way through the scenes, transfusing the blood of the novel back into the body of the play. We had a good time, and when we were done I had the script retyped and took it with me to California where I did what I had vowed I would never do again. I gave Orson the new script of *Native Son* and asked if he would like to direct it as a Mercury production—our final production together.

He called me the next day and said, "Yes, very much," as soon as he had seen *Citizen Kane* through its final editing. My feelings were mixed by this time. I had set my heart on directing this one myself. But I was eager to end my theatrical association with Welles on a note of triumph and I felt that, with the strong text of Wright's book to support him, his direction of *Native Son* would be far more dramatic than mine. I gave Wright the news and he was delighted. So was Paul Green.

It was January of 1941 before we finally got to work. *Citizen Kane* had survived Hearst's attempts to torpedo it and was receiving generally brilliant reviews, though several leading theater chains were refusing to show it. It was not until years later that it was universally accepted as the masterpiece that it is.

My relationship with Welles was somewhat different on this production from what it had been during our five-year partnership. Being less close made it easier for us to work together. Throughout rehearsals of *Native Son* he was happy, overbearing and exciting to work with. With Jean Rosenthal (who had begun to make her reputation on the outside) as our technical director, we worked out a production in which, behind a vast, permanent, brick-painted portal, ten wagon-stages of various sizes slid past and around each other with never more than a few inches to spare. It took thirty-five stagehands to move them but they worked without a hitch. And for once we had no money problems. Since *Citizen Kane,* Hollywood was suddenly full of backers eager for a piece of the action— Orson's action. Two of them, in the hope of becoming his partners in future film ventures, put up the money for *Native Son* to the tune of fifty-five thousand dollars.

Casting was a pleasure. The Mercury regulars, including those who had decided to stay on in California after *Citizen Kane,* were reassembled: Ray Collins (who played Max, the lawyer), Everett Sloane, Paul Stewart, Erskine Sanford, Jack Berry and others. New faces included Philip Bourneuf from the Federal Theatre, Frances Bavier, Joseph Pevney and Anne Burr, a complete unknown chosen in an open audition, as the girl. For our black actors we turned to old friends from the Lafayette: Evelyn Ellis, Helen Martin, Rena Mitchell, Bootsie Davis, Wardell Saunders and Canada Lee, a former prizefighter and nightclub owner who had played for us in *Macbeth* and whom the role of Bigger Thomas established as a Broadway star.

For our script we used the version Wright and I had made out of Green's script: the few added changes we

made in rehearsal were all returns to the book. Dick attended rehearsals regularly and appeared to enjoy himself. Then one day I got word that Paul Green would be in
New York for the final run-throughs. He appeared in the
theater one evening, sat in silence and left without a word
after the last scene. The next morning, the day of our first
preview, he appeared with his agent and we held an emergency meeting: Green, Wright, Paul Reynolds and I,
joined by Welles, who was rehearsing downstairs and
whom I summoned at a dramatic moment. Green insisted
that we reinstate his version—particularly the final scene.
I told him it was too late for that and, besides, we had no
intention of being parties to the distortion of a work we
admired. Richard sat silent beside his agent, who now informed us that Green's second draft (credited to Paul
Green and Richard Wright) was already in the publisher's
hands. I suggested that he get it back and change it to
conform to the acting version. Green was furious. There
was talk of enjoining the performance, which I knew he
would not do, all the more since not one word was spoken
on that stage that was not Wright's—particularly in the
last scene, where we had gone back word for word to the
book. When Orson began to howl at him, Green got up
and left, and I have never seen him again. After our successful opening I called his publisher and pointed out the
absurdity of the situation. But it was too late to do anything about the published version and, as long as it remained in print, Harper and Brothers continued to
circulate a version of the play that was substantially different from what had been performed so successfully on
the stage of the St. James Theatre.

At the final preview of *Native Son* two sets of pickets appeared on Forty-fourth Street. One, from the conservative
Urban League, was protesting the squalor of the book and
the bad light in which it put the Negro in America. The
other represented a small, rigid faction of the American
Communist Party, which could not forgive Richard

Wright for defying Party orders and refusing to rewrite certain sections of his book at their behest. Both left after an hour and did not reappear for the opening, which took place on the night of March 24th as a Mercury production presented by Orson Welles and John Houseman.

> Mr. Wright and Paul Green have written a powerful drama and Orson Welles has staged it with imagination and force. These are the first things to be said about the overwhelming play that opened in the St. James last evening but they hardly convey the excitement of this first performance of a play that represents experience of life and conviction in thought and a production that represents a dynamic use of the stage.

This from *The New York Times.* Further approval came from widely different quarters—for Wright, for Canada Lee, for Welles and for the production. Burns Mantle in the *Daily News* gave us four stars and *The Christian Science Monitor* was pleased. The *Daily Worker* was enthusiastic.

> In comparison all the productions of the current season seem dim and ancient chromos. The theater, that slumbering giant, tears off its chains in this production. From the theatrical point of view it is a technical masterpiece. As a political document it lives with the fire of an angry message.

Stark Young found Canada Lee's performance the best he had ever seen from a Negro player.

> *Native Son* also gains by the thunderous and lurid theater methods of Mr. Welles. In my opinion Mr. Welles is one of the best influences our theater has, one of its most important forces ... His talent begins with the violent, the abundant and the inspired-obvious, all of which make for the life of the theater-art, as contrasted with the pussyfooting and

the pseudo-intelligence and the feminism that have
crept into this theater of ours.

What reservations there were came mostly from those
whose admiration for the book led them to question the
wisdom of dramatizing it. Only the critic of the *Journal-
American,* loyal to his still angry master, William Ran-
dolph Hearst, detected "propaganda that seems nearer to
Moscow than Harlem" and reminded readers that Richard Wright had been a staff member of the *Daily Worker*
and of *The New Masses* and had approved the Soviet trials.

Native Son was a hit and did good business. It needed to,
for with its large cast and three dozen stagehands it was as
expensive to run as a musical. After 114 performances,
with the coming of the hot weather, our Hollywood backers decided to close the show. It reopened in the fall under
a new management and in a more economic production
directed by our stage manager Jack Berry—first in New
York and then on a national tour for the better part of the
year. It was not until they came to perform in certain
Midwestern cities, particularly Chicago and St. Louis,
that they became aware of fierce racial tensions such as we
had not encountered in New York City.

Broadway

For more than half a century Broadway meant many things to many people. For a long time it was generally admired and loved as the heart of the American theater; even in its decline it continued to represent special qualities of glamour and style.

My own feelings have always been ambivalent, colored by envy and a sense of exclusion. To me, when I entered the theater, Broadway was a rich mansion to be broken into; a citadel to be assaulted and despoiled. It was an ailing giant of whose weaknesses I must be aware and be ready to take advantage.

This led me, over the years, to write a number of articles about Broadway—about its heroes, its economic ills, its neuroses and its imminent collapse.

TWO SUCCESS STORIES

❧ Up and Down, In and Out: Josh Logan (1908–   )

THEATER PEOPLE write books for various reasons: profit, vanity or the urge to bring some artistic or pedagogic message to the world. But most often, I believe, they write to satisfy their own need to relive and, if possible, to preserve in a more durable medium, the crises and triumphs of their exhilarating but ephemeral occupation. Joshua Logan has had more than his share of both: the number of his Broadway hits exceeds that of any living American director except possibly the venerable George Abbott.

Josh (emblazoned in lights on the jacket, in harmony with the author's declaration that he is "drawn like a moth to anything outlined by lightbulbs") is the record of a hugely successful and eclectic theatrical career, engagingly and egotistically told by a man whose several nervous breakdowns have made him keenly aware of his own emotional and professional mechanism. He spent a restless childhood in which the male and female elements seem to have been in frequent conflict (mother and sister versus stepfather and military academy), moving about the country from Texas and Louisiana to Indiana and Princeton. There in his freshman year he encountered Bretaigne

Josh: My Up and Down, In and Out of Life, by Joshua Logan (Delacorte Press). Reviewed in *The New York Times Book Review,* 1976.

Windust, president of the "Theatre Intime" and later a successful Broadway director. Through him Logan met Charles Leatherbee, cofounder with Windust of the University Players, that astonishing group which in its short and disjointed existence employed—for five dollars a week less laundry—such future theatrical figures as Margaret Sullavan, Henry Fonda, James Stewart, Kent Smith, Myron McCormick, Barbara O'Neil, Mildred Natwick and Norris Houghton. It was at Princeton, at the age of nineteen, while staging *Othello,* that Mr. Logan vowed never again to direct a classic. He has kept his word—with the possible exceptions of *Charley's Aunt* and his own version of Chekhov's *The Cherry Orchard,* which he renamed *The Wisteria Trees.*

The following year he visited Russia and made his way into the presence of the great Stanislavsky who, "from a Madame Recamier-type couch, with several large pillows at his back and a crocheted throw covering his feet," was directing *Le Coq d' Or* for the Opera Studio of the Moscow Art Theater. The future director of *South Pacific* and *Annie Get Your Gun* observed Stanislavsky's use of "all the musical detail of the score, outside the singing—how he fused it to the thoughts and emotions of the characters and sought total integration of actor and music. . . . No detail was blurred or left to accident. Every transition, even the tiniest change of purpose, was fitted to a suitable phrase of music." From his visit he brought back certain ideas about musical theater and a photograph of the master with the inscription: *"Aimez l'art en vous-même et non pas vous-même en l'art."*

Logan directed his first Broadway play at twenty-six during the Great Depression, then flew to Hollywood where he served briefly and hilariously as David O. Selznick's dialogue director on *The Garden of Allah,* charged with reconciling the disparate accents of Marlene Dietrich, Charles Boyer and Joseph Schildkraut. Three years later he scored his first Broadway musical hit with *I Married an Angel,* by Rodgers and Hart, with George Balanchine as his choreographer.

In the twenty years that followed—of which the bare chronology emits a great cloud of glamorous memories—Josh Logan coauthored and/or directed two dozen Broadway shows and several films, besides getting married twice and suffering two breakdowns. Aside from these, which are described in precise and terrifying detail, and a term of service with an Air Force troop-carrier unit in the south of England during the Normandy invasion, "where death was a daily, familiar companion," *Josh* is mainly concerned with theater and, more specifically, the Broadway theater. It shows us a feverish, pragmatic world dedicated to the satisfaction of public taste—a world of miracles and disasters, of sharp deals, shifting relationships and brief, intense intimacies—whose final measure is the Box Office.

In recording the memories of his many triumphs, Mr. Logan leads us through a gallery of notable associates and collaborators—Larry Hart, Irving Berlin, Paul Osborne, William Inge, Dwight Wiman, Mary Martin, Helen Hayes, Ethel Merman, José Ferrer, Leland Hayward, David Merrick, Oscar Hammerstein and the perennially dominant figure of Richard Rodgers, among many others.

Through the dazzle of bright lights, certain figures emerge in sharp focus: from Princeton and Falmouth the impossible but irresistible Margaret Sullavan, that "lanky, drawling sophomore" Jimmy Stewart, Mary Lee and Charles Leatherbee and, above all, the straight slender figure of that petulant perfectionist Hank Fonda. Later there are full-color portraits of Nedda Harrigan (his second wife) and Merrill Moore, psychiatrist, poet and his self-appointed mental adviser. Of his Broadway collaborators, two are etched with the sharp acid of personal emotion: Oscar Hammerstein, his coauthor on the book of *South Pacific* and the shy, doomed figure of Tom Heggen, with whom he worked on the dramatization of *Mister Roberts*. It is significant (and symptomatic of show-biz's neurotic preoccupation with "credits") that the book's two most highly charged dramatic confrontations are those in which authors' "credits" and royalties are nervously discussed and haggled over. "It's going to win the Pulitzer Prize and no one will ever know I wrote a word of it!" A substantial part of *Josh* is devoted to Logan's two nervous breakdowns. Both are closely meshed with his career, and both seem to have grown directly out of his intense theatrical activity—"in disturbed conditions," as his doctor told him. The first, following the great success of *Charley's Aunt* and the collapse of his first marriage, began with a manic spiral: "I closed nightclubs, made friends with strangers with whom I could drink until it was time to make an attempt to sleep. But sleep never came. I gave out tickets like handbills, sent flowers by the carload. I began investing in plays. . . . I had a self-assurance that was incredible even to me and I seemed able to convince anybody of anything. Life was a fantasy of utter freedom."

The ecstasy was to turn sour soon, ending in a Philadelphia hotel room where he lay on a bed, his face bright with theatrical makeup: "Then it began. First a kind of chill that seemed to shoot tiny quivers through me, then that same chill mixed with a knotting diaphragm and bursting, gushing hysteria. My body shook so violently it shook the bed; I couldn't hold still. All I could do was to try to live through it, survive it and, when I did, wait breathlessly and pray it wouldn't start again. But it did, over and over."

Mr. Logan's book takes us into the 1950s, coinciding with the end of his great run of Broadway hits. He has directed more than a dozen shows since then and, happily married, lives elegantly on both sides of the Atlantic. His book recreates an era that has almost entirely disappeared—a time when New York was the center of

America's theatrical universe and a nude male torso on a Broadway stage was a subject of conversation.

Once, during a rehearsal of *South Pacific*, Joshua Logan revived Mary Martin's drooping spirits with a verse by William Blake:

> He who doubts from what he sees
> Will ne'er believe, do what you please;
> If the sun and moon should doubt,
> They'd immediately go out.

Josh is Mr. Logan's spirited reply to the uncertainties of the theater. And this time he doesn't have to worry about his author's credit.

❧ Young, Gifted and Dangerous: Jed Harris (*1900–1980*)

IN THE 1920s, before the cumulative effects of talking pictures, radio, the Great Depression, television and greed had destroyed Broadway's primacy in the American entertainment world, its business was conducted by a handful of theatrical producers—men who, with varying degrees of talent and courage, risked their fortunes and reputations presenting the shows of their choice. (Chief

Jed Harris: The Curse of Genius, by Martin Gottfried (Little, Brown & Co., 1984). Reviewed in *The New York Times Book Review*.

among them were the aging Belasco, Ziegfeld, Arthur Hopkins, Sam Harris, Brady, Miller and Ames as well as the Theatre Guild and the Shuberts.) On the night of September 26, 1926, with the New York opening of *Broadway,* they were joined by a maverick—one Jacob Horowitz—who had changed his name for professional purposes first to Jedediah ("beloved of God") and then to Jed Harris.

Within fifteen months he had eclipsed them all; he had produced three smash hits in a row: a melodrama—*Broadway;* a domestic tragedy—*Coquette,* starring Helen Hayes; and a high comedy—*The Royal Family,* each of which seemed to bear his unmistakable, personal imprint and which were bringing him, at the age of twenty-six, an income of more than one hundred thousand dollars a month.

The next year he produced another American blockbuster, *The Front Page,* followed by the effete but exquisite *Serena Blandish.* His appearance on the cover of *Time* some months later made him "famous as no other American theater person had ever been," with a legendary reputation for theatrical infallibility and for outrageous personal and professional behavior. Early in 1929, he announced his retirement "because the theater is the short pants of the arts. People outgrow them . . . it's all a hoax and I'm going away and have a long laugh over it."

The laugh lasted only a few months during which he devoted most of his energy to the conduct of tempestuous, simultaneous, transatlantic affairs with several of the theater's most glamorous ladies (one of whom bore him a son in Paris) and at the end of which he received the news that he had been wiped out in the stock-market crash.

Undaunted, he sold his newest yacht and reentered the theater with a surprising production of *Uncle Vanya.* It was his first solo appearance as a director and Broadway's first exposure to Chekhov. It received enthusiastic reviews and his choice of Lillian Gish as Elena was hailed as another brilliant piece of female casting.

There were uneven years after that with the mixed reception of *Wonder Boy, Mr. Gilhooley, Fatal Alibi* and *Spring Dance.* On the credit side there was his firm and sensitive direction of *The Green Bay Tree,* soon followed by his catastrophic presentation of Katharine Hepburn in *The Lake.*

By the mid-thirties his reputation for infallibility was fading and the bitter antagonisms he provoked among every one of his former associates were depriving him of the new successes that might have been his. A decade after his triumphal appearance on the Broadway scene he produced and directed, in close succession, *A Doll's House* and Thornton Wilder's *Our Town,* which came very near to closing in Boston but which theatrical historians will almost certainly appraise as one of the great theater productions of our time.

Later there was an unsuccessful production of Sartre's *Red Gloves* and a moderately admired version of Henry James's *Washington Square* (retitled *The Heiress*) which Harris had not originated but for whose success he was substantially responsible. Then, in 1953, following a brief association with Billy Rose in television, there was an unhappy production of *The Crucible* whose author, Arthur Miller, was finally forced to take over the production.

That was Jed Harris's last work in the theater, but the hollow shell of Broadway's former Wonder-Boy continued to haunt the scenes of his triumphs and to harass and embarrass his erstwhile associates and former lovers for more than a quarter of a century.

To writers Jed Harris has always offered the double fascination of a prodigious talent coupled with a satanic personality. Ben Hecht was the first to express his ambivalent feelings in a cruel novel named *A Jew in Love,* in which he described Jed's seductions as "a Dracula-like hunger for the blood of his victims." Wakeman's *The Saxon Charm* came next, followed by a spate of Show-Biz hero-villains of whom Harris was the obvious prototype. Martin Gottfried's is, I believe, the first serious biography. As a long-time New York drama critic he knows and understands the Broadway background and his research has been imaginative and extensive. But he too has succumbed to the fascination of the Vampire.

His book falls roughly into two parts—the sudden rise and the long fall. In the first he deals with the family history and the troubled childhood; the uneasy sojourn at Yale; the first eager, active years in the theater as a fledgling press agent in New York and Chicago; the return to Manhattan and the irrepressible drive to become the most successful producer on Broadway. For material about these formative and triumphal years Mr. Gottfried has used the personal reminiscences of survivors and the published memoirs of two of Harris's early associates—Richard Maney and S. N. Behrman. But his main and most vivid source is Harris's own *Dance on the High Wire,* which was assembled late in life when Jed was in desperate financial need. In these scattered pieces he gave the world his own subjective account of the personal crises and theatrical decisions which, in his opinion, made all the difference between the success and failure of some of his most celebrated productions. That they are egotistical and self-serving does not prevent them from furnishing some of the most vivid and dramatic material in Mr. Gottfried's book. They also leave us with a strong desire for a more intimate, objective and detailed revelation of the creative mechanism that carried this dangerous young man to the heights of his profession.

There was his notorious magnetism, which he exploited and abused and which played such a vital part in his theatrical activity. (I have known actors who had every reason to loathe and despise him but who, years later, still spoke with awe and gratitude of his intuitive understanding of their acting problems and recalled the surprising insights and the vivid metaphors with which he helped them during the preparation and performance of parts they played for him. I have known others who appeared in the same productions and feel only hatred and contempt.)

But Jed Harris was more than an actors' Svengali. He was entrepreneur, press agent, script-doctor and, in his latter days, director of the plays that bore his name. It is not easy, today, from the memory of those productions, to reconstruct the true quality of his theatrical talent. Among the contemporary testimonies quoted by Mr. Gottfried is a summation which the drama critic John Anderson wrote more than fifty years ago:

> His function encompasses the energy and intuition and thoughtful preparation with which he approaches a production . . . It encompasses his feeling for living dialogue, his conscious manipulation of his players and that injection of subtleties which take on in his general scheme the strength and body of larger design.

The playwright Arthur Miller, years later, writing after his experience with Harris in *The Crucible,* gives us a very different view:

> People thought he was brilliant; I certainly thought he was charming. But if you put it on a record and played it back, why—there was nothing there.

No such controversy complicates the latter part of Mr. Gottfried's book, in which he gives us a merciless account of the decline and fall of a man of unusual intelligence and energy who deliberately and relentlessly destroyed himself. The deterioration is effectively and sympathetically, if somewhat journalistically, described with a wealth of grim detail supplied by former associates, ex-wives and mistresses, abused relatives and exploited acolytes, most of whom seem only too willing to recall the humiliations of their former idol as he stumbled from one rejection to another and found himself finally excluded from every house and bed in which he had once been so welcome.

Once again I found myself wishing that more space had been devoted to an investigation of this creative "genius" who in his brief and brilliant career left an indelible mark upon the theater of his time, and less to the neurotic eccentricities through which he ended by destroying himself.

❧ *No Business Like Show Business*

In 1949, when inflation was still in its mild and early stages, I was commissioned by Harper's *magazine to describe the worsening condition of the Broadway theater during the recent 1947–48 season.*

During recent seasons the gradually growing unrest in the theatrical world has been frequently and variously studied and explained. The high cost of living, the wave of all-round extravagance that has been sweeping the country, the allurement and expense of the automobile, the competition of filmshows, travel lectures, cabarets, grand opera, outdoor entertainment, critics, labor unions and reckless overbuilding have all been blamed. . . . No business in the world can long endure such terrific waste. Radical readjustment is necessary and if it be not wrought by some hand with a genius for organization, it will come of itself and through trouble.

Previously published in *Harper's* magazine, September 1949

Thus *Variety*, the bible of Show Business, editorialized in December 1912 in its seventh-anniversary issue—seven years that had witnessed the birth of Show Business as we know it today: the first great theatrical building boom, the formation of the circuits and the battle of the titans (the Syndicate and the Shuberts) for control of the American theater. During those years, in every important city in this country, theater capacity had doubled or trebled. The week that editorial was written, there were playing, in New York City, thirty-eight legitimate shows; in Chicago, fourteen; in Philadelphia, ten. By the mid-twenties, the number of theaters in New York had doubled again. On New Year's Day, 1928, there were seventy-two shows open for business on and around Broadway.

That was the peak. With the coming of Talking Pictures, Radio, the Great Depression and, finally, Television, the theater's decline has been constant and accelerating. On New Year's Day, 1949, the number of shows available to Broadway theatergoers was twenty-nine; in Chicago there were eight; in Philadelphia, three. In other words, in three major cities of America, there are today *less than half* the theatrical productions of 1928 and fewer productions than there were thirty-seven years ago!

In New York City not one professional legitimate theater has been built in a quarter of a century and none is projected. Twenty years ago there were seventy-five playhouses available; today there are thirty-two—and they continue to vanish at the rate of two and three a year. The same is true the country over. Key cities like Pittsburgh, St. Louis, Baltimore, Kansas City and Cleveland boast one antiquated, cavernous structure apiece. Los Angeles, with a growing population of over two million, manages to keep one legitimate theater occupied for less than half the year.

It is of this situation and of the emergency presently

confronting the Broadway theater and the "few cities to which it ministers after a fashion" that Brooks Atkinson, in *The New York Times* last winter, wrote this devastating analysis:

> For fairly obvious reasons, the Broadway theater will never recover the festive prosperity of twenty years ago before cheaper forms of entertainment had begun to flourish on so vast a scale. Since 1929, the Broadway theater has probably gravitated to approximately the place it will always have in relation to the motion picture, radio and television. The current uneasiness derives from the suspicion that the Broadway theater may keep on dwindling and may not even be able to support the thirty theaters that are now commonly in use. The Broadway theater has been slowly becoming a neurotic ordeal. The costs of production and operation have become so high that successes have to be fantastically successful and failures have become catastrophes. . . . It is not an art, but an unsuccessful form of high-pressure huckstering. There is almost no continuity of management and no continuity of employment among actors, playwrights and allied artists and craftsmen. The whole business is conducted in an atmosphere of crisis, strain and emergency. Crisis is the normal state of affairs on Broadway.

Hobe Morrison, expressing the same thought in the more statistical idiom of *Variety,* asked bluntly: "How long can Legit take it?"

Before trying to answer that question—before probing a few of those elements of strain and crisis that increasingly harass Broadway—it is worth establishing, very briefly, just what is the Theater's present place in relation to the rest of Show Business.

It is necessary, but difficult, to remember that the entertainment business in its present form is a thing of very recent and monstrous growth. Movies, fifty years ago a technical curiosity; radio, barely a generation old; television, still in embryo—these represent, between them, a capital investment of about seven billion dollars! The five or six million which Broadway painfully raises to defray the cost of its season's productions are almost invisible next to the bankroll of four hundred million dollars expended annually on production by the motion-picture industry. Radio billings currently total about two billion a year.

Audience figures are even more striking. The theater in its peak months is likely to play host to about half a million people a week. Compare this with the *one hundred million* patrons who, during 1946, weekly attended this country's eighteen thousand movie houses. Set it, if you can, against the *one hundred and fifty million* daily listening hours over radio's eighty-five million receiving sets—and you have a rough notion of Broadway's statistical position in Show Business.

Variety, always a reliable guide to the economics of the trade, in an average seventy-five-page issue, devotes thirty-four to motion pictures, seventeen to radio-television, four to the legitimate stage and the rest to bands, music, vaudeville and nightclubs.

Considering the buffeting she takes at the hands of her overgrown sisters, it is amazing that the Theater survives at all. Here are a few of her outstanding grievances—samples of the hardships and indignities to which she has been subjected since moving pictures, radio and, now, television moved uninvited into her exclusive neighborhood:

1. With their infinite resources and their insatiable need for expansion, the new media have completely upset the housing situation. The Theater stands by helpless and humiliated, while one after another of her remaining homes are sold from under her to the motion-picture chains or hurriedly converted, with lath and chromium, into radio

and video studios (in New York City there are three more in process of transformation at this moment).

2. With their ostentatious wealth, the Mass Media have disrupted the labor market and recklessly run up the price of help. Wage scales perfectly suited to their electronic grandeurs work desperate hardships when applied to the modest operation of a legitimate playhouse.

3. The social behavior of the Mass Media has been consistently outrageous. They have treated the Theater with condescension and violence. While openly despising it for its penury and its smallness, they have never hesitated to snitch its ideas and hijack its talent. Year after year they have continued to raid and plagiarize her—without ever a word of thanks!

Still the Theater survives.

The national news weeklies, whose special business it is to assess the manifold and complex influences that go to make up the general cultural picture of our time, regularly devote to the Theater an amount of space and attention that is quite disproportionate to its economic and statistical position in our society. And for good reason. The Theater, in spite—or perhaps by virtue—of its humble economic status, enjoys one inestimable advantage over its giant competitors: it is, today, the only completely free branch of Show Business. Untrammeled by major financial commitments and stupefying overheads, it is impervious to censorship; it can defy the icy squeeze of pressure groups; above all, it can ignore futile and enervating preoccupations with its own moral responsibility. Alone in the entertainment world the Theater can, if it wishes, stay true to its creative instincts. Here, for all its manifest frailties, its excesses and its turpitudes, it has not entirely failed.

II

The Theater struggles on. And, until further notice, until something more solid or more inspiring comes along to take its place, the heart of the American theater remains Broadway. What keeps it beating? Habit, in part, and geography and *greed* and devotion and fear and the law of inertia—and money.

Last year, this year, and probably next year, between sixty and seventy shows were, are being, and will be produced on Broadway. They will cost about six million dollars. Where will this money come from? Whose money is it? How is it handled? Where does it go?

In New York today there may be ten producers capable of financing their own productions and less than half that number who are willing to do so. In this respect their methods differ widely from those of their predecessors. This is not to say that the producers of yesteryear were sedate and solid tycoons operating in the manner of Lombard Street Bankers. They took their money where they could; often they blew sky-high. They did, however, regard the business of preparing and producing and running plays as a hazardous but honorable operation in which profit and loss were balanced on their books over a period of years and from which they occasionally emerged in the black.

Today even the most constant and successful of our showmen handle each of their productions as individual ventures, with separate financing and separate books. For a number of reasons, including the I.R.S., they regard them as isolated projects, individual ventures rather than items in a continuing business. There are reasonable explanations for this:

1. *The Broadway real estate situation*—which has separated the owners of the playhouses from the men who produce the shows that fill them. In previous theatrical periods, the managers (including Shakespeare and his associates) operated their productions and the playhouses in which they played as allied and inseparable activities; the one sustained, enhanced and sometimes jeopardized the other.

In New York, since the Theatre Guild was forced to give up its playhouse on Fifty-second Street, only one or two producers regularly presents plays in their own theaters. This frees the manager from the fearful necessity of filling his theater even if he has no play to put in it but it also reduces the continuity of his operation.

2. *The tax situation,* which imposes a very special hardship on a type of business in which occasional huge profits are expected to carry the hazardous operations of less favorable years. The present pattern of theatrical financing by treating each production as a separate venture is aimed at cushioning this fiscal inequity.

3. *The drastic rise in the cost of production.* The current inflation has inured most of us to the notion of bloated prices, but theatrical costs are something quite special. One revealing example is to be found in the books of Mr. Oscar Serlin, producer of *Life with Father.* To take up the curtain on that most successful of all Broadway shows, in the fall of 1939, cost $23,000. Nine years later, with the same cast and in the same theater, *Life with Mother* cost over $85,000 to put on—more than three and a half times as much.

At present levels not only can most producers not afford to finance their own shows, even if they had the money they could not afford the risk. A director-producer who could put on a routine comedy—as George Abbott did *Room Service*—for around five thousand dollars and make six-figure profits on it, could take one or more such risks a season and think nothing of it. What he lost on the swings he could make on the roundabouts—twenty-fold. Under current conditions this is no longer true. One flop or two (they befall even the most cautious and inspired showmen) and he and his company are out of business, or, at the least, seriously paralyzed for seasons to come. At such odds, why should he risk his own substance when there are plenty of other people's dollars available, on reasonable terms, at no risk to himself, and with no entanglement for the future? The answer is: he doesn't. He goes out and finds an angel and gets "backing."

III

What is this golden stream that flows, like oxygen, through the theater's laboring heart and keeps it beating? Its nature varies with the times; so does its sources; but somehow it keeps coming.

Forty years ago it was the theater owners, eagerly competing for "product" with which to fill their expanding theater chains, who could be counted on to supply it. Nowadays the only remaining titan (the Shuberts) does not bother much with production; he has his hands full collecting the profits from the controlled contraction of his former empire; he contents himself with financing random operettas or with salvaging an occasional show in distress, on rigorous terms.

More recently it was Hollywood, on its incessant prowl for movie material, that pumped cash into Broadway— pumped it, through play purchasers, at the rate of nine million dollars in three years, plus several hundred thousand dollars a year directly invested in play production. Now that source, too, seems to be drying up. In the past year, only two major Broadway productions have been purchased or financed by Hollywood.

Today, between Broadway and total anemia there stands nothing but that small, bold band of angels who, partly as a business, partly as a hobby (some as an investment, some as a gamble, some recklessly, some with infinite forethought, some singly, and some in so-called syndicates) have taken upon themselves, in these parlous times, to act as the Theater's bankers.

The angel is a familiar figure on Broadway. He used to hover on its fringes; now he has moved dead center. His money is of many colors. It runs all the way from folding-money too hot to bank to the purest pedigreed Wall Street lawyer's check. It may be money picked up with ease over a second martini or money laboriously dredged up through dozens of tedious and embarrassing auditions and readings. It may be money from a well-heeled star eager to back his own judgment of the play in which he has decided to appear. It may be money reluctantly contributed by some theatrical supplier eager to get an order away from his competitors.

Two things these monies have in common: in the event of loss, they are tax-deductible. In the spring of last year, when a modified tax ruling threatened to upset the existent investment pattern (a "limited partnership" agreement which enables the investor to deduct his individual losses from his current year's income and to realize his gains on a basis less severely taxable than straight income) a terrific caterwauling went up along the Main Stem and all current financing negotiations came to an abrupt stop. The big angels let it be known that they were through with theatrical investment—and they probably meant what they said. Within a few weeks, a superior ruling had restored calm, but the incident revealed the very precarious base on which the present structure of play-financing rests.

That backing plays is a reasonable investment, that it is a reckless gamble—both are easily proved. Ignoring, for the moment, such legendary bonanzas as *Harvey, Born Yesterday,* or *Life with Father,* let us examine two more recent sets of figures. Consider, first, that tragic and comparatively high-brow production—*A Streetcar Named Desire.* Presented by a virgin management in the fall of 1947 with a moderate cast, one rather complex setting, an elaborate light-plot, and some backstage music, this production opened in New York, to wonderful notices, at a cost of around $85,000. By the end of the thirteenth week, this had been earned back in full. By the end of its first year, the books showed a clear profit of around 225 percent. In the next half-year, a further 100 percent was earned.

Meantime a second company had been assembled (out of the profits of the first) and sent out on the road. This one paid off its cost within fifteen weeks and continued to earn accordingly from there on. As I write, both companies are still running at virtual capacity and a big film sale is in the offing.

There are two or three *Streetcars* a year—with luck. Here, by way of contrast, is a summary of Broadway's overall financial statement for the same season: 1947–48. A total of seventy-four shows were put into production at an average cost of around one hundred thousand dollars apiece. Of these, nine were "hits"; five paid back their investment and showed a slight profit; six more, though they were listed as "hits" and ran for several months, finally paid back between five and twenty-five cents on the dollar. Of the remaining fifty-four, forty-nine were a total loss and the other five never reached town at all.

The 1948–49 figures tell the same story. Of the season's first three months, *Variety* reported that "not within human memory has so much coin been dropped in such a short period." Afterward, commenting on the season as a whole, that publication came to an interesting conclusion: of the sixty-eight shows that opened, forty-eight were straight plays (eight hits), sixteen were musicals (six hits) and four were revivals (one hit). The money spent and lost on outright flops was $4,535,000. On the fifteen hits, the sum spent was $1,940,000. Thus, "it is figured possible that when the current hits are through paying off, even excluding the possible return from film sales, the profits may equal the losses on the flops and thus balance the books for the season as a whole." This leads to the following deduction: "If an investor bought more or less standard slices of all productions of all established managements, he might be assured of a small overall profit."

There is truth in the above, and a fallacy. It is important to remember that large sums are dropped yearly, on

Broadway, on imbecilities which no competent showman and no angel in his right mind would touch with a ten-foot pole, and that such disasters affect the total balance sheet. On the other hand, assuming that an aristocracy of "established managements" really exists and that their average of success runs high, what constitutes a "more or less standard slice" of one of their shows? There are insiders and outsiders on Broadway just as there are on Wall Street. The more "established" the management the less eager it is for alien backing. The more attractive the show the thinner the "slice."

Since angels, like race-track men, habitually lie about their winnings, it is not easy to get a true mathematical picture of their operations. It is a safe guess, though, that in the portfolios of most theatrical backers the sums dropped on adventuresome projects are greater, by far, than those invested in "standard slices" with "established managements." It is sensible, but tedious, to play only the favorites. It is lucky for the Theater that this is so.

In my own experience I have never known money to be really easy to raise; conversely I know of no project—no matter how strange or wild—for whose eventual production, with enthusiasm and patience, money could not finally be found.

IV

The number of producers who have had their names on Broadway shows in the past two seasons is around two hundred. Among them were men and women who played an organic part in the preparation of the productions that bore their names. There were others who produced shows because they had nothing else to do. Any similarity between their activities and the Art of the Theater is purely coincidental.

Why anyone who is not creatively involved ever goes through the agony and humiliation of producing a show on Broadway is a mystery beyond comprehension. There are dozens of surer ways of acquiring prestige and power. There is no surer way to the madhouse.

THE BEGINNING

You want to be a theatrical producer? You have a little experience but no special skill; you are not even capable of being your own business manager. You have acquired a play for five hundred dollars down, plus a hundred a month to hold it. It calls for one set and a reasonably-sized cast and it should cost under $100,000 to produce. Armed with the script, mimeographed to the number of one hundred (you will need every one of them, for there is no honor on Broadway about returning scripts) you go into action. Your "neurotic ordeal" has begun. It may last anywhere from three months to two years.

First, the script is submitted for backing, directly and through middlemen, with an accompanying note to explain that "the author is still working on it." Next, actors must be approached, designers titillated and every effort made to entangle one of the three to four currently successful directors whose Name on the production will reassure or bedazzle the hesitant angel. (This is a tricky business, since you cannot commit these artists until you have raised your money and you cannot raise your money until you have the artists committed.)

Meantime, on promise of a job, you get someone to draw up a budget for you.

In due course, depending upon your luck, your "contacts," the state of the stock market, the quality of your script and the talent you have been able to assemble, the checks begin to arrive—money which you may not touch on pain of imprisonment. While you anxiously wait for the balance to come in, you continue, through releases to the press, to behave publicly as though you were convinced that the production was going ahead.

Sometimes it does.

EXHIBIT A
BUDGET OF PRODUCTION

PRODUCTION

Scenery (building and painting)	$8,000.00
Scenic designer	2,000.00
Costume selector	300.00
Director (first payment)	2,500.00
Furniture and props	2,500.00
Additional production (misc.)	1,000.00
Costumes, shoes & accessories	2,000.00
Electrical, perishables & supp.	300.00
Auditing	150.00
Preliminary office	900.00
Hauling (N.Y. to train)	400.00
Typing manuscripts & parts	200.00
Rehearsal halls & theaters	600.00
Photos, frames & press agent's preliminary expenses	500.00
Taxes & compensation insurance on prelim. salaries	320.00
Stage labor (dress rehearsals, etc.)	1,200.00
Legal fees & disbursements	1,250.00
Misc. (incl. N.Y. opening)	3,000.00
Preliminary salaries (up to day of out-of-town opening)	
(a) Press agent (3⅔ weeks)	740.00
(b) General and co. managers (6⅔ weeks)	1,766.00
(c) Stage crew (3 men)	400.00
(d) Wardrobe mistress (2 weeks)	170.00
(e) Stage manager (4⅔ weeks)	816.00
(f) Cast rehearsal (4 weeks)	2,500.00
Total Salaries	6,392.00
Subtotal	*$33,512.00*

EXHIBIT A (continued)

ADVANCE PAYMENTS:
(Chargeable to weekly operations)

Royalty	$2,000.00
Electrical equipment rental (3 weeks)	900.00
Furniture & prop rental (3 weeks)	600.00
Insurance	250.00
Printing	500.00
Railroad (New York to Boston)	500.00
Subtotal	$4,750.00

DEPOSITS (Returnables)

Actors' Equity—actors' bond	8,000.00
A.T.A.M.—press agent and manager bond	990.00
I.A.T.S.E.—road stage crew bond	690.00
Theater deposit a/c guarantee	3,500.00
Subtotal	$14,180.00

RECAPITULATION:

PRODUCTION	33,512.00
ADVANCE PAYMENTS	4,750.00
DEPOSITS	14,180.00
Subtotal	$52,442.00
Probable out-of-town LOSSES	7,558.00
Grand Total	$60,000.00

For all this toil, anxiety and degradation, you will receive, if and when the production comes off, the return of some of your expenses plus a niggardly allowance for office and general overhead. As producer, you will also receive 50 percent of the net profits—in theory.

In practice you will get no such thing. The agents of your talented director and your desirable leading actor demand for their clients, in addition to a handsome salary and a weekly percentage of the box-office receipts, a substantial percentage of the net, that is, a slice of *your* possible profits. Since you need them, not only for their creative skills, but also for the commercial value of their names, you have no choice but to accede. That leaves you with a sharply reduced percentage of your potential profits.

Weeks go by. Your production date approaches. You are still $25,000 (the tough $25,000) short of the sum needed to go into rehearsal. Your expenses are mounting, your commitments are piling up—and so are your anxieties. Now you start offering additional inducements to recalcitrant investors in the form of bonuses, commissions, higher percentages and preferential terms. More and more pieces are hacked out of your rapidly diminishing share. (It is not without precedent, by opening night, for the producer's only equity in his show to be the dubious pleasure of seeing his name on the billboard.)

THE END

You've made it—tonight you opened! I spare you the painful recital of the intermediate stages: the dress-rehearsals, the tryouts, the all-night conferences, the long agony of constant changes foisted between performances on a reluctant, frightened and exhausted cast. With your last spasm of energy, you have supervised the first night's seating arrangements, trying to line up an audience cordial enough to encourage your actors but not so hysterically prejudiced as to exasperate the press. Now the last curtain call has been taken (was it enthusiasm or kindness?), the theater is dark, the company is assembled in joyless alcoholic festivity in some apartment uptown awaiting the notices. It won't be long now. By 1:00 A.M., by methods known only to members of his crafty *confrérie*, your press agent will have seen or heard over the phone the reviews that will appear in the leading morning papers. As you wait, quaffing drinks and smiling falsely at your fellow sufferers, let us consider your case.

Three possibilities lie before you:

1. *Smash Notices*—unanimously ecstatic reviews, hyperbolically expressed. In that case your worries are over. You can leave for Florida in the morning, leaving your manager behind to worry about the "ice" (the illegitimate profits made by theaters and box-office men from under-the-counter sale of tickets).

2. *Flop Notices.* Now, too, you can leave for Florida—if you can borrow the fare. Your troubles are over. We shall waste no pity on you. We shall need every ounce of it for the man wretched enough to be faced with—

3. *Mixed Notices.* In the morning papers, one of your reviews is good, two are mildly favorable and one is poor. By noon the afternoon papers are out: they, too, are divided—one rave, one panning, one totally incomprehensible. At the box office, which you haunt in person or frequently consult by phone, you are told that business is "fair"—a brief word heavy with menace. Toward the middle of the afternoon you meet with your press agent, who, with typewriter, scissors and pastepot, is preparing a "display" advertisement for tomorrow's papers. In this he has skillfully smelted every superlative from the favorable reviews and tempered the adverse ones by quoting them out of context. Next day, at the expense of your last few thousand dollars, the advertisements appear; the box office reports a favorable reflex. That night there is a theater party and the house is exhilaratingly full. Encouraged, you order tickets printed for an additional month.

With this reckless act you are doomed, irrevocably condemned to weeks of hell. You will spend the next months fighting "running costs."

Though business may be mildly profitable for a week or two, a brief session with your accountant will soon convince you that never, under any possible circumstances, can you personally realize one nickel out of the production. A few more weeks go by during which your show almost breaks even—but not quite.

Then Lent begins, followed by Income Tax Day and the first murmurings of spring. By now one thing has become evident: that the overall financial situation cannot possibly get better—only worse. From here on, the only possible reasons for keeping the play running are obduracy, pride and an impulse of pure philanthropy in keeping the actors at work, the author and the director in royalties and the Shuberts in theater rental—none of which motives are likely to inspire your embittered investors.

The Easter weekend brings you false hope; then a premature heat-wave wipes out what is left of your meager reserve. Presently you give your hundredth performance and a party for the cast. You do your best to be cheerful, but it is hard, for you are living in an agonizing dilemma: to hang on and maybe get the benefit of the early summer trade or to close before another slump wipes out your last few dollars and more. When, finally, the eagerly awaited summer visitors limit their theater-going to *Streetcar, South Pacific* and *Salesman,* you give up. It is with a sense of general relief that the final closing notice is posted.

Some time later, neatly typed, you will receive your accountant's financial report from which you will learn that, after a fifteen weeks' run and the hollow satisfaction of being listed among the producers of one of the season's minor hits, your backers will get back on their investment the sum of eight cents on the dollar. As to you, the producer, the net result of *your* nine months of work and

EXHIBIT B
STATEMENT FOR WEEK ENDING _____

RECEIPTS

Box-office receipts	$15,404.65
Less theater share	5,245.39
Net receipts	10,159.26

EXPENSES

Salaries

Company	5,135.46
Producers	200.00
Crew	536.00
Stage managers	275.00
Company and general managers	250.00
Press Agents	310.00
Wardrobe and dressers	175.00

Royalty

Author	1,240.47
Director	308.09

Publicity

Share of newspaper	1,140.36
Printing & promotion	161.50
Press expense	87.02

Departmental

Props	30.95
Costume	34.74
Carpenter	25.00
Rentals	307.09
Office expense	100.00
Auditing	50.00
Payroll taxes	138.84
Insurance	40.00
New York City excise tax	10.16
League dues	10.00
Miscellaneous	15.00

Total Expenses	10,580.68
Less Net Receipts	$10,159.26
Running Loss for Week	$421.42*

* Fifteen years ago such gross receipts would have resulted in a net profit of several thousand a week. One Pulitzer Prize–winner of the thirties, in its entire long and profitable run, averaged less than $10,000 a week in box-office receipts.

worry is that your next show, if and when you have one, will be just that much harder to finance.

V

Turning our backs on this murky valley, let us climb together into the pure bright air of those sunlit hills where dwell the Gods of Olympus, the Smash Hits. Let us see what effect, if any, the rising level of costs has had on them.

To a handful of miraculous specimens the problems I have described do not apply at all. *Harvey*, with its seven-figure profits and its million-dollar movie sale, was one. Others were *Born Yesterday* and *Life with Father*. All three were reasonable shows to operate. Any rise in their running costs was more than offset by the general increase in ticket prices and the consequent rise in receipts. *Streetcar*, more recent and more expensive, is doing nicely, as we have seen. So is *Death of a Salesman*. On the other hand, one of the season's biggest dramatic hits, after half a year of excellent business, is known to have earned back less than three-fifths of its original cost—a perilous margin.

Drama, in this respect, fares better than musicals, whose costs have reached quite staggering proportions and whose receipts, contrary to the general impression, have shown no equivalent rise. *Show Boat*, in the spring of 1929, at the Ziegfeld Theatre, was playing to a top price of $6.60 a seat. That same season, another musical hit, *Follow Through*, at a $5.50 top, was reported grossing $41,000 a week at the Forty-sixth Street Theatre. Eighteen years later, in the same playhouse, *Finian's Rainbow* was taking in $42,500 a week—i.e., fifteen hundred dollars more in receipts, but with costs about double.

This helps to explain such startling items as those reported in *Variety* last fall; that *Allegro*, playing ten months to virtual capacity in one of our largest theaters, earned back less than two-thirds of its quarter-million-dollar investment; that the fabulous *Annie Get Your Gun*, doing solid capacity for eighteen months of its Broadway run, was in the black for only half of that time.* This explains why musicals, with their higher ratio of success than drama, are nevertheless viewed with reasonable suspicion by prudent investors—those same investors who are today tearing out their hair for having resisted the temptation to put money into *Kiss Me, Kate.* Here is a show that—like *Oklahoma!*—almost did not get on for lack of final backing, that cost less than $150,000 to open, and that has yielded more than $10,000 a week in profits in New York alone!

VI

For a gambler, the Theater remains full of thrills; as a business it is a poor risk. And the current inflation has aggravated its ills. Never were there such "hits," yet the number of productions continues to diminish. Never were there such long runs, yet the employment figures grow daily more desperate.

From the rising costs and the mounting receipts, one group has emerged with profit. It is not the investor, nor the producer (for all the isolated bonanzas); it is not organized labor (whose gains have just about coincided with the reduction of employment and the rise in the cost of living); nor is it the actor, whose employment continues to shrink. The theatrical element which, through these uneasy years, has steadily gained in wealth and power is, surprisingly, *the creator.*

Next time you visit one of our musical successes, take a look at the first page of your *Playbill.* Over the name of the show, you may find no less than four producers. Now let your eye run down, past the title, to where the creative elements of authorship and execution are listed. There—

---

* Another of Irving Berlin's shows, *As Thousands Cheer,* produced during the austere thirties, while regularly grossing around $27,000 (a figure that would close any current musical overnight), was able at that figure, if my informant's memory serves, to make a profit of between six and seven thousand dollars a week.

in different type and in slightly different order—are the same names as above. Of the four producers of *South Pacific*, three—Rodgers, Hammerstein and Logan—are also composer, lyricist, coauthor and director. Several of last season's hit shows were produced on this basis, with the creators (singly or in association, overtly or in silent partnership) assuming the dual function of creation and management. The material effects of this new structure have been, on the whole, beneficial. Among the disruptive and incompetent elements of today's commercial theater, these creators have shown a valuable sense of competence, of self-assurance and, above all, of continuity. But, for the Theater's deep-seated ills, this is no solution. These conspicuous successes are the thin point of a pyramid whose base is crumbling. Behind its flashy facade of occasional hits, the Broadway theater continues to shrink and wither away.

"It is a wonder that anybody stays in it. The present is intolerable; the future is very gloomy indeed." Written almost a year ago in an excess of righteous indignation by our leading drama critic, those words are still valid today. So is the thought with which Brooks Atkinson concluded his column: "The plight of the New York theater today is not merely economic. It is much more serious than that; the *fun* has gone out of it."

Extend this condition—the absence of "fun"—from the stage to the auditorium, from the theater to the public, and you have, I believe, discovered the main cause of our present theatrical crisis. The truth is that Broadway, for all its high level of talent and its great sense of technical perfection, is no longer "fun" for that section of the audience on which it ultimately depends for survival. There are, among my own acquaintances, literally dozens of educated and not completely indigent men and women who no longer attend the theater—and it is not only radio or movies or television that keeps them away.

Twenty years ago, they regarded theatergoing as a regular social and cultural habit which included, but was not limited to, the acclaimed "hits" of the season. They saw many plays, and by and large they had a good time—the good time that comes from forming one's own opinion without pressure and from that sense of personal and collective discovery that has always been one of the keenest excitements of intelligent theatergoing.

Ten years ago, in the mid-thirties, the Federal Theatre, with its nominal admission prices, seemed on the way to replacing some of the carriage-trade audience that had been lost to the Depression. Where are they today? Not in our Broadway playhouses at current prices—not more than once or twice a year. Ask them why. They will tell you that they can't afford it; they will also tell you that it isn't worth the trouble. Before making the hasty rejoinder that the theater doesn't need them anyway, that *South Pacific* and *Salesman* and *Kiss Me, Kate* are sold out months ahead with or without them, just recall a few of the figures that appeared at the front of this article. The hits may not need the regular theatergoer—being filled to overflowing with sightseers, success-chasers and expense-account chargers. But the Theater *does* need them badly. It is in a fair way to dying without them.

That it will eventually get them back I have no doubt. Whether it will reach them through Broadway or through some quite unexpected form of theatergoing, it is impossible to predict. In a similarly deadlocked situation—in the early twenties, following a similar inflation—the impetus came from below. It was the amateur intelligentsia, the longhairs from MacDougal Street and Washington Square, who cracked the hard, dry mold of the commercial theater and made playgoing one of the great excitements of that lively era. O'Neill was the prize exhibit of the Provincetown Playhouse; George Bernard Shaw and the unknown, accumulated drama of postwar Europe were the springboard from which the Theatre Guild leaped to success and fame.

No such new or compelling elements have yet appeared among us this time around. There are the British imports and there are sundry "off-Broadway" groups presenting plays of quality under conditions of great hardship; but they are little better than playgrounds on the margin of the Theater.

Perhaps, this time, the thing will not happen in New York at all. All over the country, while Broadway loses its playhouses one by one, in colleges and community centers hundreds of fine theaters are being built and equipped, in which hundreds of thousands of eager young men and women are devoting themselves to studying and practicing the Arts of the Theater. Are these the playhouses of America's next generation of theatergoers? And, if so, will we continue to describe their theatrical activities by the very American name of *Show Business?*

SHOW BUSINESS—UPDATE '86

Much has changed since this article was written more than thirty years ago. The inflation that began with World War II has continued and accelerated during the fifties, sixties and seventies, so that, today, every figure cited in that piece—including production and running costs—must be raised by *600 to 700 percent.* (At the Mercury Theatre in the mid-thirties our highest-priced ticket was $2.20, including tax. On Broadway in the forties the average ticket for an orchestra seat at a "legitimate" play was $4.40, including tax, and for a musical, $6.60. Today's prices are $30 to $42 for a straight play, $45 to $50 for a musical—not counting agency premiums. For *Nicholas Nickleby* tickets were $100 apiece and it was sold out.)

The effects of this inflation have been far-reaching and irreversible. The entire shape of the American theater is altered; it has become decentralized and its main creative activity has shifted from New York to the rest of the country. Today there are more than two hundred accredited, professional theater companies operating in major cities of the United States and twice that number performing regularly for audiences of lesser size—not including festivals and special occasions. Around twenty percent of this theatrical production is devoted to new plays.

In the numbers of its performances and in the total of its aggregate audiences, the regional theater is, of course, negligible in comparison with the Mass Media. Yet its influence on our culture is constant and considerable. Broadway, on the other hand, has virtually lost its capacity to create original theater. It has become a luxury bazaar dependent for its survival on tourists, business entertainment and deductible expense accounts. This has created a fallacious appearance of continued prosperity but the artistic consequences are calamitous. Out of every ten plays (other than musicals) successfully presented on Broadway, half are imported from Europe—mostly from London; the rest have originated in one or another of the nation's regional theaters before being moved to Broadway for exploitation. Theatrical creation in New York City is limited today to such organizations as Joseph Papp's Public Theater and to a handful of altruistic Off- and Off-Off-Broadway nonprofit theatrical groups.

Shakespeare in America

❀ <u>Lear</u> on Broadway (1951)

For more than half a century (from Harlem's Voodoo Macbeth *to the current repertory of* The Acting Company) *I have been involved in the production of Shakespeare's plays in America. Before the present renaissance, I had watched things change from the wild, creative days of the Federal and Mercury theaters to the doldrums of the forties when a professional production of Shakespeare had become a rarity in this country.*

One notable exception was the King Lear *produced in New York in the winter of 1950–51 with Louis Calhern in the leading role. It rehearsed and opened under conditions I described at the time in* Theatre Arts.

KING LEAR is not the most frequently performed of Shakespeare's tragedies. The fact that it has received two major productions this year—one on either side of the Atlantic—gives us a chance to compare the very different conditions under which they were produced and presented.

The first, with John Gielgud in the title role, was part of the annual repertory season of the Shakespeare Memorial

Theatre at Stratford in Warwickshire. The second was presented some months later, with Louis Calhern as the King, in a commercial production in New York City.

The first significant difference is that Gielgud played *Lear* thirty-two times over a period of several months; he gave an average of two or three performances a week as part of a repertory of five Shakespearean plays of widely varying moods, produced in diverse styles by different directors.

Our New York *King Lear,* in the first major production of the play to be seen in more than twenty years, was performed under standard Broadway theatrical conditions at the horrifying rate of eight shows a week including two matinees (I have never understood how Calhern—who was then in his mid-fifties—survived). The Stratford version, priding itself on the integrity of its text, ran for three and a half hours. On Forty-first Street, conforming to Broadway's current theatergoing habits, the audience was out within two hours and forty minutes of the curtain's rise.

Both productions had one thing in common: a rehearsal period of five weeks. Yet even this similarity is deceptive when one examines the actual circumstances of these rehearsals. Of the Stratford company of forty-four principal actors more than half had been with the company the previous year. (Two of their current productions were repeated from an earlier season.) Its leading actors, almost without exception, had frequently played together in Shakespeare and other classics. By contrast, of the New York company's twenty-eight actors, only three had acted together before and less than one-third had ever appeared, professionally, in a play by William Shakespeare. Finally, of the two actors playing the role of Lear, one was playing the King for the third time in his career (and was, in fact, repeating some of the stage business of his last production); the other had not appeared in a Shakespearean production since boyhood.

The technical conditions of rehearsal were no less different; members of the Stratford company rehearsed for several hours each day while appearing every evening in repertory in one of three other plays. They were able to rehearse in their own theater and on the platforms that eventually formed the basis of their own scenery. They opened after only two dress rehearsals conducted by a familiar and thoroughly routined house-staff; their premiere was given before an audience that was accustomed to opening nights performed under repertory conditions. (The truth is that John Gielgud, exhausted by his multiple duties in the company's repertory, gave an enervated and disappointing first performance of *Lear* at Stratford last summer. The dubious reviews had no appreciable effect on attendance and when the critics returned two weeks later and once again reviewed him in the role, they gave him the greatest notices of his career.)

The New York company found itself rehearsing in no less than five generally unsuitable spaces; it was not until the day of the first dress rehearsal that they finally set foot upon the step-units and platforms which formed the basis of their production. On this same occasion they encountered their technical crew for the first time in a theater that was totally strange to them all. By way of compensation, a generous management gave them three dress rehearsals and six previews before the official opening—thereby adding ten thousand dollars to the budget. This was not done out of altruism but out of desperate commercial necessity. Under the current Broadway system there is no second chance; the fate of the production—extensive run or instant closing—depends entirely on the opening night's reception and on the critics' reaction to that single performance.

As we continue to compare the circumstances of the British and the American productions their differences become more and more marked—on both the artistic and the economic levels. The Shakespeare Memorial Theatre at Stratford-on-Avon is an established and highly successful operation backed by financial guarantees which, in recent years, it has almost ceased to need. Last summer's Stratford season was attended by several hundred thousand people at ticket prices ranging (in our currency) from thirty-four cents to a dollar and a half. Broadway's *King Lear* was a straight commercial venture at a $6.60 top. Though it played almost twice as many times as its British counterpart and closed to capacity houses, its producers suffered a net loss of around seventy thousand dollars— one hundred percent of their investment.

If those strike you as sordid facts, unrelated to the art of the theater, one of the purposes of this piece is to demonstrate that they are, in fact, very closely related to the problems of serious theater in this country and at this time. Without attempting, in any way, to pass judgment upon the social or theatrical merits of the two systems— endowed classical repertory or one-shot commercial production—I hope to make it clear how widely they vary in their working conditions and how different are the functions and qualities required of their respective performers and directors.

The one—the British director—was working with a company of actors accustomed to each other's style, preparing and developing a number of well-known plays within the comparative security of a familiar stage and a predictable attendance under the economic guarantee of an assured and appreciative public. It was his function as a director to take advantage of this security and to galvanize these familiar elements into original and exciting life.

The American director has an altogether different and far more complicated and precarious assignment. At his first rehearsal he faces a troupe of strange actors painfully assembled for the occasion from every corner of U.S. Show Business: Broadway, Hollywood, vaudeville, radio, television, the most vital and doctrinaire of the theatrical studio groups—all are represented in his cast. Their experience,

their training, their habits—even their individual attitudes toward the art and practice of acting are different
and sometimes in direct conflict. To those personal and
professional diversities (which the director has a scant
month to discover, understand and assimilate into the
body of his production) must be added his cast's obvious
unfamiliarity with classical theater in general and with
this play in particular. Add to these the further fearful
economic anxieties inherent in the Broadway production
system under which he must work and the immensity of
his task becomes tragically apparent.

He starts bravely enough, stirred to vigor and enthusiasm by the challenge of a masterpiece that has not been
seen in New York in many years and by the play's unfold-
ing greatness and the gradually discovered wealth of its
parts. Then, as the days pass all too swiftly and opening
night inexorably approaches, a new and horrible anxiety
develops and begins to interfere with his work. The normal, healthy tensions, the groping and self-doubting that
form the normal hazards and benefits of rehearsal become
magnified and distorted under the pressure of what its
leading drama critic has called Broadway's "neurotic ordeal." Anxiety and fear set in—with good reason.

Each member of the American company, on signing his
or her contract, was knowingly risking an entire winter's
living on the slender chance of commercial success to be
expected from the performance of one of the most no-
toriously difficult plays in the English language. Free en-
terprise and the profit motive are no respecters of the
Classics. Unlike their British colleagues our actors can
hope for no guaranteed engagement and no assured audience. Their alternatives are disaster and instant closing or
the limited run that awaits even the most successful of
classical revivals on Broadway. For the sheer satisfaction
of sharing in what they hope will be a great theatrical experience, they have engaged themselves, individually and
collectively, in what they know to be a desperate ven-

ture—with the odds overwhelmingly against them. Caught in a deliberately contrived shortage of Broadway playhouses, Shakespeare's greatest tragedy finds itself struggling for stage space in direct, ruthless competition with whatever modern melodrama, drawing-room comedy, farce or musical spectacle happens to be in production and to have the price of a house guarantee. And, in its fight for survival, it is judged by exactly the same commercial standards of "entertainment."

No wonder that, as opening night draws near (that single performance upon which they must stand or fall, "run" or "fold"), a mounting fever of anxiety and fear sweeps over the company. Only the very experienced or the very inspired are immune to it. In those last precious days of rehearsal, when the final dramatic discoveries are made and the long agony of creation melts into sudden clarity and assurance, the director of a Broadway production is apt to find himself sharing his actors' attention with the agency tipsters and the box-office prognosticators. How to deal with this spiraling anxiety is not the least of his responsibilities to his company and to himself. On his energy and skill will depend whether these pressures act as a stimulating challenge or a disastrous diversion at this most crucial stage of the play's production.

Whether it is proper to submit Shakespeare to the tensions that result from these obsessive commercial preoccupations is a matter for argument. Under conditions prevailing in America today, we have no choice.

POSTSCRIPT

King Lear opened on Christmas night with a good but nervous performance. The press was generally favorable:

> "A magnificent cast in a fine production." . . . "Forceful, vivid drama . . . acting of virtuoso brilliance, carefully planned and rich in detail." . . . "An altogether splendid revival of this formidable work."

These golden opinions failed to stir Broadway theater-goers. *King Lear* played to good houses throughout the holidays; then, during the usual late-January slump, business fell off. Following the grim Broadway tradition that a show is either a "hit" or a "flop," a "smash" or a "dog," our management panicked and allowed another show to be booked into our theater for mid-February. As soon as our closing was announced business bounced back: for the last three weeks of our run we sold out. At our four final performances police were summoned to control the crowd that was besieging the theater for standing room. The usual desperate but futile last-minute attempts were made to extend the run, but by then it was too late. New York's *King Lear* closed after fifty-six performances—twenty-four more than had been presented in Warwickshire during the entire summer and fall.

❧ *Julius Caesar on Film* (1952)

In 1952, as a reward for producing two successful motion pictures for the studio (The Bad and the Beautiful *and* Executive Suite), *MGM allowed me to undertake a filmed production of Shakespeare's* Julius Caesar.

As part of a campaign intended to prepare film audiences for the first American Shakespearean movie since Reinhardt's Midsummer Night's Dream, *I wrote a number of articles of which this is a composite.*

PLATFORM STAGE or proscenium arch, radio, TV, or motion picture—no matter what medium you employ, the problems of effectively presenting an established master-piece to contemporary audiences are essentially the same.

You must, without distorting it, adapt the text and intention of the dramatist to the technical resources and the psychological climate of your own time and of the medium you have decided to employ.

Of all Shakespeare's tragedies *Julius Caesar* benefits from one very specific advantage—the empathy it evokes in modern audiences, to whom gang-war among the great is an habitual subject of melodrama and to whom the tragic conflict between personal ambition and the democratic ideal is a painfully and dramatically familiar one.

> *Julius Caesar* has about it the immediate ring of today's headlines. One man brooding against Caesar's ambition finds another until they stand around a single man to strike him down to save their liberties. Then one man emerges to stand alone against them and the mob rises and they must answer for what they did singly. . . .
>
> Shakespeare's language presents no incongruity. It is simply released to work its supreme magic in terms of theatre, as if this method had renewed its vouchers of immortality, as if, in fact, a great poet had risen in our midst only yesterday.

So ran one of the enthusiastic reviews that greeted Orson Welles's Mercury Theatre modern-dress, bare-stage production of *Julius Caesar* in 1937. For audiences whose daily news-diet was being poisoned by the unchecked growth of fascist and Nazi power in the world, Welles had prepared a script that was as sharp and intense as his production. Since it was clearly impossible to bring the pomp of the Roman state, the city-mob's organized violence and, above all, the changing tide of battle onto our small Mercury stage, they were all handled impressionistically. Out of darkness into the crude electric glare of innumerable projectors, dark-uniformed figures appeared in conflict and vanished again with stylized and shocking suddenness. Like all the best of Welles's work, it was magically and brilliantly theatrical.

Now, fifteen years later, I found myself in a different association, faced with an even greater challenge—that of working with Joseph Mankiewicz to transfer *Julius Caesar* to the motion-picture screen. When Shakespeare wrote

> ... how many ages hence,
> Shall this our lofty scene be acted o'er
> In states unborn and accents yet unknown ...

he was, as we have seen, prophesying accurately for our time. It remained for us to reproduce his "lofty scene" with all of its content and excitement, no longer on one small stage but on hundreds of theater screens in terms that would be moving and comprehensible not only to a few thousand experienced playgoers, but to audiences of millions the world over.

In preparing this project, we started with two assets: first, that the historical climate for such a drama is particularly favorable; second, that, in this new medium of motion pictures, we had no fustian to strip away, no hardened tradition of Shakespearean production to inhibit us.

This left us free to attack our main artistic problem— that of translating Shakspeare's bloody and turbulent melodrama into a medium where both mass effects and personal conflict could be more closely observed and more fully developed than under the fixed, unchanging focus of a playhouse stage. Yet, while exploiting the camera's brooding mobility, we had to be careful never to substitute effect for tension; never to lose—as some Shakespearean films have—the dramatic unity of the work as a whole.

PRODUCTION

Of the problems that arose over the filming of *Julius Caesar,* some were solved in conference before production began; some on the soundstage during production; some in cutting- and dubbing-rooms after production was closed.

The question as to whether we should make *Julius Caesar* in black and white or in color was among the first to come up—and to be answered. We picked black and white. Our decision, like Laurence Olivier's for *Hamlet* (following his success with his Technicolor *Henry the Fifth*) was guided by esthetic and not by economic considerations.

It is possible, under ideal conditions, to use color for its dramatic value—as, for example, in the deeply moving nocturnal camp scenes in *Henry the Fifth.* Yet color continues to be used, in Hollywood today, principally for irrelevant and spectacular show. For all its mass scenes, violent action and historic background *Julius Caesar* remains, basically, a tragedy of direct, personal strife. Its scenes call for intensity, rather than color or grandeur, and should be concerned primarily with the interplay and conflict of character and personality expressed through words in the mouths of individual actors. That is why we chose to work in the powerful simplicity of black and white.

Having made this decision, we carried it to unusual lengths. Unlike most productions which are designed in bright colors and then photographed in black and white, *Julius Caesar* was designed and executed in monochromes. We denied ourselves the idle pleasure of admiring our many-hued pre-production sketches and models and saw our production, from its earliest stages, pretty much as it would finally look in the positive print of Joe Ruttenberg's strong and moody photography.

We were influenced by one further ephemeral consideration. *Julius Caesar,* when effectually performed before modern audiences, enjoys one clear advantage over most classical dramas: the instant and almost automatic emotion that this history of political strife engenders in audiences which, in their time, directly or indirectly, by remote or immediate experience, have suffered or witnessed analogous scenes of political conflict, demagoguery and mass violence. It was for us to encourage this empathy.

Without ever deliberately exploiting the historic parallels, there were certain emotional patterns arising from political events of the immediate past that we were eager to evoke—Hitler, Mussolini and Ciano meeting at the Brenner Pass, Molotov and Ribbentrop signing the Pact and other similar smiling conference-table friendships that soon ripened into violence and death; also, memories of Hitler at Nuremberg and of Mussolini on his balcony addressing that same docile mob that later watched him hung up by his feet outside a gas station. These sights are as much a part of our contemporary consciousness—in the black and white of newsreel and TV screens—as, to Elizabethan audiences, must have been the personal and political conflicts and tragedies of such political figures as Essex, Leicester and the Cecils.

Having decided, from the start, not to clothe our actors in modern dress, it was all the more essential that our costumes and backgrounds be totally credible. Our costumes, while authentically Republican-Roman in style, had to be simple and functional. Formal or informal, civilian or military, we would try to give the impression, at all times, that our actors were wearing the clothes of their various occupations—not characters wearing costumes.

The same rules would govern the design of our settings. They would be solid and architectural; large or small, public or intimate, they had to be at the same time credible and dramatically affective. Our main setting—the Roman forum with the "pulpit" and the long, steep flight of steps leading up to the pillared porch of the Capitol where the tyrant is murdered, would have the line and scope of great stage design. For years we had all been admiring Appia's and Gordon Craig's magnificent theatrical conceptions while regretfully realizing that, noble as they may look on a drawing board or in an album, their proportions could never be satisfactorily contained within the restricted frame of even the largest of our modern proscenium arches. In this filmed *Julius Caesar,* we hoped, to some extent, to realize these designs. Through the magic power of lens and microphone, registering every syllable and every facial expression no matter how whispered the voice or how intimate the secret thought, the actors and their conflicts would never be dwarfed, even within settings of great size and scope. Rather, they should profit from our set's heroic size and their own changing and controlled dramatic relation to it.

In sharp contrast to the official magnificence of the Capitol was the sweaty congestion of our Roman slums. Here, as in the later military scenes, it was action we were after, not spectacle. Always, it was dramatic effect we were striving for rather than archeological realism. (How pleased we were the afternoon Vittorio De Sica came onto our set and, walking along one of our dark and crooked streets, asked if we hadn't copied it from an existing alley in present-day provincial Ferrara rather than from imperial Rome!)

There was another challenge of which we were aware, but of which, no matter how carefully we planned, little could be learned until we got into production: the proper visual and acoustical treatment of Shakespearean dialogue on the screen.

In one respect we were fortunate; the action of *Julius Caesar* is swift, concentrated, intense. Thus, we were spared some of the grievous problems that beset the filmmaker who undertakes a *Hamlet,* a *Macbeth* or a *Lear.* The cinematic treatment of the soliloquies in *Julius Caesar* presented no hazard—for there are none. The words of Cassius as he watches Brutus's retreating figure and plans his next move to enmesh him, and of Brutus in his orchard at dawn awaiting the coming of the conspirators and reluctantly conceding the necessity for Caesar's murder, were not treated as soliloquies (with sound track riding over a frozen close-up or the camera wandering across irrelevant scenery), but as highly charged dramatic scenes.

The basic problem, of course, was how to transfer the dramatic action of a great playwright whose primary instrument of communication is the spoken word, to a medium in which the auditory is habitually subordinate to the visual. Beyond that, there was the problem of fixing in a permanent print, for projection before diverse audiences separated by time and place, words intended to be spoken directly by living actors to living audiences whose daily mood the actors could gauge and whose measure they could take at each performance. Transferred through camera and microphone to a flat, rigid screen, Shakespeare's words would have to resound through the surrounding darkness with an impact and a meaning no less immediate and intimate than they had in the resonant "Wooden O" of the Elizabethan playhouse for which they were intended.

No matter how carefully and cautiously we rehearsed, with camera and sound crews present, a new hazard faced us when we came to shooting. The layman is probably not aware of the extent to which Hollywood studios have come to rely on voice tracks corrected and put together long after the actual shooting is over. Does a boom squeak or a dolly-track rumble, an arc-light hum or the natural-gas flame in a fireplace hiss? Does distant traffic or a plane overhead or the whir of a ventilator on the next stage throw a faint but pervasive rumble under your most intimate scene? Does an actor fluff a line in a long speech, or mar an otherwise thrilling reading with some slight verbal error? Rather than retake the scene, it is cheaper and more convenient to correct the voice track in the sound department by an ingenious system known as "looping," whereby the actor, standing before a microphone in a dark room, matches a new voice track, phrase by phrase, to his original image. For routine action with realistic dialogue this system usually works: after careful technical treatment the match between new voice and old image is sufficiently close for an audience not to be aware of the correction.

For the classic dialogue of *Julius Caesar* it soon became apparent that such corrective measures could not be counted on. The dramatic curves were too long, the tension too high, the speeches too carefully phrased and plotted for them to be splintered into arbitrary fragments. Technically, the proper dramatic delivery of iambic pentameter requires of an actor, in his breathing and in his thinking, a rhythm and a flow that cannot be checked or suspended at the whim of a sound engineer. The necessity to secure a perfect and final voice track *on the set* during shooting, added several days to our schedule. Precious hours were consumed while rails were adjusted, uneven stage floors leveled, and microphones maneuvered into the ideal, rather than the easiest position. These precautions paid off. In the picture as released, there are less than a dozen lines of "looped" dialogue. Every speech is clear and firm, we hope, with the quality of its original delivery.

Despite all our planning and precaution it was inevitable, in making such a picture, that new problems, visual and aural, should have been encountered right through to the last phases of editing and preparing the film for release. We discovered, for instance, that a Shakespearean scene, no matter how conventionally shot, is not subject to the normal laws of film cutting. With the intuitive skill of a sensitive editor watching film running through his moviola, Jack Dunning soon discovered that a Shakespearean scene had certain editing rules of its own, differing from those of other movies.

The reaction-shot, for instance, which has long been the basis of dramatic cutting in both silent and talking pictures, becomes a tricky thing to use in editing Shakespearean dialogue. Silent reactions, even when carefully planned by the director to fall in predetermined places during a long speech, were rarely used by our editor, who developed a strong reluctance—born not of veneration for the classics but of sound cutting instinct—to interrupt the line and cadence of a speech in the mouth of one character by cutting away to the reaction of another. It struck him as arbitrary and false. And he was right. The film, as he worked on it, seemed to develop its own proper cutting rhythm and form. The result was no less sharp or dramatic than regular film editing—only different.

Special problems arose for Robert Shirley, our chief sound-mixer, when he came to make the final composite sound track for *Julius Caesar*—perspective, volume, coloration, the balance of voice and sound and music, to mention only a few. Time after time, the conventions of realistic voice recording and mixing, as generally practiced in dramatic pictures, had to give way to a more sustained and lyric treatment. The Forum scene, with its acoustical and dramatic problem of a single human voice fighting and riding the roar of a great mob while constantly changing not only its volume but also its relation and perspective to the crowd below it, took days of trial and error and tentative combinations of tracks at various levels, before it finally jelled.

The place of music in a work of this nature, and the general and particular decisions we made as to the use or omission of scored music under sustained dramatic speech—were the result of debates that I cannot reproduce here. Suffice it to say that here, again, we planned and worked with one dominant artistic aim, and that everything else was subordinated to its fulfillment: to bring to our audiences, by the best means at our disposal, in their full energy, beauty and sustained emotional impact, the *words* of Shakespeare's *Julius Caesar.*

CASTING

There are various ways of casting a classic drama, depending on circumstances and on the theatrical fashion of the time. Henry Irving, quoted by his grandson, explained his own position on *Julius Caesar* frankly and sensibly. He confessed that he would like to play Brutus. "That," he said, "is the part for the Actor, for it needs acting. But the Actor-Manager's part is Antony. And when the Actor and Actor-Manager conflict in a play . . . I think it's wiser to leave it alone." And leave it alone he did, as did Garrick and Kemble and Kean before him. Booth played Brutus often, consenting in his later years to share billing with Barrett as Cassius. Beerbohm Tree, on occasion, made a bravura piece of Antony's oration; Gielgud, at the height of his fame, played Cassius in repertory at Stratford. All of which indicates that this is not a one-man show like *Hamlet* or *Macbeth,* nor even a two-man show like *Othello. Julius Caesar,* in performance, is as great as the sum of its parts.

Casting, therefore, became our first and most pressing care, once the decision had been made to bring Shakespeare's great political melodrama to the screen. Unencumbered by tradition, commitments or financial problems, we were free to recruit our company from among the best available players of the English-speaking world. And in this very freedom there lay a hazard.

On August 8, 1952, our principals assembled around a long table in the vastness of MGM's soundstage 25, in Culver City, for a first reading of the play. Having brought them together from Britain, from Broadway and from Hollywood, from theaters and soundstages, from among actors with classic backgrounds and actors whose achievements had been mainly in the realistic mode, we now had exactly three weeks of rehearsal (this, in itself an unprecedented luxury in movie-making) in which to turn this aggregation of distinguished players into an acting company. To meet this challenge and to aid us in achieving a unity of style in our production, without reducing the variety or the vitality of the individual performances, we had two substantial allies in our midst.

Joe Mankiewicz is a director known for his intelligent and subtle handling of dramatic dialogue in films. The freshness of his approach to Shakespeare's tragedy, his sure sense of the dynamics of a movie scene and his insistence, at all times, that every resource of motion-picture technique be employed to enhance the clarity and energy of Shakespeare's dramatic text—these, in themselves, proved a strong, unifying force.

To John Gielgud, too, our debt was incalculable. Of Gielgud as a theater star, a critic wrote recently, "You always have the impression that he not only tolerates his colleagues but inspires them." To this latter quality our entire company of *Julius Caesar* can bear witness. He contributed to our production not only his great qualities as a classic actor; he gave us a constant example of that dedication and virtuosity that have made him the world's most brilliant speaker of Elizabethan theatrical verse. From Mason and Brando to the last of our citizens and spear-carriers, the whole cast gained confidence and spirit from Gielgud's presence. He, in turn, working under Mankiewicz with such experienced film actors as Mason, Calhern, O'Brien, Garson and Kerr, soon gained, for the first time in his career, the habit of playing to the camera, without loss of force or color, in a voice no longer projected into the resonant distance of an auditorium but adjusted to the mechanical proximity of camera and microphone.

Out of such exchanges and collaborations and such diverse elements fused together in the heat of work, the unity of our film was achieved. Too often, under our prevalent methods of film production, personality is confused with performance. I like to think that we avoided this error and that the characters whom Shakespeare took over from Plutarch and fired with his own genius before he sent them out on the wooden platforms of the Elizabethan stage, found on our MGM soundstages a new, individual and tragic reality within the frame of our twentieth-century movie screen.

James Mason's Brutus is the hero of our tragedy, the man whose decisions concern us most deeply and whose fate fills us with pity. It is for him, in Hollywood parlance, that you should be rooting. Brutus is said to be "noble." Nobility and honor are the goal and the essence of his life; they are his strength and his undoing. I have seen Brutus played as a ponderous prig with all the outward show of smug self-righteousness and solemn virtue. I had seen him played by Welles with a rigid, remote nobility—huge and powerful and sad, with the blindness and clumsiness that are the tragic accompaniment of a consistent moral superiority. As Mason plays him, he is less an "antique Roman" and more of a modern man whose nobility lies not in grandiose sentiment but in the sincerity of his thinking and living. A man of reason in a world of violence, he makes us think of that tragic figure of our times, the liberal man, torn between his principles and the need to vindicate them with bloodshed, if that is necessary. Brutus is Shakespeare's first draft for Hamlet. Like Hamlet, it is his virtues, as well as his faults, that destroy him.

It is not until late in the play, in the great tent-scenes at Sardis, that we become fully aware of the human depths that lie behind the traditional "lean and hungry" mask of Cassius. As Gielgud plays him, this is no common conspirator; the soul that is "envenomed with his spleen" is that of a man who "reads much," of a "great observer who looks through the deeds of men"—including his own. The frayed nerves that whipsaw him between self-pitying tears and idle boasting never distort his practical judgment. Herein lies the fatal irony of his relationship with Brutus. In every disagreement between them (i.e., the permission granted Antony to speak in the Forum and the strategy at Philippi that leads to certain defeat and death) Brutus's mistaken notions are hotly disputed by Cassius, whose boast that he is "a better soldier, older in practice, abler" than Brutus "to make decisions" is tragically justified by events. Yet, each time, he gives in under the irresistible pressure of Brutus's moral superiority. For Cassius is a man who hates himself no less than he does Caesar; the fever of destruction burns hottest in his own body; he is the first and surest victim of his own discontent.

Mark Antony as he appears in this play (but not in another of Shakespeare's plays and not in history) is the very antithesis of these two. Shakespeare reveals him always in action, never in thought. He is shrewd, ruthless, energetic and ambitious. He loves Caesar, but he loves him better dead than alive. His loyalty is to Caesar's corpse; he leaves Caesar, living, to the tender mercies of the conspirators within the Capitol while he passes the time of day with Trebonius in the Gallery. His triumph in the Forum is for himself, not for Caesar. He cannot wait to sit on Caesar's throne.

Marlon Brando as Antony was generally regarded as our most controversial piece of casting. It never seemed so to me. There were skeptics who suggested that "Friends, Romans, Countrymen," might become "Kowalski Variations on a Theme by Shakespeare." We never had a moment's doubt. Brilliance and power are the outstanding qualities of Caesar's favorite cavalry leader. Of all the young actors in America Brando has these qualities in fullest measure; he also possesses a powerful voice and speech on whose training he has worked long and hard. His Antony is younger than history makes him, but he is the proper age for running foot-races on the Lupercal and appearing clear-eyed at breakfast after a long night's revel.

In Antony's famed "eloquence" lies the greatest obstacle to making him live as a character within the play. His oration over Caesar's body is taken almost verbatim from Plutarch; it is not a recitation but a scene of dramatic action—a passionate dialogue between two protagonists—Antony and the Mob. A man on a flight of steps facing a huge and murderous crowd does not address them in the manner of a baritone taking center stage to render a familiar and difficult aria. He works on them as best he can, using every trick he knows to sway them—alternately cajoling, threatening, bribing, flattering, shaming and yelling them into subjection. The dramatic test of Antony's oration is the extent to which you believe in its efficacy. For twelve and a half minutes the Roman mob in the Forum and the spectator, in the darkness of the theater, should become one.

Casca is a real horror of a man: ward-heeler and gossip-monger, coward and hatchet-man. Edmond O'Brien plays him with grim relish. But it is in the performance of the man against whom Casca strikes the first blow—the tyrant himself—that we made some of our most exciting and rewarding discoveries. Too often Julius Caesar has been played as a noble but pompous figurehead. By going deeper into Shakespeare's text Calhern shows him to us as a great man, burned out with ruling and fighting and a long surfeit of power. His grandiloquence becomes tragic, for he is pontificating for no ears but his own and his wife's; his superstition is the last refuge of an aging man with the taste of fear in his mouth, who knows that death is waiting for him on the steps of the Capitol.

Having assembled such a disparate aggregation of talent and temperament we were prepared for trouble. There was none. Whatever the cause—the surprise and pleasure of speaking noble and well-rehearsed lines on a movie set,

Joe Mankiewicz's expert and sensitive direction, the pure excitement of the play itself—the agreeable truth is that we could not have had a happier or more dedicated company. When one of our actors was not on call for a day's shooting, the chances were that one might find him, on the set or on a broiling location, watching his colleagues play their scenes. When Brando finished his speech in the Forum, nine hundred extras applauded—and John Gielgud, who was not working that day, was leading them!

❖ Stratford, Connecticut (1956–1959)

By 1956 the state of classical theater in America had undergone drastic changes. The first of the new subsidized, professional, nonprofit "Festival" companies had been formed and opened by Tyrone Guthrie at Stratford, Ontario. The second was Joseph Papp's Shakespeare Theater in New York City. The third was the American Shakespeare Festival Theatre at Stratford, Connecticut, of which I was Artistic Director from 1956 to 1959.

The four articles that follow have one thing in common: each combines the functions of an artistic manifesto with those of a publicity release. They appeared, in successive years, in the Sunday drama section of The New York Times *and each celebrates the launching of a new Stratford Festival Season.*

These pieces reflect my changing moods: the nervous bravado of our first hazardous season; our reaction to success and our mounting self-confidence in our second and third years; finally, in our fourth year, my own growing, obsessive preoccu-

pation with the creation of a permanent American Classical Repertory company of which the Festival Theatre at Stratford would be the base.

Stratford '56 (The First Year)

IT WON'T BE LONG NOW. For more than a month we have been rehearsing in a hall on Broadway that recently witnessed the birth-pains of such musicals as *Most Happy Fella, New Faces* and *The Ziegfeld Follies.* Tomorrow we move to the banks of the Housatonic River where, for the next two weeks, we shall be holding our final rehearsals in our own theater and on our own stage. On June 26th we open the 1956 season of the American Shakespeare Festival Theatre in Stratford, Connecticut.

There, on successive nights, we shall present the massive and violent tragedy of *King John* and that most modern and tantalizing of Shakespeare's comedies, *Measure for Measure.* Five weeks later, from his improvised bed, Christopher Sly will look down on the familiar but ever fresh and lusty antics of *The Taming of the Shrew.*

For the production of three such widely different plays a new and flexible stage has been devised within the handsome existing structure of the Festival Theatre. Here we hope to combine the blunt immediacy of the Elizabethan platform stage with the visual variety that lies within the depth of a dramatically lighted proscenium arch. This is no unit set but a functional stage-form within which each production will be free to develop its own individual quality—its size and shape and color—and above all its own particular style, through which it can most clearly and eloquently communicate its message to a contemporary American audience.

Similar considerations guided us in the formation of our acting company. We have not limited ourselves to specialized "Shakespearean" actors, nor can we boast of one single star of the high-powered, mass-publicized class. Instead, we have worked hard to recruit a company from among the best and most vital elements in the contemporary American theater. Within the range of these three so varied plays we hope they will find a wide and rewarding scope for those same qualities of energy, variety and professional skill for which American audiences have admired them over the years in the leading parts of such assorted theatrical successes as *Cat on a Hot Tin Roof, Chalk Garden, Bus Stop, King Lear, John Loves Mary, Death of a Salesman, Skylark, Awake and Sing, Candida* and *The Garrick Gaieties.*

We have been rehearsing two plays at once and for many of us this is a new and stimulating experience. Even this does not entirely explain the air of concentrated dedication with which the work of preparation goes on. These are skilled and experienced professionals preparing for a demanding project. Yet there is more to it than that. Without being in the least solemn about it, there is among us the unspoken but inescapable realization that, in preparing this Festival season, we have assumed a particular responsibility and must meet a rather special challenge.

In England, with its long and honorable classical tradition, unbroken since the Restoration, the production of a season of Shakespeare's plays may be regarded as a normal, proper and vaguely patriotic procedure. For us this is not so. For many years America's professional production of Shakespeare has been fitful and irregular—an altruistic and capricious operation, existing outside the mainstream of the American theater. Only recently has there appeared a revived and rising enthusiasm together with a rapidly growing audience for the works of William Shakespeare. In popular editions the sale of his plays has reached astronomical circulation. All over the United States Shakespeare festivals are springing up—Ashland, Oregon; San Diego, California; Yellow Springs, Ohio, to mention only a few. Even in New York City, that almost impregnable stronghold of the naturalistic and speculative theater, there may be observed a growing appetite for and an ever-increasing preoccupation with Shakespeare's plays.

This general surge of enthusiasm is more than a passing fancy. It is a significant manifestation of certain strong and irresistible tendencies in our contemporary theater. For some years now, among actors as well as playwrights, directors as well as critics, there has been a growing impatience with the limitations of the naturalistic theater, a general desire for a freer, more fluid and more lyric communication between stage and auditorium, between the theatrical creation and its audience. In none of the great dramatic periods of the past have these virtues been so clearly marked as in the Elizabethan theater—above all, in the works of William Shakspeare. A season of his plays, if it is to justify its existence, cannot fail to contribute, on both sides of the footlights, to the development of that richer and more dynamic kind of theater, the desire for which seems to hang so clearly in the American air. It is our hope that in some small measure the American Shakespeare Festival at Stratford, Connecticut, may be part of this evolution.

Indeed, this is one of several reasons which prompted us to open our season with two of Shakespeare's least known plays, *King John* and *Measure for Measure.* It is a cultural characteristic of our time that we tend to repeat certain accepted masterpieces at the expense of the main body of the artist's work. This was not always so. *King John* was for many years in the repertory of the great actor-managers; Edmund Kean played it, so did the Kembles, MacCready, Booth the elder and Tree. And the part of Constance was judged by Sarah Siddons to be the greatest of all Shakespeare's women's roles.

As to *Measure for Measure,* always a controversial piece, it has recently and for obvious reasons found great and special favor in the English theater. Charles Laughton, Flora Robson and Roger Livesey played in it at the Old Vic in the middle-thirties; more recently the two Stratfords (Warwickshire and Ontario) have presented it in very different forms.

Though neither play belongs in the list of Shakespeare's most finished masterpieces, both *King John* and *Measure for Measure* are filled with their own variety of theatrical excitement; and their very unfamiliarity gives them a special virtue in our eyes. Unfettered by tradition and free from precedent, actors can work on them and audiences can view them with fresh eyes and clear minds, almost as they would a new play opening on Broadway tonight.

For the greatest enjoyment of such unfamiliar works, should members of the audience read the play before they see it? My first reaction is to say Yes. Shakespeare's work is crammed with riches and there is no question that the spectator who knows the play will, at performance, perceive subtleties of language and details of action which cannot be appreciated by one who is encountering it for the first time. However, in this very richness lies a trap. Shakespeare's plays are not suitable for hurried reading (it is not until after several readings that you begin to perceive what *Lear* is really about and *Coriolanus* is virtually impenetrable at the first three attempts). Add to this the inevitable strangeness, for the casual reader, of the Elizabethan form and language—and, on second thought, my advice would be No! Don't try to read the plays first. Come to Stratford of a fine summer evening, sit in our beautiful theater beside the Housatonic and let the impact of a theatrical performance prepared for your pleasure and excitement do its work. The closer your emotions come to those of the audiences which, in Shakespeare's day, had themselves ferried across the Thames and paid their entrance fees at the Rose, the Swan or the Globe, the happier you and we will be! After that—go home and read the text at leisure. Probably, like most members of the audience, you will have your own views about what should have been done with the plays. If you do, come a second time and check your findings. We shall be most happy to see you.

Stratford '57 (The Second Year)

EXACTLY ONE YEAR AGO in these columns, with a bold front and deep inner trepidation, I tried to describe the hopes and fears, the opportunities and the inhibitions facing the American Shakespeare Festival Theatre. Now, as our 1957 season gets under way, I avail myself of this same hospitality to reaffirm some earlier hopes and to indicate certain new anxieties attendant upon the continued operation of an American classical acting company. If that seems a presumptuous name for our organization, may I point out, with pardonable pride, that by this summer's end (including our winter season at the Phoenix in New York City), the core of our company will have worked and played together in no less than seven major classical productions that have afforded consecutive employment for eleven out of the past fifteen months. Under prevailing American theatrical conditions, this is an unusual achievement—one that gives us added confidence as we embark on our new festival season.

In several ways our situation has changed since last year—mostly for the better. First—materially. We opened in June 1956 amid profound public apathy, with an advance sale that was not merely small but, quite literally, nil. We played our previews to half-empty houses, and in spite of a generous press and generally favorable word of mouth, it was not until our fourth week that we began to do substantial business. From then on, till Labor Day, we enjoyed good houses during the week and capacity on weekends. Some of these gains appear to have stuck. We are opening our 1957 season with an advance sale which, while it certainly doesn't spell S.R.O., goes far toward ensuring us good audiences all season long and toward protecting our repertory from the hazards of critical preferences. Artistically, our present season differs considerably from that of 1956. Last summer, with recklessness born of dire necessity, we opened our festival season with two of the Bard's least known and most consistently "unpopular" plays: *King John* and *Measure for Measure*. (That *Measure* turned out to be a huge success, first in Stratford and later in New York, surprised no one more than it did ourselves.) Not till mid-season did we present the tried and familiar *Taming of the Shrew*. This year we go to the other extreme. *Much Ado About Nothing* will open early in August, but before that we shall already have presented two of Shakespeare's great, accepted masterpieces. *Othello* is, deservedly, one of the most frequently and successfully performed of Shakespeare's tragedies. As for *The Merchant of Venice,* in a questionnaire which we submitted to our last summer's audiences (and which also included the titles of *Romeo and Juliet, Macbeth* and *A Midsummer Night's Dream*) *The Merchant* surprisingly received 40 percent more votes than its nearest competitor.

With the selection of these three plays there has followed, almost inevitably, our next deviation from last year's practice—the incorporation of "stars" in our festival company. Let it not be supposed that this decision was taken lightly. We think of ourselves as a permanent company and we are proud of our young troupe and of its first year's achievements; we are also well aware of the disruptive effects that might result from the temporary addition of powerful outside elements to a company still in its formative stages. After careful consideration we decided that the incorporation of Katharine Hepburn and Alfred Drake into the festival company this summer would be of clear and mutual advantage. To the company it offers an exciting association with two professionally outstanding actors of acknowledged skill and distinction; and to those stars it offers the opportunity—unique in this country—of playing great and taxing roles in collaboration with the regular members of an organized and cohesive classical troupe; Drake's Iago to Earle Hyman's Othello; Miss Hepburn's Portia to Morris Carnovsky's Shylock. For Miss Hepburn, classical repertory is no novelty; she toured Australia with the Old Vic in 1955 with a repertory that included *The Merchant of Venice*, playing the same role she will play with us.

It is worth noting that both she and Drake made it a condition of their coming to Stratford this summer that they would each appear in two plays, in repertory. Here, if further proof were needed, is a welcome confirmation of our own strong and constant belief that our main (if not our only) hope for survival and growth as an acting company lies in our continued and firm adherence to the practice of repertory.

In Stratford this presents no particular problem other than the rigors and expense of opening three large Shakespearean productions within a period of five weeks under standard Broadway commercial conditions. Repertory is regular procedure at most theatrical festivals—on the theory that persons making the pilgrimage (in some cases, a long one) to the site of the festival should have the opportunity to enjoy the greatest possible number and variety of plays within the short span of their visit. In Stratford-on-Avon, by August, this amounts to no less than five; in Stratford, Ontario, three; in our own theater in Stratford, Connecticut, we are arranging our schedule in such a way that, during the last six weekends of our season, three plays may be seen in the course of any two days.

The effect of this rapid and constant rotation is vastly stimulating to audiences no less than to actors. Seven years ago, when the American Shakespeare Festival was no more than a twinkle in Lawrence Langner's eye and Louis Calhern was pounding his heroic way through eight

weekly performances of *King Lear,* I asked Sir John Gielgud how he could possibly have played Lear at Stratford-
on-Avon at the same time as he was performing Cassius,
Benedick and Angelo. He replied that he had played Lear
on an average of twice a week and that, far from being a
distraction or a strain, the multiplicity of parts had helped
him not only to conserve his energy but also to enrich his
performances.

Assuming, then, that the virtues of repertory are fairly
generally recognized during the Festival season, what
happens next? It is when summer is over and we find ourselves hopefully facing the hazards of a year-round operation that the maintenance of a repertory policy presents a
truly vexing and frightening problem. It is one thing for
the Old Vic Company with an old and honorable name
(and a government subsidy) to present its accumulated
repertory for a limited season in New York and a handful
of major American cities. It is quite another for a native
American company to survive the commercial hazards of
repertory, to achieve stature and build a roster of plays
and players fit to compare with that of its foreign competitors. If you believe, as we do, that only through the continuing disciplines and satisfactions of repertory can a
strong and resourceful acting company be formed and
held together, then you must also face the harsh fact that
repertory conflicts with most current American theatergoing habits and runs directly counter to almost every apparent tendency in American show business.

Nevertheless we continue to dream of an American
classical acting company and we are obstinately convinced that repertory, in one form or another, is one of its
essential conditions. We have no illusions about the difficult nature of the road ahead and we suspect that we may
have to change our course several times before we attain
our fully developed and effectively functioning form. Two
things we do realize as we prepare to open our second season: without our Stratford Theatre as a permanent base,

this dream of an American classical theater would not exist at all; without our Festival stage as an artistic workshop and our Festival audiences as an inspiration, our company could never have reached even its present stage of growth.

Stratford '58 (The Third Year)

TIME WAS, not so long ago, when summer was regarded as a long, idle siesta during which the performing arts snoozed happily in the sun and stored up their energy for the agitations of the season to come. Air-conditioning, population shifts, new leisure habits and, above all, drastic developments in transportation have changed all that. Today, all over the world, summertime is Festival time. In parks, arenas, bowls, tents and specially constructed and reconstructed edifices from Reykjavik to Avignon and Spoleto, from Ashland, Oregon, to Kingston, Jamaica, the public is flocking to music festivals, jazz festivals, art festivals, film festivals and theater festivals of various sorts and sizes.

At the least these activities are accompanied by a rise in local employment and tourist activity. At their best, they mark a rebirth of the kind of enjoyment and excitement that has been steadily and regrettably disappearing from the contemporary metropolitan theatrical scene, where entertainment is normally presented in worn and shabby surroundings following theatrical habits that were stale two generations ago. It is worth noting, moreover, that the most consistently successful of these festivals have been those that presented "classical" rather than "popular" entertainment and that the most widely attended theater festivals in the English-speaking world today are those three Stratfords which are exclusively devoted to performing the dramatic works of William Shakespeare—in repertory.

How has this come about? What does a festival offer that is lacking in the average metropolitan entertainment? First, there is an atmosphere—a spaciousness and leisure that are in welcome contrast to the cramped and depressing condition of most of our city playhouses. From their natural and pleasing surroundings these performances seem to take on a color and a panoply that harks back to the happiest days of our theater, when it was a real and vital part of the cultural life of the country—not just of one section of one city. In those days the theater traveled the length and breadth of America; today, America travels to the festivals.

This sense of pilgrimage gives festival-going special direction and purpose. The festival audience makes an effort; it plans its day or its weekend around its performances and this restores some of that individual and collective excitement and anticipation that was once a natural part of theatergoing. The audience, many of them "repeaters," knows what it has traveled to see; it comes much better prepared than when it attends a Broadway production, of which it usually knows little more than whether it is a "hit" or a "flop." Often a visit to a festival becomes a family affair at which children see their first play and many adults their first classic, and this sharing of an artistic experience undoubtedly contributes to the audience's pleasure.

These are a few of the obvious reasons for the growing popularity of the festival habit. But there is one further respect in which the Shakespeare festival marks a significant development in the American theater. For years there has been much talk and some agreement that our theater, if it is to survive at all in its unequal competition with the giants of the Mass Media, must find a means of achieving a measure of artistic and economic continuity. No such theatrical continuity seems possible if it is not built upon the rich and solid foundations of a classical repertory. To date, the festival has proved the most viable format for the achievement of these two long-cherished aims.

The Festival Theatre at Stratford, Connecticut, was conceived, built and staffed in pursuit of a dream that has come closer to realization in a shorter time than there was any reason to expect. On the solid foundation of a twelve- to fifteen-week festival, we shall, with the opening of this season, have produced eleven full-scale Shakespearean productions that have been seen by almost half a million people; we shall have given a company of thirty-five actors (not counting students, apprentices, and technicians) continuous theatrical employment for no less than *twenty out of twenty-seven months.* Of our present Festival Company, all but seven are regular members who have been with us for one or more of our previous seasons.

This achievement has been made possible by two things—first the firm basis offered by the nature of the Festival itself; second, and no less important, by our use of and adherence to the principle of *Repertory*—which we have taken to mean the production of a continuous and alternating cycle of plays performed by a stable company of actors, accustomed to working together in a wide variety of roles. To open three major productions within a period of five weeks presents not only an artistic but also a logistical challenge. We have found it worth the effort— not only for what it has done for us in the way of forging a company, but also for what we feel it has done in building and consolidating our audience.

There is something in the passion it takes to mount such a repertory that quickly communicates itself to the front of the house. Audiences sense the shared creativity; their imaginations are stimulated by seeing the same artists appear in not just one but a number of great roles. The continuity of such an institution is like a ready-made memory to thousands who have seen play after play, year after year. And the satisfaction that the audience derives from this continuing diversity is more than matched backstage. From the rawest apprentice to the veteran of three seasons there is a constantly renewed sense of participation in a rich and varied experience for which the "neurotic ordeal" of Broadway has no equivalent. The fact is that each of Shakespeare's plays reflects on every other; and just as an audience gets a special kind of pleasure from seeing three of his plays within two days, so our actors, working on these plays, are enormously enriched by the interplay between them.

Beyond this, there is one very concrete reason why Repertory (a word which still strikes terror in the stoutest Broadway heart) has proved to be our strongest weapon in the challenging task of keeping both audience and company together. No play I know of—not even an Elizabethan play—offers enough great parts to satisfy a company of thirty ambitious and energetic actors. Repertory takes care of this. (*Item:* Morris Carnovsky played three small parts in 1956; Shylock and old Leonato in 1957; King Claudius and the low comedy role of Quince in 1958. *Item:* Last summer John Colicos played an eight-line part in *Othello,* Gratiano in *The Merchant of Venice* and replaced Carnovsky in *Much Ado About Nothing.* On our winter tour he replaced Alfred Dake and played Benedick to Katharine Hepburn's Beatrice. This summer he plays Laertes in *Hamlet,* one of the young lovers in the *Dream* and the jealous monarch Leontes in *Winter's Tale. Item:* Richard Easton's roles with us include two Claudios, young Gobbo, Roderigo, Osric, Florizel and Puck. *Item:* Earle Hyman played Othello last year; this year he does Horatio and Autolycus. *Item:* In 1956 Hiram Sherman played a penitent murderer in *King John* and an impenitent pimp in *Measure for Measure;* in 1957 he was absent; in 1958 he is playing Polonius, bully Bottom and the Old Shepherd in *Winter's Tale. Item:* Richard Waring played Cassio, Antonio and Don John last year; this year—Fortinbras,

Oberon and Polixenes. *Item:* Fritz Weaver played Casca in 1955; Faulconbridge and Gremio in 1956; he was absent last season; this summer he is Hamlet.)

Weaver is one of the nineteen actors, seven actresses, twenty apprentices, two directors, one choreographer, four stage managers, two lighting experts with their aides, two designers, five costume-makers, one wardrobe mistress, two composers, one countertenor and one conductor (complete with harpsichord) who, this week, have augmented the population of Stratford, Connecticut, in preparation for the 1958 season of the American Shakespeare Festival Theatre.

Stratford '59 (The Fourth Year)

THE AMERICAN THEATER has energy and talent; it has material and human resources that make its future rich with promise. Yet it continues to suffer from an open wound that has been draining its vitality and endangering its life for more than a quarter of a century—a total absence of continuity in its economic, artistic and human affairs. Not only is this undermining many of our theater's best talents; it has also decimated our audiences, as the habit of regular theatergoing for pleasure has given way to the enervated thoughtless hit-chasing pattern of current show business.

That many of our most devoted and talented workers in the theater are concerned with this problem is proved by the numerous actors' groups that have sprung up in recent years and sought to find in studio and scene work an active but limited substitute for the missing continuity of performance—limited because from all such activity one essential theatrical element, the audience, is inevitably absent.

How can we deal with this depressing situation before the damage to our theater becomes irreparable? To date, no more propitious and hopeful conditions have been found in which to reestablish habits of theatrical continuity on both sides of the footlights than those of a repertory company planted and nurtured in Festival soil. Our experience with the American Shakespeare Festival Theatre offers eloquent proof of this.

This summer at Stratford, Connecticut, the Festival Theatre is presenting a repertory of four plays to audiences which (including the preseason School Program) are expected to total more than two hundred thousand. For the last six weeks of our 1959 season, our schedule has been so arranged that anyone spending the night in Stratford may see three of these four productions: *A Midsummer Night's Dream, Romeo and Juliet, The Merry Wives of Windsor, All's Well That Ends Well.* Such a repertory is rare in the American theater; it puts on every member of the Festival organization—actors, directors, stage crew, technical staff, musicians, maintenance men, business and box-office personnel—a burden of work that goes far beyond the call of normal theatrical duty.

On the production level, each of our four plays (three new and one—*Midsummer Night's Dream*—a repetition of last season's outstanding success) requires exactly the same amount of acting, technical and musical rehearsal as a full-scale Broadway production. Yet some of these dramatic and technical rehearsals must be held during weeks in which five evening and three matinee performances are being presented to the public. Under our repertory schedule, none of our plays is ever presented twice in succession. That means that each day our stage manager and crew (not to mention wardrobe, wig-makers and other technicians), after working the current show, must take it down, store it and prepare and check the scenery, light cues, props, costumes, wigs and musical scores for the next. On matinee days they must do it twice! At the same time, besides rehearsing our new productions (sometimes two at one time) directors and actors must keep a vigilant eye on the quality of the running performance. This involves constant rehearsals—plus understudy rehearsals to the full limit permitted by the Equity repertory contract.

On the other side of the footlights, our box office handles a volume of business equal to that of the biggest Broadway hit—but with this difference: under our repertory system, it is not handling *one* ticket but *four,* subdivided into season tickets, theater parties, student rates, phone reservations and all the other special accommodations that a growing festival must offer its clients. Why do they do it? Why do they beat their brains out in this relentless grind that lasts the full length of a festival season that now runs for close to twenty weeks?

To reply that most theater people are crazy is an ungracious and inadequate acknowledgment of their passionate and devoted service. Nor is it enough to point out that the Festival offers its members, in all departments, a continuity of employment and involvement (from show to show and from year to year) that is unheard of in the commercial theater. This is an important element in Festival morale; so is the obvious fact that no other form of theatrical endeavor offers its creative elements such consistently rewarding challenges and opportunities as classical repertory.

Eloquent as they are, these considerations still supply only part of the answer. The other, and not the least significant, may be observed at any evening or matinee performance, during the season, in and around the American Shakespeare Festival Theatre at Stratford, Connecticut. It is the Festival audience.

Here lies the great incentive and satisfaction of the Festival operation. Here something is being created in the present and for the future that has no equivalent in the tense, competitive atmosphere of the Broadway theater. What most impresses new visitors to Stratford—besides the beauty of the grounds and the theater and, we hope, the particular quality of the Festival performances—is the extraordinarily warm and direct communication that has sprung up between the stage and the auditorium, the public and the plays. There, so pervasive and palpable that there is no escaping it, is a feeling of shared excitement and pleasure, derived from the performance and enjoyment of some of the world's greatest plays. There is something deeply thrilling in being part of a theater through which pass more than ten thousand people a week, most of whom have come from considerable distances and many of whom have become regular patrons, repeating the visit from play to play and from season to season. For many of them, this is a rare opportunity to enjoy living theater in agreeable surroundings; for many more, it is the discovery of the deep, rich satisfaction to be derived from the works of the world's greatest playwright. This it is that justifies our backbreaking toil and gives us the incentive for the further efforts which the future developments of the Festival operation entail.

There is something in the passion it takes to mount such a festival that quickly communicates itself to the front of the house and vice-versa. Audiences sense the labor, and the shared satisfaction which the audience derives from this diversity is more than matched backstage. From the rawest apprentice to the veteran of four seasons there is a constantly renewed sense of participation in a rich and varied event, for which the "neurotic ordeal" of Broadway has no equivalent. Each of Shakespeare's plays reflects on every other; and just as a spectator gets a special kind of pleasure from seeing four of his plays within three days, so we, in organizing, producing and mounting these plays, are enormously enriched by the interplay between them and the audiences that are enjoying our repertory in ever-increasing numbers.

POSTSCRIPT:

There was no fifth season.

For all my sanguine statements, satisfying reviews and

the best attendance so far, the summer of 1959 was marked by a steady deterioration of my relations with my Board of Trustees. Three weeks before the end of the Festival season, following a particularly stormy meeting with the Board, it became clear to me that my dream of a year-round Festival Company would never be realized.

Late in August I resigned. According to *The New York Times,*

> The points of disagreements include the continued failure of the Board of Trustees to provide the necessary organization and working funds to extend the activities of the Festival Company on a year-round basis with national scope.

The American Shakespeare Festival folded some years ago. For my part, it took me a dozen years to achieve, in a modified form, what I had hoped to accomplish at Stratford. THE ACTING COMPANY was created in 1972 as the country's only permanent touring classical repertory company. Its formation coincided with the national acceptance of institutional theater and the need for actor training and ensemble playing in the American theater.

In fifteen years The Acting Company has performed a total of fifty-nine plays for audiences of close to two million people in two hundred and ninety-five American cities—not counting a six-week tour of Australia in 1979 and a month's engagement at London's Old Vic Theatre in the summer of 1985.

This year The Acting Company will enter upon a new phase of its development when it assumes occupancy of its own theater in New York City.

BOOK TWO

HOLLYWOOD

Raymond Chandler

❀ Lost Fortnight: The Blue Dahlia

In the spring of 1944, on my return to Hollywood after two years with the Office of War Information's Voice of America, I found myself working with Raymond Chandler at the Paramount Studio in Hollywood, "polishing" a routine minor mystery movie entitled The Unseen. *Our second collaboration was on* The Blue Dahlia—*a film starring Alan Ladd, Bill Bendix and Veronica Lake with a screenplay by Raymond Chandler based on his own unfinished novel. Years later, in* Harper's *magazine, I recalled the unusual circumstances of our collaboration.*

> *Just don't get too complicated, Eddie.*
> *When a guy gets complicated he's un-*
> *happy. And when he's unhappy—*
> *his luck runs out. . . .*
> — *Raymond Chandler,*
> The Blue Dahlia

Previously published in *Harper's* magazine, June 1965.

RAYMOND CHANDLER was fifty-seven when he risked his life for me. By then most of his books had been written—some of them twice; first, long ago, for a pittance from the pulps; then, again, when they were combined and expanded ("cannibalized" as he called it) for publication as hardbacks and, later, as paperbacks. His creative days were almost over, but his great success was just beginning; royalties were coming in now, followed by movie sales. For the first time in many years—since he ceased to work as an executive for a Los Angeles oil company—Chandler and his wife were able to enjoy such modest Southern California comforts as they desired.

Ray appeared at the Paramount Studio in Hollywood soon after I got there; he came at the invitation of Joe Sistrom to work with Billy Wilder on dialogue and to supply the Los Angeles atmosphere for a movie called *Double Indemnity,* which (as played by Edward G. Robinson, Barbara Stanwyck and Fred MacMurray) made a lot of money and received an Academy nomination. By then two of his books had already been made into films (*Farewell, My Lovely* and *The Big Sleep*) but Ray had not been invited to work on the screenplays. He grumbled about that—as he did about a number of things that happened to him in Hollywood. Sometimes he did more than grumble.

I hardly knew Ray when he issued his first ultimatum to the studio. Typed on a long sheet of yellow paper, it listed the numerous indignities which he claimed he was suffering at the hands of his collaborator and demanded their instant redress. I remember two of his grievances. *Item:* Mr. Wilder was at no time to swish under Mr. Chandler's nose or to point in his direction the thin, leather-handled malacca cane which Mr. Wilder was in the habit of waving around while they worked. *Item:* Mr. Wilder was not to give Mr. Chandler orders of an arbitrary or personal nature, such as "Ray, will you open that window?" or "Ray, will you shut that door, please?"

Apparently his demands were met, for he stayed on to finish Wilder's script. It was during this time that our friendship began, based on the surprising premise that he and I alone, of all those currently employed at Paramount, were British Public School men—and, consequently, Gentlemen. It lasted till his death in 1959. It is not always easy to remember that Chandler, whose literary territory was bounded by Malibu on the west, Long Beach on the south and San Bernardino on the east, and whose writing gave the world some of its most ruthless documentation on the seamier aspects of Southern California society in the twenties and thirties of this century, had spent most of his adolescence in England and had been educated in the classics at Dulwich. When he appeared in my office at lunchtime, seeking relief from the pressures of the glib and forceful men with whom he was working, I think he was hoping to recapture with me, for a few moments, some of the sounds and memories of his boyhood.

It was one of the basic inhibitions of that Public School system that you did not ask questions about your companion's past; consequently, I never got to know much about Chandler's life. There was a story around the Studio that he had once been an executive in an oil company and that later he had earned his living for a time stringing tennis rackets; there was also a rumor that he had, for many years, been an alcoholic. This was easy to believe, for the first impression Ray gave was one of extreme frailty; it was not till later that you discovered the peculiar strength that lay beneath his ashy, burnt-out look and his querulous hypochondria.

In life he was too inhibited to be cheerful; too emotional to be witty. And the English Public School system that he loved had left its sexually devastating mark upon him. The presence of young women—secretaries and extras around the lot—disturbed and excited him. His voice was normally muted; it was in a husky whisper that he uttered those juvenile obscenities at which he would have been the first to take offense if they had been spoken by others.

Soon after he had finished *Double Indemnity* Ray came to work with me on what was to be my first film. Charles Brackett had just produced a successful ghost story called *The Uninvited;* what more natural than that the Studio should change the title of the banal thriller I was preparing to *The Unseen?* It was felt that the script needed added strength; who was more qualified to toughen a script than Ray Chandler? At a thousand dollars a week, Ray was agreeable. The fact that neither of us was under any delusion as to the merit of the project on which we were engaged helped to make the seven or eight weeks of our association relaxed and pleasant.

After that "polish job" was over we continued to see each other occasionally. We dined together several times during the summer, and one Sunday afternoon Ray drove the monumental, gray-green vintage Packard convertible of which he was so proud up the steep dirt road that ran around the edge of the hill between King's and Queen's roads, high above Ciro's and the Hollywood Strip. From my terrace, to the right, we could see the Pacific and Catalina; far off to the left, still visible above the smog, the pyramidal tower of City Hall; directly below, the long thin line of La Cienega (before it became the Fifty-seventh Street of the West) stretching directly ahead till it got lost among the oil wells of Baldwin Hills—all Chandler territory.

With him on these visits—with him, in fact, wherever he went, except to the Studio, was his wife, "Cissie." In Hollywood, where the selection of wives was frequently confused with the casting of motion pictures, Cissie was an anomaly and a phenomenon. Ray's life had been hard; he looked ten years older than his age. His wife looked twenty years older than he did and dressed thirty years younger. Later, after she had died, "not by inches but by half-inches," Ray wrote to me of their "thirty years, ten months and four days of as happy a marriage as any man could expect."

He was writing then from the loneliness of his big house overlooking the sea in La Jolla, where he and Cissie had hoped to retire. The letter ended:

> Before I stop talking about myself—I don't really want to, but a lonely man does it too much, I know—I do like to remember what I worked on for you. We once wrote a picture called *The Blue Dahlia*, remember? It may not have been the best but at least we tried. And the circumstances *were* a bit difficult . . .

It was early in 1945, not long after Buddy deSylva's stormy resignation, that the front office of the Paramount Studio came to the horrifying realization that Alan Ladd, Paramount's top star (at that time the highest-rated male performer in the U.S.) would be reentering the Army in three months' time, leaving behind him not one single foot of film for the company to release in his absence. At our next producers' meeting we were given to understand that anyone coming up with an Alan Ladd vehicle ready to go into immediate production would earn the undying gratitude of the Studio and of Mr. Balaban, its chief stockholder.

Two days later Ray Chandler, lunching with me at Lucey's Restaurant across the street from the Studio, complained of being stuck on the new book he was writing and muttered that he was seriously thinking of turning it into a screenplay for sale to the movies. After lunch, we went to his house—a small, Spanish-style stucco bungalow west of Fairfax, where Cissie was lying in a cloud of pink tarlatan with a broken leg—and I read the first hundred and twenty typed pages of his book. Forty-eight hours later Paramount had bought *The Blue Dahlia* for a substantial sum and Ray Chandler was at work on a screenplay for Alan Ladd. I was to produce it, under the supervision of Joseph Sistrom, a lively second-generation Hollywood movie man who, with his pink cheeks and his stiff, black golliwog hair, looked like a schoolboy of fourteen.

In those lush days, it usually took about a year and a half to turn out an A picture. The average writing time for an adaptation was around five months; for an original, rather more. After that, there was a period of gestation to allow everybody to criticize and tamper with the script; this created the need for revisions which took another three months. Then came the casting. And while we had not yet reached the fantastic level of titanic negotiations that came later (as the business began to fall apart) it often took three or four months to find the right actors for a picture. Finally, a director having been chosen and having almost certainly demanded rewrites which might take another eight to fifteen weeks, production would start.

Raymond Chandler delivered the first half of his script—about forty-five minutes of film—in less than three weeks, at the rate of four or five pages a day. This was no miracle; the scenes and the dialogue were already written, with transitions which Ray carried directly into the screenplay. After the first seventy pages had been mimeographed, a shooting date was set—three weeks away. Everyone was overjoyed and busy taking credit.

Our director was one of the big maestros of Hollywood—George Marshall, who had been in movies since their earliest days, first as an actor, then as a director. He had never become one of the giants, but he held a solid and honorable position in the industry. His most famous picture was *Destry Rides Again,* which, according to him, he had practically created on the set. This and similar successes resulted in a state of mind (which he shared with many of his colleagues at the time) in which the director showed absolutely no respect for the script and made it a point of prestige, justifying his high salary, to rewrite it as he went along. It took a lot of earnest talk from me (though, since I was a beginner, George didn't pay much attention) and from Joe Sistrom to convince George Marshall that *The Blue Dahlia* was an inspired script which he was forbidden to rewrite or improvise on the set.

Casting presented no serious problem. The leading part, as written by Chandler for Alan Ladd, was perfectly suited to the special qualities of that surprising star, who had played a part, so small that I barely remembered it, in *Citizen Kane* and had continued to work as a stagehand, between jobs, until the lucky day on which he appeared in *This Gun for Hire,* playing a professional killer with a poignant and desolating ferocity that made him unique, for a time, among the male heroes of his day.

As a star, Ladd had some say in the choice of the persons with whom he worked. Since he himself was extremely short, he had only one standard by which he judged his fellow players: their height. Meeting another actor for the first time, if his glance hit him or her anywhere below the collarbone, Ladd was sure to explain as soon as we were alone that he didn't think he or she was exactly right for the part and would we please find someone else.

Veronica Lake was the perfect size for him, but we had trouble over the part of his dissolute wife, in which I had cast a beautiful, dark-haired girl named Doris Dowling. Since she was a full half-foot taller than Ladd, he made a determined attempt to get rid of her; we placated him in their scenes together by keeping her sitting or lying down. Also in the cast were William Bendix and a troupe of those lowlife types with whom motion pictures, and now television, have always been so plentifully populated.

Shooting of *The Blue Dahlia* went well from the start. By the end of our first week we were a day and a half ahead of schedule. In the next fortnight we gained another day. It was not until the middle of our fourth week that a faint chill of alarm invaded the studio when the script girl pointed out that the camera was rapidly gaining on the script. We had shot sixty-two pages in four weeks; Chandler, during that time, had turned in only twenty-two—with another thirty to go.

Ray's problem with the script (as with the book) was a simple one: he had no ending. On page 83 of his shooting script he had reached the following impasse: Ladd's wife (all five-foot-seven of her) had been found shot—in a position that suggested, but clearly was not, suicide. Our hero was suspected (by the police, but not by anyone else) of having knocked her off in a rage on discovering the kind of life she had led during his absence in the South Pacific. Of the members of his bomber crew, with whom he had returned from the war, one was a dull and devoted friend; the other (Bill Bendix), who had a large silver plate in his head and convenient moments of total aberration, was under very serious suspicion which he was doing everything possible to aggravate. Obviously, he was innocent. There was a villain, lover of the hero's wife; as the main suspect he, too, was clearly above suspicion. There was also the villain's estranged wife (Veronica Lake), who had picked up our hero, at night, on the Pacific Highway; but since she had immediately fallen in love with him and he with her (in a nice way) it was quite clear that the murder couldn't possibly be her work. Other characters and suspects included a professional killer, a number of petty crooks, two blackmailers, an ambulance chaser, a house detective, a bartender and a night watchman, each of whom could very plausibly, with one or two added close-ups and a few planted lines, assume responsibility for the shooting.

Still, I was not worried. Ray had written such stories for years and I was quite confident that sooner or later (probably later since he seemed to enjoy the suspense) he would wind up the proceedings with an "artistic" revelation (it was his word) and a caustic last line. But as the days went by and the camera went on chewing its way through the script and still no ending arrived, signs of tension began to appear. Joe Sistrom, who shared my faith in Ray but who was being tortured by the front office, called a couple of meetings in his quarters on the ground floor of the main Paramount office block, with its Elizabethan timbering and casement windows, to discuss the situation and to review our various suspects. And it was during one of the meetings, early one afternoon, that a man came running down the studio street, stopping at the various windows to shout something we could not hear to the people inside. When he reached us, he shoved his head in and told us that President Roosevelt was dead.

I remember that we sat stunned for a while. One by one, we said all the obvious things: how ill he had looked, already, in the photographs from Yalta; how reckless it had been of him to take that ride in the pouring rain through the New York streets; how he had looked and sounded on that morning of his first inauguration almost exactly twelve years before—all the things that everyone was saying, in that moment, all over the world and would continue to say in the days and the years to come. Finally we fell silent and sat there gloomily for a while. Then, gradually, we drifted back to our story conference; half an hour later, we were deep in the intricacies of *The Blue Dahlia,* looking for the least likely suspect and trying to decide on whom it would be most satisfying to pin the murder. We went through all the tired alternatives, using them to smother the realities of the world outside, and Ray sat listening, only half there, nodding his head, saying little.

Two days later I was sitting in my office when my secretary hurried in to say that Mr. Chandler was outside and was asking to see me. I was not used to this formality and there was something strange about the way she said it. When Ray came in, he was deadly pale and his hands were trembling. She made him a cup of coffee and, piece by piece, I heard his story: Late the night before, Ray's agent had called him to say that Paramount's head of production would like to see him, privately, in his office, at nine-thirty the next morning. Ray spent a sleepless night; he was a timorous man and his agitation was increased by the admonition that he should, under no circumstances, mention the appointment to me.

When he appeared in the paneled executive office with the English hunting prints and the cream wall-to-wall carpet, Ray was told that the future of Paramount would be seriously imperiled if the rest of *The Blue Dahlia* script was not delivered on time. If it *was*—such would be the Studio's gratitude and appreciation that a check for five thousand dollars would be exchanged, there and then, for the final page of script.

It was the front-office calculation, I suppose, that by dangling this fresh carrot before Chandler's nose they were executing a brilliant and cunning maneuver. They did not know their man. They succeeded, instead, in disturbing him in three distinct and separate ways: *One,* his faith in himself was destroyed. By never letting Ray share my apprehensions, I had convinced him of my confidence in his ability to finish the script on time. This sense of security was now hopelessly shattered. *Two,* he had been insulted. To Ray, the bonus was nothing but a bribe. To be offered a large additional sum of money for the completion of an assignment for which he had already contracted and which he had every intention of fulfilling was by his standards a degradation and a dishonor. *Three,* by going to him behind my back they had invited him to betray a friend and fellow Public School man. The way the interview had been conducted ("sneakily") filled Ray with humiliation and rage.

These accumulated grievances had reduced Ray to a state of nervous despair, the depth of which it took me some time to realize. Finally, when he assured me that his creative mechanism had been wrecked and that he had no choice but to withdraw from a project to which he had nothing more to contribute, I found myself believing him.

After he had gone—to lie down and, later, to discuss the matter with Cissie—I tried to evaluate my situation. The latest word from the soundstage was that we would complete page 93 before night. That left us with seven pages of unshot script plus an estimated twelve more pages still to be written. And in ten days' time Alan Ladd would vanish beyond hope of recovery into the U.S. Army—forever. The front office called in the afternoon over the executive intercom and I ignored the call. Soon after that, word came from the soundstage that almost seemed like good news. During a scene of mayhem, one of our heavies had let a massive oak tabletop fall upon and break another heavy's toe. But when we reached the set, George Marshall told us not to worry; he had found a way for the injured heavy to play the rest of his scene from the floor. He also asked where the rest of the pages were.

The next morning, true to his promise, Chandler appeared in my office, looking less distraught but grimmer than the day before. He said that after a sleepless and tormented night he had come to the unalterable conclusion that he was incapable of finishing *The Blue Dahlia* script on time—or ever. This declaration was followed by a silence of several minutes during which we gazed at each other, more in sorrow than in anger. Then, having finished his coffee and carefully put down his cup on the floor, Ray spoke again—softly and seriously. After some prefatory remarks about our common background and the esteem and affection in which he held me, he made the following astonishing proposal: I was certainly aware (or had heard it rumored) that he had for some years been a serious drinker—to the point where he had gravely endangered his health. By an intense effort of will he had managed to overcome his addiction. This abstinence, he explained, had been all the more difficult to sustain, since alcohol gave him an energy and a self-assurance as a writer that he could achieve in no other way. This brought us to the crux of the matter; having repeated that he was unable and unwilling to continue working on *The Blue Dahlia* at the Studio, sober, Ray assured me of his complete confidence in his ability to finish it, at home—*drunk*.

He did not minimize the hazards: he pointed out that his plan, if adopted, would call for deep faith on my part and supreme courage on his, since he would in effect be completing the script at the risk of his life. (It wasn't the drinking that was dangerous, he explained, since he had a doctor who gave him such massive injections of glucose that he could last for weeks with no solid food at all. It was the sobering up that was parlous; the terrible strain of his return to normal living.) That was why Cissie had so long and so bitterly opposed his proposed scheme, till Ray had finally convinced her that honor came before safety, and that his honor was deeply engaged, through me, in *The Blue Dahlia*.

My first reaction was one of pure panic. Such is my own insecurity that contact with a human brain that is even slightly out of control frightens, repels and finally enrages me. On that ground alone I was horrified by Ray's proposal. I also knew that if I was mad enough to take this risk, it would have to be entirely on my own responsibility and without the Studio's knowledge. At this point Ray produced a sheet of yellow foolscap paper (of the same format as that on which he had drawn up Billy Wilder's ultimatum) and showed me the list of his basic logistical requirements:

A. Two Cadillac limousines, to stand day and night outside the house with drivers available for:
   1. Fetching the doctor (Ray's or Cissie's or both)
   2. Taking script pages to and from the Studio
   3. Driving the maid to market
   4. Contingencies and emergencies
B. *Six* secretaries - in three relays of two each - to be in constant attendance and readiness, available at

all times for dictation, typing and other possible emergencies.

C. A direct line open at all times to my office by day, to the Studio switchboard at night and to my home at all times.

I took the paper from him and asked him for an hour to think it over. With great courtesy and understanding, Ray agreed. For half an hour I walked the studio streets. I visited the set, where George infomed me, not without satisfaction, that he'd be out of script by evening of the following day. I went to Sistrom's office by the back way. I showed him Ray's demands and told him I had decided to take the risk. Joe approved. He said if the picture closed down we'd all be fired anyway.

I thanked him and went back down the hall to my office where Ray was sitting, reading *Variety*. With all the Public School fervor and esprit de corps I could dredge up from the memory of my ten years at Clifton, I accepted his proposal.

Ray now became extremely happy and exhilarated. It was almost noon, and he suggested, as proof of my faith in him and of my confidence in the efficacy of our scheme, that we drive to the most expensive restaurant in Los Angeles and tie one on together immediately. We left the Studio in Ray's open Packard and drove to Perino's where I watched him down three double martinis before eating a large and carefully selected lunch, followed by three double stingers. I then drove the Packard, with Ray in it, back to his house, where the two Cadillacs were already in position and the first relay of secretaries at their posts.

Early next morning when I drove past his house on the way to the Studio, I found the limousines in place and shining in the sun. The drivers had been changed: so, inside the house, had the secretaries. Ray lay, passed out, on the sofa in his living room. On the table beside him was a tall, half-filled highball glass of bourbon and water; beside

it were three typed pages of script, neatly corrected—
Ray's work of the night. As one of the black limousines
rushed me back to the Studio, I learned, without undue
surprise, that the murderer of Doris Dowling was, in fact,
Newell, the house detective. At some time in the night
Ray had given him a death scene:

NEWELL:

Cheap, huh? Sure—a cigar and a drink and a cou-
ple of dirty bucks—that's all it takes to buy me!
That what *she* thought—
  (*His voice suddenly grows hard and savage*)
Found out a little different, didn't she? Maybe I
could get tired of being pushed around by cops—
and hotel managers—and ritzy dames in bunga-
lows. Maybe I could cost a little something. Just for
once—even if I do end up on a slab.
  (*He jerks a gun out of his pocket*)
Anybody want to go along with me? It's nice cool
country. No offers, huh?
  (*To Lloyd*)
All right, you! Get out of my way.

LLOYD:

Sure—anything you say.
  (*He puts his hand on the knob of the door.*
  There is the sound of a gunshot.
  Newell staggers.)

NEWELL:

  (*As he starts to collapse—keeping himself upright by*
an effort)
Just a minute, gentlemen—you got me—all—
wrong . . .
  (*As he falls—*)
DISSOLVE

I was on the soundstage when a boy on a bicycle arrived
with the mimeographed pages, still damp from the ma-

chine. George Marshall read them, found them acceptable and set about shooting them. (I think George had looked forward to saving the day by improvising the last week's work on the set and that he was disappointed and perhaps a little hurt that we preferred the work of a man in an advanced stage of alcoholism to his own. But he behaved admirably. So did everyone else.) The film was finished with six days to spare and Alan Ladd went off to the Army and Paramount made a heap of money.

During those last eight days of shooting Chandler did not draw one sober breath, nor did one speck of solid food pass his lips. He was polite and cheerful when I appeared and his doctor came twice a day to give him intravenous injections. The rest of the time, except when he was asleep, with his black cat by his side, Ray was never without a glass in his hand. He did not drink much. Having reached the euphoria he needed, he continued to consume just enough bourbon and water to maintain himself in that condition. He worked about a third of the time. Between eight and ten every evening he sat in Cissie's room and they listened together to the Gas Company's program of classical music on the radio. The rest of the day and night were spent in a light sleep from which he woke in full possession of his faculties and picked up exactly where he had stopped with whichever of the rotating secretaries happened to be with him. He continued until he felt himself growing drowsy again, then dropped back comfortably into sleep while the girl went into the next room, typed the pages, and left them on the table beside him to be reread and corrected when he woke up. As his last line of the script, Ray wrote in pencil: "Did somebody say something about a drink of bourbon?"—and that's how we shot it.

Ray had not exaggerated when he said he was risking his life for *The Blue Dahlia*. His long starvation had seriously weakened him and it took him almost a month to recover, during which his doctor came twice a day to administer mysterious and reviving shots which cost him a lot more than the "bonus" he was to receive. During his convalescence he lay neatly dressed in fresh pajamas under a silk robe; when I came to see him he would extend a white and trembling hand and acknowledge my gratitude with the modest smile of a gravely wounded hero who had shown courage far beyond the call of duty.

In the years that followed we talked and wrote a lot about doing another movie or a television show together. It never happened. We remained friends for thirteen years, even through a short period in which Ray pretended to be angry with me. I had written disparagingly, in *Vogue*'s annual "American" issue, of the current Bogartian hero and bracketed him with Chandler's Philip Marlowe whom (paraphrasing Ray's own words) I described as a drab, melancholy man of limited intelligence and mediocre aspiration, who is satisfied to work for ten bucks a day and who, between drinks, gets beaten up regularly and laid occasionally. Ray wrote me a sharp letter in which he said that my piece, though well written, was typical of the glib thinking and crummy values that made him detest Hollywood producers and all their works. In his opinion, Marlowe and his kind were the last honest men left in our society; they did their assigned jobs and took their wages; they were not acquisitive nor did they rise in the world by stepping on other people's faces; they would never try to take over the earth nor would they compensate for their own weakness by pushing other people around. Marlowe's was, in fact, the only attitude that a self-respecting, decent man could maintain in today's rapacious and brutal world.

I saw less of Ray after he went to live in La Jolla. And it was only in the last two years of his life, after Cissie was dead and Ray was commuting between La Jolla and London, that we once again began to exchange letters. It was in one of these that he wrote on a subject which, till

then, I had always found him reluctant to discuss—his life
as a writer:

> What should a man do with whatever talent God
> happened in an absent moment to give him?
> Should he be tough and make a lot of money like
> me? Of course, you don't get it just by being tough.
> You lay your neck on the block in every negotia-
> tion. And for some reason unknown to me I still
> have my head. A writer has nothing to trade with
> but his life. And that's pretty hard when other peo-
> ple depend on you. So how much do you concede? I
> don't know. I could write a best-seller, but I never
> have. There was always something I couldn't leave
> out or something I had to put in. I don't know
> why . . .

> I am not a dedicated writer. I am only dedicated as
> a person. . . . Most writers are frustrated bastards
> with unhappy domestic lives. I was happy for too
> long a time, perhaps. I never really thought of what
> I wrote as anything more than a fire for Cissie to
> warm her hands at. She didn't even much like what
> I wrote. She never understood, and most people
> don't, that to get money you have to master the
> world you live in, to a certain extent, and not be
> too frail to accept its standards. And, also, they
> never understood that you go through hell to get
> money and then you use it mostly for other people
> who can't take the punishment but nevertheless
> have needs.

At the end, as a sort of postscript, he added:

> I hope you know that I never thought of myself as
> important and never could. The word itself is even
> a bit distasteful. I have had a lot of fun with the
> American language; it has fascinating idioms, is

constantly creative, very much like the English of
Shakespeare's time; its slang and argot is wonderful, and so on. But I have lost Los Angeles. It is
no longer the place I knew so well and was almost
the first to put on paper. I have that feeling, not
very unusual, that I helped create the town and
was then pushed out of it by the operators. I can
hardly find my way around any longer . . .

❧ *Today's Hero*

In 1947 I reviewed a film for the Hollywood Quarterly
that was based on a novel by Raymond Chandler—The Big
Sleep. *Later, under the title "Today's Hero," I expanded my
critique into an article for* Vogue, *which caught Chandler's
eye and caused the only brief rift in our long friendship.*

EVERY GENERATION has its myths—its own particular
dreams in which are reflected the preoccupations of its
waking hours. In years of high artistic activity these myths
become absorbed into the intellectual and emotional life
of their time. In a period of general anxiety and low cultural energy such as ours the dream reveals itself naked
and clear. Then we witness the fascinating and shocking
spectacle of a nation's most pressing fears and secret desires publicly exhibited in whatever art form happens, at
the moment, to be the most immediately accessible to the

Previously published in *The Hollywood Quarterly,* 1947.

largest mass of its people. Today, this art form is the Hollywood-made motion picture.

I have argued elsewhere against the notion that Hollywood enjoys any real free will in the choice of its subjects. The best it can do, in the general run of its product, is to reflect as honestly and competently as it can the interests and anxieties of its hundred million customers. That this reflection is at the moment a rather frightening one can hardly be blamed on the entertainment industry. The current "tough" movie is no lurid Hollywood invention; its pattern and its characteristics coincide too closely with other symptoms of our national life. A quick examination of our daily and weekly press proves quite conclusively, whether we like it or not, that the "tough" movie, currently projected on the seventeen thousand screens of this country, presents a fairly accurate reflection of the neurotic personality of the United States of America in the year 1947.

The current American Legend, like all such myths, assumes varying forms. It shifts, changes, and feeds upon itself, grows more outrageous and fanciful, until it finally bursts of its own absurdity. Since this might be happening any day now, I believe this is the proper time to analyze our "tough" movies at the moment of their fullest and ripest development. From among the motion-picture advertisements of any current big-city newspaper, a perfect specimen presents itself.

The Big Sleep is based on a not very recent detective story by Raymond Chandler. Its plot is complex—too complex to be understood by most of its audiences, and far too complex to be related here. In one essential respect the picture differs from the book. The latter is a narration, the unraveling of an elaborate tangle of interrelated events. The movie by its very nature is a *dramatization*. Thus its values are automatically changed. The book was cynical, hardboiled and quick-moving—a slick, atmospheric job of detective fiction written by Chandler with a

fine contempt for his characters and the sordid world they
inhabit. Marlowe, in the book, is an instrument of the
plot; the other characters are colorful signposts in a complicated maze. In the movie the approach is basically *romantic.* Marlowe is played by an important male star. He
makes love to a rising and very lovely female star. To millions of paying customers this spells Romance, and Marlowe and his exploits become the stuff of contemporary
American Legend.

Let us examine him then—today's Hero, this fellow
who follows Heathcliffe, Mr. Rochester, Buffalo Bill,
Horatio Alger and Little Caesar into the dreams of the
English-speaking world. He is not young; he is somewhere
in his middle thirties. He is unattached, uncared-for, and
irregularly shaved. His dress is slovenly. His home is a hall
bedroom and his place of business is a hole in the wall in a
rundown office building. He makes a meager living doing
perilous and unpleasant work that condemns him to a solitary life. The affection of women and the companionship
of men are denied him. He has no discernible ideal to sustain him—neither ambition nor loyalty nor even a lust for
wealth. His aim in life, the goal toward which he moves
and the hope that sustains him, is the unraveling of obscure crimes, the final solution of which affords him little
or no satisfaction. For this he receives twenty-five dollars a
day (plus expenses) and he certainly earns it. His missions
carry him into situations of extreme danger. He is subject
to terrible physical outrages, which he suffers with dreary
fortitude. He holds human life cheap, including his own.
The sum of his desires appears to be a skinful of whiskey,
an occasional fornication and a good sleep. In all history I
doubt there has been a hero whose life was so unenviable
and whose aspirations had so low a ceiling.

In the Heroine he has a worthy mate. She is by Arlen
out of Hemingway, a sister under the skin to Iris March
and Brett Ashley, who drifts through life in a hopeless,
smoldering kind of way. Some obscurely disgraceful event

in her past overshadows her present and inhibits her from intelligent behavior. Unlike her more vital sisters, who swept glamorously up and down the continent of Europe in Blue Trains and Hispanos, she sits moping discontentedly in her father's house. Her shady entanglements are not with members of the international fast set, but with an obscure and melancholy gangster operating in the San Fernando Valley. Like the Hero, she is utterly lacking in hope and ambition.

At certain intervals throughout the picture, Hero and Heroine are left alone together to conduct their joyless and ill-mannered courtship. When, in the end, they get together, one wonders whether they do so under some mysterious working of the laws of natural selection or whether their merging is simply due to the fact that everyone else in the movie is dead, in irons, or on the lam.

These, then, are our protagonists. Surrounding them is a whining herd of petty chiselers, perverts, halfwits and nymphomaniacs—poor, aimless creatures without brains, without skill, without character, without strength, without courage, without hope. Not only are they totally lacking in moral sense; they seem to have no sense of anything at all—except fear. From first to last they move through the story with one single desire—to be left alone. "We know we are no good," they seem to say, "we are sad, futile, foolish people. But our crimes are petty. We do not really hurt anybody much except ourselves and each other. After all, this is a free country. Let us be."

In one of the current "tough" pictures, technically one of the best, the Hero, finding himself spotted by his enemies, lies in bed waiting for them to come and finish him off under the blankets. And here, I think, is the key to the nature of the present American Legend. The howls of certain critics and ladies' organizations notwithstanding, it is *not* violence or spasmodic savagery that are the outstanding features of the "tough" movie. Violence is a basic element in American life and has always been an important component of American entertainment. What is significant and repugnant about our contemporary "tough" films is their absolute lack of moral energy, their listless, fatalistic despair. In this respect they are in direct contrast to the gangster film of the thirties, which was characterized by a very high vitality and a strong moral sense. The vitality may have been antisocial, the moral tone may have stemmed from a false morality bred of power-hunger, lust and greed, but at least the energy and the morality were always present; and so, consequently, was the tragic sense. The Hero (*Little Caesar, Scarface,* et al.), misguided, arrogant and brutal though he may have been, rose triumphant, by his own will, against fearful odds. When he finally fell, he did so with a sort of tragic grandeur, paying the price of his sin. The inevitable and deeply moral lesson of the gangster picture was: crime may be profitable, glamorous and lots of fun, but in the end you pay the price with your life! The moral of our present "tough" picture, if any can be discerned, is that life in the United States of America in the year 1947 is hardly worth living at all.

It is not by chance that so many of the successful pictures of our time, those which attract our highest professional talent and technical skill, are whodunits and thrillers in which the tension is entirely external and mechanical. The "tough" movie, generally speaking, is without personal drama and therefore without personal catharsis of any kind. It almost looks as if the American people, turning from the anxiety and shock of war, are afraid to face their personal problems and the painful dilemmas of their national life.

Chandler took sharp exception to my review and to a statement I had made in another piece about "the new American hero—a drab, melancholy zombie of limited intelligence and mediocre aspiration; a man who is satis-

fied to work for ten bucks a day and who, between drinks,
gets beaten up regularly and laid occasionally."

Ray found my piece "well written but artistically pa-
tronizing, intellectually dishonest and logically unsound."

> Marlowe's is the struggle of all fundamentally hon-
> est men to make a decent living in a corrupt so-
> ciety. It is an impossible struggle; he can't win. So
> he can be poor and bitter and take it out in wise-
> cracks and drinks and casual amours or he can be
> corrupt and amiable and rude like a Hollywood
> producer! The bitter fact is that there is absolutely
> no way for a man of this age to acquire a decent af-
> fluence in life without to some degree corrupting
> himself, without accepting the cold, clear fact that
> success is always and everywhere a racket . . . Mar-
> lowe is a more honorable man than you or I. Not
> because I created him. I didn't create him at all.
> I've seen dozens like him in all essentials except for
> a few colorful qualities he needed to be in a book.
> They were all poor; they will always be poor. How
> could they be anything else?
>
> When you have answered that question, you can
> call him a zombie.
>
> Love, Ray

His next letter to me was shorter and showed that he
did not bear a grudge:

> I may do a picture in the near future and would
> rather do it with you than with anyone else. Shall I
> hold off or don't you care?

❧ *"Too Personal"*

I'm afraid this letter may seem to you too per-
sonal. If so, forgive me. Sometimes I feel terribly
lonely.

THIS FINAL SENTENCE of a letter to a virtual stranger sup-
plies the key to much of the material included in this collection of letters written by Raymond Chandler during
the last twenty years of his life.

This is particularly true of the first part of this volume
which contains correspondence from the forties and early
fifties when Ray's wife Cissie was in her seventies and ailing and he himself had reached his mid-fifties. His life had
been uneven and hard. A hybrid, born in Chicago of an
American father and an English mother, he was educated
in England where he attempted a brief, unsuccessful literary career. After World War I, in which he served in com-
bat with the Canadian Army, he migrated with his
mother to California and made a meager living for some
years before achieving substantial success as an accountant and office manager for independent oil companies. It
was not until after he left his job for reasons that included
restlessness and alcoholism that, in desperation, he turned
once again to writing. He approached the task methodically and, before long, he had sold his first story to the
pulps—eighteen thousand words for $300. Soon he had

Letters of Raymond Chandler, edited by Frank McShane (Columbia University Press). Reviewed in the *Washington Post* Book World, 1981.

become a regular contributor to *Argosy* and *Black Mask.* These were, in fact, the most creative years of his life. Most of the books that later brought him fame and unexpected wealth—among them, *The Big Sleep* (1939), *Farewell, My Lovely* (1949), *The Long Goodbye* (1953)—were combinations, expansions and refinements of stories he had written years earlier for the pulps.

Further prosperity came when he began to work in films, but this added success did not seem to bring him satisfaction or peace. "I have been praised too much . . . I live a lonely life and have no hope of anything else from now on." The letters he wrote in those years are the ruminations of a man sitting alone in his study at night—some typed with aching hands (he suffered from an allergy that caused the tips of his fingers to crack and bleed) and some dictated onto discs for transcription by a secretary in the morning. In them this frail, irritable man gave expression to his dreams and resentments in letters that are more like a writer's notebook than ordinary correspondence. They are the soliloquies of a man fighting "that horrid blank feeling of not having anyone to talk to or listen to."

In contrast to the desperate, repetitive garrulity of the letters written years later after Cissie's death, these communications of Chandler's middle age are generally impersonal; they are addressed to a small number of professional recipients, almost all male: publishers, editors, agents and, occasionally, fellow writers. What passion they reveal is almost all literary; his most intimate autobiographical confessions are made in a letter to his tax lawyer in which—for the benefit of the Internal Revenue Service—he gives a frank and detailed account of the cannibalization of his early novellas into the books that made him rich and famous.

Throughout, there is a recurrent and almost obsessive preoccupation with his own position in the world of letters and with the status of the detective story as a literary genre. He has no illusions about the kind of writing he is practicing:

> For Christ's sake let's not talk about honest mysteries—they don't exist. The novel of detection little by little educates the public to its own weaknesses which it cannot possibly remove because they are inherent.

Yet he is remarkably eloquent in its defense: "When a book, any sort of book, reaches a certain intensity of artistic performance, it becomes literature. The intensity may be a matter of style, situation, character, emotional tone . . . It may also be perfection of control." And he finds a "peculiar kind of satisfaction in taking a type of literature which the pundits regard as below the salt and making it something which the fairminded among them are forced to treat with respect."

> The Detective Story (I prefer the term mystery story) is a completely integrated thing if it is any good; most novels are sloppy by comparison. It has the elements of tragedy without being tragic and the elements of heroism without being heroic. It is a dream-world which may be entered and left at will and it leaves no scars . . . It allows you to live dangerously without any real risk. If you have to have significance (the mark of a half-baked culture) it is just possible that the tensions of a novel of murder are the simplest yet the most complete pattern of the tensions in which we live in this generation.

Among the causes of Chandler's irritability was a growing awareness that he was being widely plagiarized and a constant concern with criticism, particularly from "the mob of snob-fakers" who, in his view, had misunderstood or underestimated his work and who showed a "constant haste to deprecate the mystery story as literature for fear the writer of the piece should be assumed to think it important writing."

In a letter to Erle Stanley Gardner in 1946, Chandler wrote, "The critics of today are tired Bostonians like Van Wyck Brooks or smart-alecks like [Clifton] Fadiman or honest men confused by the futility of their job, like Edmund Wilson." Wilson, who once classified him in a *New Yorker* piece as "sub-literary," is also variously described as "ill-natured and bad-tempereed," a "fat bore" and "a damp fart." Even W. H. Auden fared little better: "Here I am halfway through a Marlowe story and having a little fun (until I got stuck) and along comes this fellow Auden and tells me I am interested in writing serious studies of a criminal milieu."

He writes a fawning letter to Somerset Maugham (whose *Ashenden* he sincerely admired) and his references to Hammett are consistently friendly, but his estimates of his peers and competitors, most of whom he regards as "smooth and shallow operators," are generally caustic and ungenerous. "Very likely they write better mysteries than I do, but their works don't get up and walk. Mine do." Of Graham Greene's *The Heart of the Matter* he reports that "it has everything in it that makes literature except verve, wit, gusto, music and magic; a cool and elegant set-piece, embalmed by Whispering Glades."

His appraisal of his own writing is egotistical but realistic:

> I am not just a tough writer. I am tough only incidentally as a matter of projection. Substantially I am an original stylist with a very daring kind of imagination. . . . As a mystery writer I am a bit of an anomaly, since most mystery writers of the American school are only semi-literate and I am not only literate but intellectual . . . It would seem that a classical education might be a poor basis for writing novels in a hard-boiled vernacular. I hap-

pen to think otherwise . . . I had to learn American
like a foreign language; I had to study and analyze
it.

In fact, his most creative period was over before most of
these letters were written. By the fifties his energy was
flagging. "I write when I feel like it. I am always surprised
at how easy it seems at the time and by how tired I feel
afterwards." Indeed this problem of inertia and atrophy of
the inventive powers (coinciding with the progressive deterioration of his own and his wife's health) preoccupy
him increasingly with the years. The despair he often feels
is "no mood in which to produce writing with any lift and
vitality." In one letter he reports that his greatest problem
in life now is to do any work; in another, that the last doctor he saw told him he would probably die of exhaustion.

After Cissie's death in 1954, "by half-inches," a sudden
change occurs in Chandler's life and, even more, in his
letters. His first reaction to his loss was an attempted suicide followed by a nervous breakdown. Then, almost
overnight, this tired and sedentary man is transformed
into an eager, tireless traveler, shuttling between La Jolla
and London (about which he still had strangely ambivalent feelings). He reverts sporadically to his drinking and,
after years of ascetic fidelity, becomes an active and ardent ladies' man: "I have been married so long and so
happily that after the slow torture of my wife's death it
seemed, at first, treason to look at another woman, and
then suddenly I seemed to be in love with all women."

His correspondents were now mostly female; his letters
were addressed to: "Darling Jessica," "Darling Helga,"
and "Darling Deirdre." (Deirdre was a young Australian
girl whom he never met; Helga Greene, for whom he developed intense respect and affection, became his literary
agent and, later, his executrix and heir.)

The tone of these letters, written not long before his
death, is completely different from that of the earlier ones.

They are sentimental, frivolous, intimate and nostalgic—laced with yearning tributes to the dead wife-mother who was 17 years his senior and with whom he had lived "for 30 years, 10 months and four days":

> She was the light of my life, my whole ambition. Anything else I did was just the fire for her to warm her hands at ... It was my great and now useless regret that I never wrote anything really worth her attention, no book that I could dedicate to her.

Howard Koch

Howard Koch occupies a special place in my life. He and I have been collaborators and friends for close to fifty years, beginning in the fall of 1938 when he wrote his first radio scripts for the Mercury Theatre on the Air.

Since then we have worked together on a Broadway play, on a documentary film for the Office of War Information and on one of my favorite films—Letter from an Unknown Woman.

The following piece was written as a foreword to Howard Koch's Hollywood memoir, As Time Goes By. (Harcourt, Brace, Jovanovich, Inc. 1979.)

❊ *Candide in Hollywood*

ONE AFTERNOON, almost exactly forty years ago, I was sitting in the third-floor cupboard that was humorously known as the executive office of the Mercury Theatre at Forty-first Street and Broadway when the phone rang and the woman in the box office reported that there was a man on his way up to see me. It was a long and complicated climb to the second balcony and then up some more iron steps to what had once been the electrician's booth—a narrow, airless room with two large holes in the wall through which arc-lights had been aimed at the actors, singers and dancers whose performances had made the Comedy Theatre Broadway's most distinguished small musical theater. They served now as spy-holes through which, with growing anguish, I could observe the awful excavations that my partner, Orson Welles, was perpetrating in our expensive stage floor in preparation for Buechner's *Danton's Death*—the first offering of our second, disastrous Mercury repertory season.

When my visitor appeared he turned out to be a tall, spindly, hollow-eyed, rather shy young man. He was armed with a letter from one of our principal backers to whom he had been recommended by the wife of the Governor of New York State—Herbert Lehman. His name was Howard Koch; he was a struggling lawyer in Hartsdale, New York, who had decided to come to the city and attempt to make a living by writing for the theater. Could we help him in any way?

He was not a total stranger, as it happened. A play of his—*The Lonely Man*—had been done by the Federal Theatre of the W.P.A. in Chicago with a young, unknown actor named John Huston in the leading part. (Typically it concerned an idealistic, reincarnated young Lincoln and his tragic fate in the contemporary world.) I had read it and liked it. And in the forty minutes that we talked I found its author pleasant, well-informed, serious and literate. Since he was also destitute and desperate I judged him to be eminently eligible for employment by the Mercury.

In fact he could not have chosen a better time to climb those stairs. In the summer of 1938, following our first triumphal repertory season, Welles (who had become something of a radio star with *The Shadow* and the *March of Time* and the voice of Chocolate Pudding) was offered a radio show of his own on the Columbia Network, to be known as *First Person Singular,* which he would produce, direct, narrate and play the leading part in stories of his own choosing—preferably adventures. He asked me to work with him on the series as editor-writer and associate producer.

Our first show was a radio version of Bram Stoker's *Dracula,* which Welles and I scrambled and pasted together during one continuous seventeen-hour session held in Reuben's Restaurant (which boasted that it never closed) between the hours of 6 P.M. and noon of the following day. During the next two months we broadcast a show each week: these included adaptations of *A Tale of Two Cities, The 39 Steps,* short stories by Saki and Sherwood Anderson, *The Count of Monte Cristo,* Drinkwater's *Abraham Lincoln, The Affairs of Anatol, Julius Caesar* and *The Man Who Was Thursday.*

Due mostly to Orson's prodigious voice and charismatic radio presence the show became a success—so much so that the Columbia Network decided to continue it into the fall season with a further series of thirteen. Our name was changed to *The Mercury Theatre on the Air* and our time was moved to Sunday evening where we competed with Edgar Bergen and his dummy. This renewal coincided with our preparations for our second Mercury Theatre repertory season so that, between the theater and the radio show, Orson and I were working a minimum of twenty hours a day.

In desperation we decided to add two new figures to our staff: Paul Stewart came in as associate producer and remained in that position throughout the life of the show. And I engaged a writer in the person of Howard Koch. His starting salary was fifty dollars a week for which he was expected to turn out sixty or more pages of script plus the numerous alterations and rewrites demanded by Welles and myself. According to Koch we had "exacting standards" and considered sleep a luxury which we denied ourselves and our staff. To aid and guide him in this unfamiliar work I lent Howard my ash-blond secretary—an attractive, tireless "college-girl-of-all-work from Smith." He never returned her.

Koch's first assignment for the Mercury was an Arctic epic—about the ill-fated De Jong expedition to the North Pole, known as *Hell on Ice*. He did so well with this, followed by Booth Tarkington's *Seventeen*, *Jane Eyre* and *Oliver Twist*, that his stipend was raised to $65.00 and, later, to $75.00. In his fifth week he was ordered to make a radio show out of that well-known English classic *Lorna Doone*. For all his apparent mildness Howard has always been a man of firm opinions. He read it and objected that it was unalterably boring. Since neither Orson nor I had the faintest notion of what it was about we did not argue with him. In its place we decided the time had come for a touch of science fiction. We considered Shiel's *Purple Cloud*, then settled on H. G. Wells's Edwardian *War of the Worlds* which Koch was given six days to adapt.

The panic of October 30th, 1938, has been described from many angles by many people, including Koch and myself. At 9:05 P.M. we believed ourselves to be mass murderers; next day we were on the front page of every paper in the country but learned with relief that there had been no deaths—only one broken arm and several miscarriages. During the next few days we were grilled and ostracized amid rumors of expulsion from the network; the following week, as a direct result of our outrage, and on the theory that if we could sell a Martian invasion we could also sell tomato soup, we signed a contract with Campbell Soups, went "commercial" and became the Campbell Playhouse at a huge increase in emoluments. Koch benefited from this bonanza to the tune of an additional $50.00 a week. Three months later, as a result of his Martian script, he departed for Hollywood where his volume of memoirs begins.

There is something of Candide in Howard Koch; his experiences in Hollywood bring to mind the adventures of Voltaire's innocent in the land of El Dorado. Like him he finds himself—sincere, trusting and optimistic—moving in continuous wonder from one crisis to another. Unlike him, he emerges with flying colors; time after time success is thrust upon him. For his first assignment this modest, mild intellectural is ordered to fashion a vehicle for that swashbuckling "macho" Errol Flynn; he studies moral history, Elizabethan politics, the geography of the Spanish Main and comes up with *The Sea Hawk*—a winner! This is followed by a melodrama of tropical adultery— Maugham's *The Letter*—to which he finds it necessary to add an element of expiation. Another winner!

Next this earnest pacifist is set to writing a screenplay based on the lethal exploits of America's Number One Hero of World War I—a rednecked marksman by the name of Alvin York. Koch objects that he is the wrong man for the job; he is not interested in shooting—turkeys or Germans. The Studio is adamant. Koch perseveres. His pivotal scene becomes York's inner struggle to reconcile his religion with his patriotic duty. The commandment "Thou shalt not kill" was in direct conflict with his participation in an endeavor whose purpose was to kill. To dramatize this subjective process, we had York find his solution in Christ's words, "Render unto Caesar what is Caesar's and unto God what is God's." (Looking back after more than thirty years Koch observes somewhat wryly that "this solution worked well enough at the time and under the circumstances. But, appraising it from today's perspectives, it seems less convincing. If you render unto Caesars, past and present, what they demand of us, God comes out on the short end.") *Sergeant York,* as played by Gary Cooper, was the biggest box-office success of the year. Eighteen months later came *Casablanca* and, later still, our production of *Letter from an Unknown Woman.*

Unlike Candide's, Howard Koch's optimism seemed to be fully justified. Within five years this sincere, conscientious man had moved from being an indigent lawyer and a fifty-dollar-a-week literary drudge to recognition as one of the most successful and highly regarded screenwriters in the film business. He collaborated with such formidable Hollywood figures as Flynn, Cooper, Curtis, Huston, Bette Davis, William Wyler, Howard Hawks, Bogart, the Warner and Epstein brothers, Goldwyn and many others, and he came through these associations with his integrity untarnished and his pride intact. He would be needing both in the years ahead, for he was about to enter the dark period of the Hollywood Witch-hunts. Yet, even here, Koch's story takes on a strange and special turn. His experience with the film *Mission to Moscow* is a grotesque and horrifying example of the sort of thing that went on during that incredible and shameful era.

Weary from three years of uninterrupted scriptwriting, Howard had reluctantly declined this project when it was first offered him in the summer of 1942. The Warner brothers—Harry and Jack—begged and bludgeoned him into doing it; they assured him that he was uniquely qualified to undertake a patriotic project which, they informed him, was dear to the heart of the President of the United States. Five years later these same Warners denounced him as a Red to the inquisitors of the Un-American Activities Committee, citing his work on that pro-Russian film as evidence of his Communist sympathies.

Koch flew to Washington as one of the Hollywood Eighteen—nineteen, including Brecht—but he was not one of the Hollywood Ten. (There was a technical but significant difference there: membership in the Communist Party of America, which Howard had been too "lonely" and independent ever to have joined.) But his name had appeared on the letterhead of countless organizations, formed out of concern with the future of mankind, that were now suddenly pronounced subversive: organizations such as the Hollywood Writers' Mobilization (of which he was chairman and I vice-chairman), the Hollywood Independent Citizens' Committee for the Arts, Sciences and Professions (HICCASP) and, later, the California Arts, Sciences and Professions Council (A.S.P.). As a result he was known as a "sympathizer" and "fellow traveler" with the result that offers of work were still coming in but in diminishing numbers. His transition to the Blacklist occurred later, following an incident that is Voltairean in its tragic absurdity.

To escape the deteriorating political climate of Hollywood, Howard and Ann had moved to Palm Springs. On his departure he had resigned as chairman of the moribund Arts Council but agreed to let his name be used until a replacement could be found. In his absence the office was run by a zealous and foolish secretary. The Korean War was at its height; U.S. and South Korean troops under MacArthur were pushing the North Koreans back toward the Chinese border where the Chinese Army was massed ready to join the North Koreans. In a final effort to negotiate the conflict the Chinese flew a delegation to the United Nations in New York. Without Koch's knowledge or consent his "well-intentioned" secretary met the plane at the Los Angeles Airport and, in a gesture of good will, presented the head of the delegation with two dozen red roses—in Howard Koch's name! That night China entered the war and Howard was splashed over the front page of the *Los Angeles Times* as a Benedict Arnold who was giving aid and comfort to his country's enemies.

Deprived of his livelihood at home, he spent time in Europe, was ripped off by a fly-by-night producer in Rome and worked on some good pictures in England. By the time he was rehabilitated, the motion picture business had drastically changed; he was never able to regain the position he had occupied in Hollywood in the early forties.

Undefeated and undaunted he continues to work and, like Candide, to cultivate his Hudson Valley garden (located up the river from mine) in Woodstock, New York. Here he turns out books, film scripts and plays which, since they're about serious and controversial subjects, he has trouble getting produced. He retains his essential faith in the perfectability of man. In spite of much personal evidence to the contrary, he believes that "new people" are coming who will help to make this the best of all possible worlds.

I doubt if Howard Koch qualifies for sainthood but I know that he ranks high among the pure in heart.

Four Giants:
Hitchcock, Chaplin,
Griffith, Brecht

My acquaintance with these four giants, whose biographies I reviewed at various times, varied greatly. Hitchcock was a personal friend. I worked with him on the early stages of The Saboteur *when we were both under contract to David Selznick and we remained close for many years after that.*

Chaplin was a social acquaintance in Beverly Hills; I played tennis with him and attended his parties. I also got into serious trouble on his account during the Witch-hunts for asking him to play the theme song of Limelight *on a record about Hollywood I made in French for the Voice of America. As a result I was denounced as a "notorious red" by Senator McCarthy during one of his investigations of subversion in government.*

I met Griffith briefly while he was shooting his last disastrous film, The Struggle, *of which my first wife, Zita Johann, was the principal victim.*

My personal and professional contact with Brecht runs from 1935 to 1948.

❖ Hitch

NOT LONG AFTER Alfred Hitchcock's death in 1980 a letter was circulated among his friends and former associates
apprising them of a forthcoming biography in which certain intimate and forbidding aspects of his life were about
to be exposed. It was surmised that some of these revelations were being supplied by one or more aggrieved former employees, and these apprehensions were confirmed
by an appended publisher's "proposal" for the book in
which the author promised to deliver "dark and terrible
and grotesque and surprising revelations." In the circumstances we were all urged not to meet him or in any way to
collaborate with him.

That book—*The Dark Side of Genius*—has now been
published. It is the work of Donald Spoto, director of the
Film Studies Department of New York's New School for
Social Research, and it is, without doubt, the fullest and
most elaborately researched Hitchcock biography to date.
It is not quite the scandalous exposé that had been promised even though, in his anxiety to justify his title,
Mr. Spoto—particularly toward the end of his book—becomes increasingly concerned with the more shocking and
unattractive aspects of the great filmmaker's life and
work.

It is Mr. Spoto's thesis that Hitchcock, "as a macabre
joker, a frightened child and a tyrannical artist, lived in
the grip of fantasies so obsessive that his work can now be

The Dark Side of Genius: The Life of Alfred Hitchcock, by Donald Spoto
(Little, Brown & Co., 1983). Reviewed in the *Chicago Tribune* Book
World.

seen as astonishingly autobiographical." Beyond his meticulous expertise and his unique capacity for creating suspense,

> The unassailable genius of Alfred Hitchcock and the source of his enormous popularity can be explained by the fact that he drew so deeply from the human reservoirs of imagery and dreams and fear and longing that he achieved universal appeal. . . . In giving form to these fantasies he was exploring and exposing things not only in himself but also in others. . . . He expressed elusive images and half-remembered dreams in terms that moved and astounded and delighted and aroused awe for millions around the world.

In the more than five hundred pages of his book Mr. Spoto relentlessly pursues these fantasies and attempts to trace them to their source in the circumstances of his subject's life—the familiar facts of his lower-middle-class English origin and upbringing, his Catholic education and the sense of social and physical inferiority for which he compensated throughout his career. Yet, for all its abundance of significant and sometimes indiscreet detail, I am not sure how much *The Dark Side of Genius* really adds to our understanding of Alfred Hitchcock's life and work beyond what has already been established by his earlier biographers. (Among them must be included the French filmmaker Francois Truffaut, whose taped interviews with the master, for all their consistent attitude of respect and admiration, constitute the basic material for any serious consideration of his oeuvre. It was Truffaut who first pointed out that Hitchcock filmed scenes of murder as if they were love scenes and love scenes as if they were murders.)

A previous biographer, John Russell Taylor, in his semiauthorized book written in 1978, two years before Hitch's death, made the following telling analysis of the emotions underlying his work—to which the subject, to my knowledge, made no overt objection.

It is not for nothing that the pervasive theme of his work is anxiety: fear had been instilled by his strict father and his formidable mother, by his Jesuit teachers, by his own early experience of life. He likes to quote Sardou's recipe for drama, "Torture the heroine!" but despite this classic authority, the attitude toward sex in his films seems inspired by a fearful fascination with and an extreme nervousness before the unknown. His typical cinematic ill-treatment of his heroines has nothing to do with personal misogyny but a lot to do with devising a ritual to control the uncontrollable, a way of working out otherwise unmanageable impulses and emotions—not dislike of women but fear of himself, the good Catholic boy, in relation to women.

And he added his own interpretation of Hitch's lifelong predilection for frequently tasteless and often cruel practical jokes:

Anxiety is even at the bottom of his sense of humor. His practical jokes are a means of communicating and of fixing things in such a way that the deviser has the whip-hand, is always in control.

Except in style, this does not differ substantially from Mr. Spoto's postmortem version:

It was as though he could, by playing the prankster, prevent the eruption against himself of the terrible or the dehumanizing; his high-jinks could pawn off the dreadful on others and, by a kind of sympathetic magic, go scot-free.

In developing his somber scenario, Mr. Spoto has enjoyed the advantage of posthumous writing. Unlike his predecessors he has been able to follow Hitchcock's life and career through to his final, tragic decline. And he has made the most of it. The cutback in Hitchcock's production during these last years can be explained by his wife's and his own failing health, by his growing isolation and by the inevitable attrition of his creative energy. Mr. Spoto has chosen to focus on the emotional changes that followed the departure of Grace Kelly, the anguish of his subsequent rejections by Vera Miles and Audrey Hepburn (both of them had the disloyalty to get pregnant just as they were about to start a film with him), followed by his protracted and frustrated passion for Tippi Hedren, the heroine of *The Birds* and *Marnie*. "After that," according to Mr. Spoto's scenario, "something hardened in Hitchcock; something closed over his always limited capacity for warmth," and he attributes the decline and final sterility to "something inside him that changed everything—a sad and ultimately destructive passion pursued from behind a mask of love and motivated with increasing indiscretion. . . . He never recovered from this period. It seems forever to have killed something in him."

This psychological analysis is spiced with in-house and presumably authentic blow-by-blow accounts of the great filmmaker's repeated and embarrassing attempts to seduce his leading ladies, from which he emerges as an obese, pathetic and somewhat malignant Svengali.

Not everyone will agree with this melodramatic and simplified version of those final years and it is to the somewhat prurient tone of this part of the book that Hitchcock's friends will no doubt object. To trace the disintegration of genius is a tricky and ungrateful task. By concentrating on the more titillating and sinister aspects of Hitchcock's final years, Mr. Spoto tends to overlook other elements that were equally significant and corrosive. Chief among these was Hitchcock's lifelong and highly neurotic preoccupation with money, which found its culminating expression in his ambivalent relationship with his agent, employer and partner—the Music Corporation of America—under whose protection he had become a multimillionaire and whose head, Lew Wasserman, had become a second father-figure with all the attendant mingling of love and guilt, gratitude and resentment. Fear of displeasing him by failure to deliver his new film on time and the dread of being punished by the withdrawal of favors such as his prestigious bungalow suite at Universal Studios loomed no less "dark" toward the end than the anxieties of sexual frustration and had an equally destructive effect on Hitchcock's work.

The Dark Side of Genius ends up as a serious book—one that will be of interest to scholars and film buffs. Unfortunately Mr. Spoto is neither the first nor the last to explore the murk of Hitchcock's tragic last days. Some of his informants have branched out on their own: articles have already appeared in magazines and a book is promised on the subject. In his lifetime Hitch eschewed revelations about himself while encouraging a personality cult that fed his vanity and helped to promote his films. As long as he was around he was able to control and manipulate it. It was inevitable that, after his death, the vultures would gather.

❧ *Chaplin*

I REMEMBER A WINTER in the early fifties when three well-known writers were biting their nails around Beverly Hills, all seeking interviews with Charles Chaplin, each

My Autobiography, by Charlie Chaplin (Fireside, 1978). Reviewed in *The Nation,* October 1964.

trying to wring out of him some authentic account of his early years—to be used in books they were hoping to write about him. He was charming to them all, listened politely to the results of their painstaking research, which he neither confirmed nor denied, and bade them a smiling farewell.

"Writers are nice people," declares Mr. Chaplin in his autobiography, "but not very giving. Whatever they know they seldom impart to others; most of them keep it between the covers of their books." As though to prove his point, after so many years of stubborn silence here, finally, between the covers of his own book, is the wild, tragic and improbable drama of his life, consciously and unconsciously revealed in words which, for better or for worse, are unmistakably his own.

"To gauge the morals of our family by commonplace standards would be as erroneous as putting a thermometer in boiling water." Charles Chaplin was born into a broken theatrical family. His father, a quiet, brooding man with dark eyes who looked like Napoleon, was a talented but alcoholic baritone on the Variety stage; his mother, a successful "soubrette" until she lost her voice in her late twenties, was herself the child of a broken home, the daughter of a half-gypsy and a cobbler from County Cork. The first and most affecting part of Mr. Chaplin's book is, in fact, a memorial to Lily Chaplin, his "gay, spirited mother with the violet-blue eyes and long, light-brown hair that she could sit upon," who through the years of their blackest misery managed, with her racy elegance and theatrical literacy, to make her sons Sydney and Charlie feel that they were "not the ordinary product of poverty, but unique and distinguished."

Yet the circumstances of her life and theirs were tragic, almost beyond belief; an unbroken decline from gentility to poverty and then, as her health gave way, to an indigence so complete that it drove him through the Lambeth Poorhouse to the Hanwell School for Orphans and Destitute Children and, later, when Lily had her first mental collapse, led the doctors to attribute it in large part to chronic malnutrition. These grim years are described in a style that is deliberately dramatic but not oversentimental. There are scenes consciously constructed for irony and pathos; others, like the story of his and his brother's ten-hour truancy from the poorhouse, the sheep's escape from the slaughterhouse and Charlie's association with the wood-choppers—are told with a vividness that leaves you blinking with amusement and pity. When his father died,

> Mother, being the legal widow, was told to call at the hospital for his belongings, which consisted of a black suit spotted with blood, underwear, a shirt, a black tie, an old dressing-gown and some plaid house-slippers with oranges stuffed in the toes. When she took the oranges out a half sovereign fell out of the slipper onto the bed. This was a godsend . . .

Returning home from a guilty meal at a less impoverished neighbor's, Charlie first learned, from some children in the street, of his mother's insanity: "She's been knocking at all our doors, giving away pieces of coal, saying they're birthday presents for the children." Later, when he and Sydney were allowed to see her at the Cane Hill Asylum:

> . . . she just sat there listening and nodding, looking vague and preoccupied. I told her that she would soon get well. "Of course," she said dolefully, "if only you had given me a cup of tea that afternoon, I would have been all right."

When a man's art is as intensely personal as Chaplin's, the life and the work become inseparable. This gives the first part of his book the curious and fascinating effect of double exposure. As he draws us back to the turn of the century, across Westminster Bridge to Lambeth and along the Kennington Road, we find ourselves following him with a strange recollection of having been there before. On page 65 are two fading photographs, one of "The garret at Pownall Terrace, Kempton Road" and one of the back street "where we lived behind Kennington Cross, next to the slaughterhouse and the pickle factory . . ." It becomes clear, studying the production stills of Charlie and Jackie Coogan in *The Kid*, that except for the formal presence of an American cop (with 1905 on the badge of his cap), the set which Chaplin created in his studio at the corner of La Brea and Sunset in Hollywood in 1920 not merely suggests but *is* the alley "behind Kennington Cross, next to the slaughterhouse and the pickle factory." The corner where the sheep escaped on its way to death and the back street to which Charlie and the Kid return from their window-smashing expeditions are one and the same; so are the little room where they try to forget their hunger and the garret at Pownall Terrace ("a little over twelve feet square . . . and in the corner, snug against the wall, an old bed") where Lily Chaplin sat listlessly staring out of the window on the afternoon she became ill.

Once this correspondence is established it is a rare page that does not reflect some well-remembered episode from one or other of the films. The many odd occupations which Chaplin followed before and during his teens: newsboy, flower vendor, doctor's boy, glass blower, wood chopper, old-clothes peddler, page boy and operator atop a giant printing machine of whose innards he was totally ignorant—we have seen them all, in some form, dramatized and transmuted by the richest comic talent of our time.

Those were interludes. With his heritage and environment there was only one way for Charles Chaplin to go— into Show Business. He made his professional debut (for wages of half a crown a week and a "bread-and-jam breakfast") as one of the Eight Lancashire Lads, a juvenile song-and-dance troupe managed by a devout Catholic couple. At 12½ (pretending to be 14) he played his first dramatic role as Billy, the Baker Street page boy in *Sherlock Holmes*. At 21, after years of touring with Fred Karno's comedy companies, he was a seasoned professional, in and out of work, having known triumphs and disasters, with a fair chance—if he played his cards right—of one day joining the ranks of Britain's leading Variety performers. The moment of decision came when Karno offered him an American tour as principal comedian of a foolishness known as "The Wow-Wows."

> The night before sailing I walked about the West End of London with the wistful feeling that it would be the last time I would see London ... In the morning I did not bother to wake Sydney but left a note on the table stating "Off to America. Will keep you posted. Love, Charlie."

Charlie's conquest of America was not instantaneous. There were many months of touring (with his violin, his cello, Bob Ingersoll, Ralph Waldo Emerson and Schopenhauer), two more Atlantic crossings and a 25th birthday, before he finally summoned up the courage to enter the Keystone Studio in Ellendale, California, and appear before his new employer, Mack Sennett, who had hired him to work in one-reel film comedies at a starting salary of $150 a week. On his first morning before the camera, Chaplin displayed that ruthless, egomaniacal self-assurance that distinguished great men at the critical stages of their rise to fame—fame, in Chaplin's case, so overwhelming that it made him, for a time, the best-known and most beloved performer in the history of the world.

Mr. Chaplin gives us his version—which we might as well accept as definitive—of his creation of the Little Tramp, though one detects an element of hindsight in his elaborate and rather selfconscious analysis of the Tramp's personality at birth. Elsewhere he writes more simply of the figure who was

unfamiliar even to myself. With the clothes on I felt
he was a reality, a living person. In fact it ignited
all sorts of crazy ideas that I would never have
dreamed of till I was dressed and made up as the
Tramp.

And he quotes a barroom acquaintance of his early California days: "The guy has baggy pants, flat feet, the most miserable, bedraggled-looking little bastard you ever saw; makes gestures as though he's got crabs under his arms— but he's funny!" And funny is what America, and then the world, found him—funny and affecting and irresistible.

By fiscal standards (to which Mr. Chaplin himself attaches great importance) his rise was astronomical. In twelve months his earnings rose from $150 to $1,250 a week; his next contract was for $670,000, the next for $1,250,000. It has always been a moot question whether it was the Little Tramp's special and fantastic popularity that lifted the American movie industry from Side Show to Mass Medium, or if he was just lucky enough to ride in on the crest of the public's sudden, ravenous and insatiable passion for movie entertainment. Either way, the Little Tramp did, without question, add a new, human element to the mechanical novelty of the medium. Out of the acting tradition that he had absorbed with his mother's milk, and from the British Variety stage where he had practiced its techniques, Chaplin brought into movie comedy, for the first time, the concept of character or, as he prefers to call it, *personality*. His early conflicts at Keystone—and later at Essanay—were all on this theme. "We have no scenarios," Sennett explained to him that first morning. "We get an idea, then follow the natural sequence of events until it leads to a chase, which is the essence of your comedy." To which Chaplin replied that he hated a chase: "It dissipates one's personality; and, little as I knew about movies, I knew that nothing transcends personality." The personality of Lily's boy Charlie developed freely in the heady sunshine of the new world and was metamorphosed on tens of thousands of screens the world over into the mute, universal figure of the Little Tramp.

In the third and central part of his book Chaplin covers the quarter-century of his greatest renown: the period in which he made most of his most famous, longer pictures, from *Shoulder Arms* to *Modern Times*. As the movies grew longer and their creator more sophisticated, certain inevitable problems arose:

> In the Keystone days the Tramp had been freer ... His brain was seldom active then; only his instincts, which were concerned with the basic essentials: food, warmth and shelter. But with each succeeding comedy the Tramp was growing more complex. Sentiment was beginning to percolate through the character.

In *The Kid* and *The Gold Rush* the new blend of slapstick and sentiment, drama and comedy was brilliantly achieved: in later works, with the coming of sound, the problem was to arise again, in aggravated form.

This period also witnessed two unsuccessful marriages, several celebrated amours, the formation of United Artists with Doug and Mary and a series of triumphal visits to New York, London, Paris, Berlin and Tokyo, which occupy the least satisfying section of the book. The urge to "cash in on this business of being a celebrity" was, in the circumstances, a natural and respectable one, but it makes for tedious and frequently embarrassing reading—especially when it is couched in a jargon that seems derived, in equal parts, from Cholly Knickerbocker and Roget's Thesaurus:

> Having skimmed over the surface of New York society, I now desired to penetrate the intellectual subcutaneous texture of Greenwich Village.

Or again:

It was an affluent potpourri: Prince George of Greece, Lady Sarah Wilson, the Marquis de Talleyrand-Perigord, Commandant Paul Louis Weiller, Elsa Maxwell and others.

Plowing through pages that are crammed with the names (and snapshots) of the world's most illustrious figures, bristling with cute faux-pas and snappy quips ("And with this cryptic remark I said goodbye!"), I found myself unkindly recalling the words of the song with which Charlie had made his theatrical debut:

I've no fault to find with Jack at all.
Not when 'e's as 'e used to be.
But when Jack has come into a little bit of cash,
Well, 'e don't know where 'e are.

Finally Mr. Chaplin leads us back to California, to work, and to the fourth, most melodramatic act of his life. "A holiday is at best an empty pursuit; I had dallied around the resorts of Europe long enough . . . I knew why I was aimless and frustrated—I could not determine my future plans." With the reluctant but universal adoption of sound in films, Chaplin faced serious esthetic and commercial problems. Squeezed between the "depressing fear of being old-fashioned" and the conviction that "if the Tramp talked, the first word he ever uttered would transform him to another person," he took his dilemma so seriously that at one time he considered moving to China where he could "live well and forget motion pictures!" History, finally, provided a solution. In 1937, Alexander Korda had suggested a Hitler movie based on mistaken identity. Now, two years later, it suddenly struck him— "Of course! As Hitler I could harangue the crowds in jargon and talk all I wanted to. And as the Tramp I could remain more or less silent."

It came about that the film with which he had hoped to

lay the bugbear of sound ended by raising a whirlwind more violent than anything Chaplin had yet encountered. At the time of its release, *The Great Dictator* got a mixed reception. It disturbed not only Bundists and isolationists, but also a number of passionate anti-Nazis who found it frivolous. Among Leftists it became entangled in the confusion of loyalties that followed the Nazi-Soviet Pact. But not until much later was it officially classed as a clear and flagrant example of "premature antifascism" and used, as such, to swell the case against Chaplin.

The elaborate, shameful drama of the Red purge reached a virulent and spiteful climax in Hollywood during the late forties. Chaplin was one of its many victims. Marked from on high as one of the nation's most prominent and vulnerable fellow travelers, of whom an example must be made, his lynching was carried out over a period of several years, with weapons that included an organized press offensive, personal and professional blackmail, an economic boycott, the superannuated sex laws of the State of California and the direct intervention of the government of the United States.

Chaplin's main offense lay in three flamboyant, highly publicized speeches (one in San Francisco, one by telephone to Madison Square Garden and one in Carnegie Hall) in which he praised the Russian war effort and urged an opening of the Second Front. Though they were delivered at a time when every major Hollywood studio (not to mention the U.S. Signal Corps) was making "pro-Soviet" movies either for money or to promote the war effort, it is difficult to understand what drove a resident alien, an avowed antinationalist, a war-hater and a jealous individualist to involve himself in a spontaneous (but thrice repeated) act of direct political pressure in favor of a military operation of which he was woefully ignorant and which unquestionably involved the risk of a hundred thousand American lives. Was he driven to it by "a genuine hatred and contempt for the Nazi system" and an overwhelming fury against those who blandly recommended that we "let them both bleed white"? In part, I'm sure he was but now, after almost twenty years, Mr. Chaplin himself has attempted a complicated analysis of his secondary motives:

> Would I have entered this quixotic adventure if I had not made an anti-Nazi film? Was it a sublimation of all my irritations and reactions against talking pictures? How much was I stimulated by the actor in me and the reactions of a live audience?

Reading that final sentence, I found myself thinking back half a century and 200 pages to his account of those simpler and happier days of the First World War when he and Doug and Mary (all in the full flush of success) were rushing around the country on their third Liberty Bond tour, and how Charlie "bounded onto the platform and let fly with a verbal machine-gun barrage: 'The Germans are at your doors! We've got to stop them! And we *will* stop them! If you buy Liberty Bonds!' "—to tumultuous applause and congratulations from the Assistant Secretary of the Navy, Franklin Delano Roosevelt! Now, for appearing in a dinner jacket and addressing a cheering audience as "Comrades," he was to be hounded out of the country in which he had lived and worked for forty years by those same legal devices which the government employs to get rid of murderers, bootleggers, dope peddlers and pimps.

All's well that ends well. As the curtain rises on the last act—but by no means the epilogue—of Mr. Chaplin's history, the old maestro is discovered against the background of the Swiss Alps, surrounded by his beautiful, talented and ever-growing family. And the paradox of this astonishing life goes on: on the one hand, "we live relatively near the Queen of Spain and the Count and the Countess of Chevreau d'Antraigues, who have been most cordial to us"; on the other, "I am still very ambitious; I could never retire; besides having a few unfinished movie scripts, I should like to write a play and an opera—if time will allow." It probably will.

 *Griffith*

RICHARD SCHICKEL has subtitled his biography *An American Life*—with good reason. David Wark Griffith was born in Kentucky where his mother was a minor heiress and from which his father went off to the California gold fields in the eighteen-fifties, later returning to fight for the Confederacy and living out his life "giving orations and telling tales," playing fiddle, gambling, drinking and womanizing. Griffith's own early manhood was spent as an unsuccessful actor in a typically American form of feckless wandering from coast to coast before achieving sudden, overwhelming success in a field which he helped to create and which was predominantly (though by no means exclusively) American. Even his decline and fall followed a familiar American pattern.

The true story of this man with whom "begins the history of film as a self-conscious art, as a magic financial institution, as a significant shaping force in the modern mind and the modern world," is not an easy one to tell. Like certain other filmmakers I can think of, he was "both secretive and a mythomaniac." It is the depth and fullness of Mr. Schickel's research that makes his book what I be-

D. W. Griffith: An American Life, by Richard Schickel (Simon & Schuster, 1984). Reviewed in the *Chicago Tribune* Book World.

lieve to be the definitive biography of this complicated, tragic, exasperating yet supremely important figure. For the casual reader it may seem at times overloaded with detail but it is from this complete documentation that the truth emerges, free at last of the myths and legends with which its subject chose, for so many years, to surround himself. Among the misconceptions dispelled is the one that, having made an overnight killing with *The Birth of a Nation,* Griffith lost it all with *Intolerance* and spent the rest of his life paying off the debts he had incurred building the walls of Babylon. The true story is more complicated and mundane. Griffith's career in motion pictures was, in fact, a long series of manipulations and disputes complicated by his own egomania and his inability or unwillingness to work within the complicated and dangerously mobile structure of a monstrously growing and shifting industry in which he was forced, if he wanted to survive and go on making pictures, to mortgage each of his successive films to pay for the next until he finally ran out of inspiration and credit. All this is fully and convincingly described in Mr. Schickel's book together with a meticulous account of the man's truly enormous volume of work.

David Wark Griffith was no precocious wonder-boy. After a dozen years of dreary and precarious subsistence as an actor he entered the film business in desperation as a writer. Soon he was creating most of the improvised one-reelers that were the staple output of the Biograph Company, for which he worked, and of which no less than sixty were ground out in 1908 and more than twice that number in 1909. By 1913 he was expanding them into two-reelers and then finally (with *Judith of Bethulia*) to four. Critics have examined these early potboilers for evidence of Griffith's genius and of the technical and artistic innovations with which he is generally credited. A catalogue of this enormous output makes clear, however, what a gigantic leap—artistically and commercially—was achieved when Griffith, in 1915, wrote, directed, edited and sold to the American public the twelve reels of *The Birth of a Nation* with a cast that included such future film figures as Lillian Gish, Mae Marsh, Henry B. Walthall, Miriam Cooper, Robert Harron, Wallace Reid, Donald Crisp and Raoul Walsh.

With great care and detail Schickel takes us, critically and commercially, through the more than two dozen full-length films which Griffith made between 1916 and 1931, when his disaster with *The Struggle* finally ended his career as a filmmaker—seventeen years before his death.

Parallel to this is the full, perceptive treatment of the man's personal story. It is impossible to understand the flaws, the sentimentality, the frequently dubious taste, the sexual attitudes and, above all, the prejudices (that created racial problems in *The Birth of a Nation*, of which Mr. Schickel gives us the fullest account I have seen) without a comprehension of his Southern background and, particularly, of his father's influence upon him. Although—or perhaps because—he died in David's tenth year, Jacob Griffith left behind "a powerful yet confusing image of masculinity" and a pattern of "histrionic behavior" that his son carried with him for the rest of his life.

Not only does this help to clarify certain recurrent themes and characteristic attitudes in Griffith's films and public utterances, it explains much of his own personal behavior, including his relations with women. The private, highly protected area of his two marriages and the series of romantic-professional attachments (of which that with Lillian Gish is the most celebrated example) are explored by Mr. Schickel with a combination of tact and a zealous investigator's persistence, but they remain vague and incomplete—the least satisfying part of this detailed and perceptive biography.

I was struck, while reading Mr. Schickel's book, by certain similarities between this and another recent American biography. Jed Harris and David Wark Griffith were the two most flamboyantly successful showmen of their day; both were innovators and megalomaniacs. Otherwise they were unlike in every respect—background, education, experience, intelligence—and they worked in different generations, in two very different dramatic media. Yet their lives were tragically alike in one respect: sudden, overwhelming fame followed by tragic, irreversible decline.

Both, at what should have been the peak of their careers, seemed to lose their magic touch and their creative control of a world they had once dominated. For the final third of their lives neither was able to practice his art: each lived on in reduced circumstances in which the fame he had once enjoyed served only to accentuate the depth of his fall and the extent of his final impotence.

Does this, I wonder, raise certain general questions concerning the hazardous and ephemeral nature of popular and artistic success in America today?

Griffith and Harris both triumphed in a world dominated by mass comunication—a world in which success and money have become virtually synonymous; in which fame can be achieved without honor and reputation without respect; one in which the most eloquent proof of accomplishment seems to be *Variety*'s weekly box-office score and last night's Nielsen ratings.

When the tide turned against them, it represented more than an artistic, critical or commercial reverse. In the lives of both Griffith and Harris, it was as though the gods had suddenly and inexplicably withdrawn the favors upon which their very lives had come to depend. With nothing to fall back on, they accepted their fate, turned their faces to the wall and waited for the end.

❧ Bertolt Brecht:
Exile in Paradise

I met Brecht in New York in the mid-thirties when the Theatre Union was producing his version of Gorki's Mother. *We discussed the possibility of staging another of his plays,* Roundheads and Squareheads, *for the Negro Unit of the W.P.A.'s Federal Theatre in Harlem. That scheme fell through but seven years later, as head of Radio Programming for the Voice of America, I engaged him to prepare and direct a weekly broadcast, to be transmitted by shortwave to the German people. The program consisted of his own poetry and scenes and songs from his plays with music by Weill, Dessau and Eisler. Some beautiful works came out of it, including several original poems. But, besides the problem of transmitting such delicate stuff by shortwave through organized enemy "jamming," it turned out to be unsuitable propaganda material: no communication seemed possible between Brecht and the listeners of Hitler's Nazi Third Reich.*

My next encounter with Brecht was in California in 1947, when I produced his Galileo *with Charles Laughton in the leading role. I have described that production in* Front and Center; *Brecht wrote about it extensively in his own preface to the German edition of the play.*

THERE ARE A NUMBER of works written and in progress dealing with the sojourn of Western European émigrés in the United States, and particularly in Hollywood, before,

Bertolt Brecht in America, by James K. Lyon (Princeton University Press, 1980). Reviewed in the *Los Angeles Times* Book Section.

during, and after the Second World War. I doubt if any will be more comprehensively researched or more intelligently and sensitively written than James K. Lyon's *Bertolt Brecht in America*.

Mr. Lyon is faithful to his title; his focus is mainly on the events and attitudes that relate to Brecht's visits to this country. But early in his book he makes a fascinating comparison between the mythical America of Brecht's imagination in the twenties and the realities of the society in which he came to spend six unhappy years in the forties.

> No sociologist can accurately measure what the idea called "America" did to the consciousness of a certain young counterculture in Germany. For many this exotic word carried a thousand overtones: gangsters, flappers, boxing and the latest dance steps, Prohibition and Chaplin films, auto racing and labor violence, jazz, the Wild West and runaway technology ... America was an exciting alternative to the Europe which they thought to be depleted of its imaginative resources.

(Half a dozen of Brecht's plays of that period contain "American" characters and locales—though in reality they were little more than superficially Americanized portrayals of contemporary life in Berlin.)

In fact, no two worlds could have been more different than this mythical "America" and the scene of Brecht's enforced exile—the Southern California suburb in which he lived in penury and frustration and which he variously described as a "sewer" of capitalism, a "marketplace where lies are bought," "a place where it is impossible to buy decent bread," where "the houses are built onto garages," where "cheap prettiness" prevails and culture is nonexistent—an "undignified city where men shoot their inconstant wives, teenagers axe their fathers, who beat their mothers."

Most of the book covers the period from July 1941, when Brecht and his entourage arrived from Finland via Moscow and Vladivostok, until late 1947 when Brecht returned to Europe on the eve of the New York production of *Galileo* and on the day following his interrogation in Washington by the House Un-American Activities Committee. Using sources that include Brecht's dead and living German and American associates, together with his own journals and the recently released files which the F.B.I. kept on him during his stay in this country, Mr. Lyon writes with sympathy and understanding but without illusion of the ordeal of this prickly but indomitable genius in a world in which (unlike many of his compatriots) he was determined to regard himself as a political "exile."

The first year was the hardest. Living on the charity of his fellow émigrés, many of whom he disliked and despised (none more than Thomas Mann), he was able to do almost no creative writing. Instead, he tried desperately to share in the spoils of a film industry he detested.

> Brecht looked on filmmaking as many people do on gambling. He knew the odds against him, but knowing that he stood to win big money for a small expenditure of time and effort, he went right on playing.

Finally, with the benevolent cooperation of two fellow exiles (Fritz Lang and Lion Feuchtwanger) who had made the transition more easily than himself, he participated in two moderately lucrative sales to film studios that enabled him to buy a house and live in comparative comfort for the rest of his California exile. Neither did much to enhance his reputation or to soften his attitude toward members of the Hollywood film industry. Of his American fellow filmwriters he declared, "the sight of such intellectual deformity makes me physically ill. I can scarcely stand to be in the same room with these intellectual cripples and moral casualties."

Films were not the only field in which Brecht attempted unsuccessfully to make the big-time in American Show Business. Spurning all attempts by earnest but obscure theatrical groups to produce his works, he employed every possible ruse—flattery, manipulation and personal maneuvers—to secure a Broadway production of one or more of his plays. None of them worked—though one of these vain attempts did, in fact, result in the writing of what has become one of his most frequently performed works—*The Caucasian Chalk Circle.*

Yet his years here were not all bitter or somber. Brecht did, during his exile, enjoy a number of personal friendships with fellow émigrés and with Americans—including several young poets and intellectuals. But his most agreeable and productive association seems to have been the one he developed with Charles Laughton, which resulted in the reworking, translation and eventual production of *Galileo* during his last year in California.

Much has been written by Brecht and others about that production, of which I was one of the producers and which I have described to the best of my own recollection in *Front and Center.* Mr. Lyon seems to have put the facts into their proper perspective. He has done the same for Brecht's final appearance before the Un-American Activities Committee in Washington, of which Dalton Trumbo felt that "Brecht took the right balance between belligerence and passivity." But the chief merit of Mr. Lyon's book lies in his patient and scrupulous exploration of Brecht's states of mind during those difficult years. In sections titled "Brecht and Feelings," "The Charismatic Brecht," "The Ideological Brecht," he analyzes the secretive, obdurate, intellectual and emotional workings of this egomaniacal genius who, regardless of frustrations and hardship, never for one moment doubted his present and future theatrical preeminence or his influence on posterity.

In an epilogue entitled "America Before and After,"

Mr. Lyon summarizes Brecht's continued and perversely hostile view of the America in which he lived, constantly complaining, for six years, but which he had, in fact, chosen as the scene of his exile over the Marxist state which he consistently favored in his writings. Commenting on the award Brecht received in 1948 from the prestigious American Academy of Arts and Letters—"in recognition of the international value and import of his work . . . together with his contributions to our culture," Mr. Lyon observes that although he had not contributed directly to American culture,

> Brecht was too far ahead of his time and too uncompromising in presenting his kind of theater in his own way to have succeeded in an alien environment like America. Only after his leaving did his influence begin to make itself felt. And only in his absence did American theater gain perspective on the genius of this writer whom it had harbored during a productive but bitter "exile in paradise."

Life Among the Natives

Budd Schulberg *worked for David O. Selznick shortly before my time and left to become a novelist.*

Irene Mayer Selznick, *Hollywood's original "Jewish Princess," was generally recognized as a force in her husband's films (including* Gone With the Wind) *before she established herself, independently, as one of Broadway's most intelligent and successful producers. She remains a close friend.*

My acquaintance with Nunnally Johnson *came mostly through his affectionate association with my dear friend Herman Mankiewicz.*

❖ *Buddy in Wonderland*

IN *Moving Pictures* Budd Schulberg has attempted not one autobiography but two. In his nostalgic memoir he offers us parallel and concurrent accounts of his own birth, childhood and adolescence synchronized with the phenomenal rise of the film industry of which he considers himself a coeval and an organic part.

Born in 1914 (two years after his father, B. P. Schulberg, went to work for Adolph Zukor to help create Famous Players), the angels flying around his crib included such illustrious film figures as Charles Chaplin, Theda Bara, the Keystone Cops and Mack Sennett's Bathing Beauties. His first baby carriage was presented to him by Mr. Zukor (so were the milk and fresh eggs that were delivered daily from the Zukor estate) and he received a fine wool blanket from Mary Pickford, who could afford it since her salary had recently risen from $500 to $10,000 a week. (Her title of "America's Sweetheart" had, in fact, been bestowed upon her by Buddy's father.)

The Schulberg family's move to the West Coast coincided with Hollywood's emergence as the film capital of the world. In the second section of his memoir Mr. Schulberg combines film history with a child's reminiscences of life in the "celluloid cocoon." The reader soon finds himself on avuncular terms with the new tycoons—Zukor, Lasky, Mayer, Selig, Selznick, Goldfish and Laemmle—and receives personal introductions to such mythical figures as Clara Kimball Young, Bronco Billy, Katherine MacDonald, Olive Thomas, Anita Stewart, Mickey Neilan, Pola Negri, Gloria Swanson, William S. Hart, Lon Chaney, Erich von Stroheim, Blanche Sweet and the un-

Moving Pictures: Memories of a Hollywood Prince, by Budd Schulberg (Stein & Day, 1981). Reviewed in the *Chicago Tribune* Book World.

fortunate Roscoe Arbuckle, not to mention the child stars of Buddy's own generation—Jackie Coogan, Baby Peggy and Mickey Rooney—all of whom worked for his father.

In the next section, "The Prince of Paramount" (where B. P. Schulberg, as head of production, was now solely responsible for fifty or more films a year), we are offered intimate glimpses of a new crop of stars: March, Bancroft, Cooper, Colbert, Velez and, above all, the "It" girl, Clara Bow, with sufficient inside stories, anecdotes, romances, scandals and disasters to please the most avid fan. On a personal level, too, we learn more about the Schulbergs' family life; we get to know Buddy's strong, intelligent, devoted, ambitious mother Ad (short for Adeline), who was for years one of the film colony's dominant taste-making matrons before becoming its first and most successful female talent agent. But the dominant figure in the boy's life remains his father—"a prodigy in all departments," a man of enormous energy at work and at play, a stutterer (like his son), a prize-fight aficionado, a gambler, a drinker and a womanizer who combined substantial culture with monstrous vulgarity—as when, in his first opulence, he acquired "a town car with the body of an 18th-century coach, laced with gold bric-a-brac, incongruously placed on a Lincoln chassis with a sixteen-cylinder engine and two genuine antique lanterns over its doors."

As Master Schulberg moves through his mid-teens at the wheel of his Duesenberg, two themes emerge and assume increasing importance in the little prince's life. The first is a growing and disturbing awareness, which will stay with him for the rest of his days, that he is a Jew. (This is in no way diminished by his having been expelled at an early age from the Temple B'nai Brith by the formidable Rabbi Magnin for irreverent and scatological impertinence.) The second is his growing problem with sex. Close contact with the "Hollywood Dream-and-Sex Machine," in the creation of which Buddy had watched his father play such an active professional and personal part, seems to have driven his son into a state of puritanism and timidity so deep that, in spite of all temptation, he retained his innocence far beyond the Southern California norm.

By the mid-thirties the industry has become too complex to be encompassed in a personal memoir and Mr. Schulberg turns away from the Studio life which had been "not only my nursery and my kindergarten" but had offered him "an advanced course in psychodrama and pathological insecurity," to concentrate on the problems of his own tortured adolescence. This change of focus, reinforced by quotations from a previous and revealing diary, coincides with a decline in B.P.'s fortunes and the breakup of the Schulberg family life, followed by open domestic quarrels, separation and divorce.

The book ends with his father on the way down, his mother on her way up and Buddy himself, still a virgin, on the way to Dartmouth and a writing career which, before long, was to produce that sharp and authentic examination of predatory behavior in Hollywood—*What Makes Sammy Run?*

❧ *The Golden Days*

HER FATHER was the most powerful man in the film industry. Her husband, whom she married in Hollywood's most glamorous dynastic union, produced the world's most successful motion picture for which—as wife, part-

A Private View, by Irene Mayer Selznick (Knopf, 1983). Reviewed in *USA Today.*

ner and adviser—she received partial but unofficial credit.

After their separation and divorce, alone, as an independent Broadway producer, she presided over one of the theatrical triumphs of our time (*A Streetcar Named Desire*); her personal relationships have included close and lasting friendships with many of the outstanding men and women of her day.

It is a tense, crammed life of which Irene Mayer Selznick writes subjectively and with substantial candor in *A Private View*. Her most detailed and revealing portraits are those of her father, MGM's Louis B. Mayer, and husband, David O. Selznick. The former, who remained to the end the most potent influence in her life, emerges as a blend of a willful, sentimental, conventionally moral patriarch and a ruthless tycoon.

Although her attitude toward him remains that of a dutiful and protective daughter, her final portrait is probably closer to reality than some of the other more lurid journalistic accounts that have been published about this formidable and unlovable figure.

Toward David Selznick (for whom I worked as associate producer in one of his least fruitful years) her attitude throughout is affectionate but critical. In describing their courtship and their matrimonial and professional vicissitudes with a full awareness of his gradual deterioration, she manages to convey a sense of the intense excitement she derived fom their tumultuous and eventful years together.

Irene Selznick describes herself quite rightly as a child of Hollywood. For all her constant traveling and East Coast residences, there is a special quality about her early California memories that changes somewhat when she leaves that lunatic state and becomes a citizen of the world.

Her uncompromising account of her experience as a New York and London theatrical producer (particularly her dealings with Williams and Kazan) contains some new and fascinating material; it also reveals a slight hardening of her ego and a persistent need to convince the reader of her perspicacity and consistent rightness—of which the first part of her book is remarkably free.

A Private View is a fascinating and historically important account of the great era of Hollywood written by an unusually intelligent, sensitive and emotionally mature woman. Fate and her own initiative placed her in a perfect position to observe it all more closely, more authoritatively and more intimately than almost anyone of her generation.

❉*Pepys in Hollywood*

MORE THAN HALF a century has passed since Nunnally Johnson first swam into my ken as the author of a humorous column in the *New York Evening Post* and of sundry pieces in the *American Mercury* and the *Saturday Evening Post*. By the time I arrived in Hollywood he had written the screenplay for *The Grapes of Wrath* and established himself as a successful filmwriter and as one of the handful of educated Wasps on whom Darryl Zanuck counted to write, produce and, occasionally, to direct the more sophisticated items in his vast annual output of motion pictures. I knew of him, too, as a fellow wit and favorite drinking companion of my beloved friend, Herman Mankiewicz who, incidentally, first lured him to the fleshpots of California. Yet in all those years our personal acquaint-

The Letters of Nunnally Johnson, selected and edited by Dorris Johnson and Ellen Leventhal, with a foreword by Alistair Cooke (Knopf, 1981). Reviewed in *The New York Times Book Review*.

ance has been unilateral and posthumous—established mostly through a reading of *Flashback*, his daughter's affectionate but merciless account of their intense father-daughter relationship.

With the publication of this new collection of Nunnally Johnson's letters, I was hoping to gain deeper insights into the fascinating personality of this gifted, much-loved and loving man. In that respect I was disappointed—unjustly perhaps, since this selection of letters (written between 1944 and 1976) seems to have been made with the limited but deliberate intention of presenting him to the world as a humorous, sophisticated and objective commentator on the Hollywood scene. It offers the reader, in the words of his friend Alistair Cooke, "an insider's diary of the fun, the guile, the allegiances and enmities, the social habits and pretensions of the movie colony for thirty years or more in the middle of the twentieth century."

These are letters anyone would be overjoyed to find in his mailbox. Except for an occasional flare of irritation provoked by such visiting celebrities as Clare Luce and Walter Winchell ("a perfectly splendid fellow with but one weakness—he thinks you are glad to see him"), they are without illusions but their tone is tolerant of the frailties they describe: "In a flashy and cynical society," to quote Cooke once again, "Nunnally rendered himself no threat to anybody by adopting, as second nature, the air of a bewildered mouse in a world of tigers."

The events recorded by this latter-day Pepys include a croquet game in which a bouncing mallet draws blood from Zanuck's Olympian brow; the introduction of tamales into the Studio commissary; a feel-out followed by a punch-out at Romanoff's involving the Levants, the Wangers and "Dangerous George Raft"; a topless gymnastic exhibition by Darryl Zanuck in a nightclub on the Strip; Bogart's funeral; and his own son's antiestablishment wedding. We are also treated to frequent bulletins on the courtship of John Huston and Olivia de Havilland

and reports of the latest absurdities uttered by Spyros Skouras.

This correspondence, from which personal and emotional reactions have been almost entirely excluded, is addressed mostly to Johnson's professional associates: producers, directors, actors (Burton, the Bogarts, Helen Hayes, Groucho Marx, Fredric March, Monty Woolley, etc.) but there is a special warmth in his letters to fellow writers, including Thurber, Frank Sullivan, Arthur Sheekman, Liebling, Cooke, Steinbeck and George Kaufman, for whom he has an admiration bordering on reverence. Indeed, of the six longest and most carefully written pieces in this collection, four were sent in response to requests for information from the biographers of Ed Howe, William Faulkner, Scott Fitzgerald and Charles MacArthur. Of the remaining two, one is a sympathetic and perceptive account of his working experience with the love-goddess Marilyn Monroe; the other, in the form of a letter to *The New York Times,* is a witty, non-political and devastating exposure of the inanities of Hollywood's Un-American investigations (though it is worth noting that his protest was not made until the box-office receipts of one of his own films—*The Senator Was Indiscreet*—appeared to be threatened by the Witch-hunt).

The few intimate letters included in this collection and the memory of some that were quoted by his daughter in *Flashback* made me regret that there were not more of the same quality in this selection.

❧ *Grub Street, California*

HOLLYWOOD HAS NOT been kind to writers over the years. It has paid them lavishly but it has rarely given them the feeling that they played an essential, creative part in the production of film. The writers have reciprocated: for all its highly publicized glamour and the desperate energy of its personal relationships, Hollywood has still not furnished the background for a single major American novel or play. Even the best of them lack body. *What Makes Sammy Run* is a slick, knowledgeable first novel; Fitzgerald's *The Last Tycoon* remains an impressionist, uncompleted work, and *The Big Knife* is one of Odets's least imaginative plays. *The Day of the Locust* is about Los Angeles rather than Hollywood; Mailer's *Deer Park* (not to mention Robbins and Susann) show inadequate digestion of their overabundant source material.

There are obvious reasons for this: it is difficult to impose artistic form on a society which lives in a state of violent and perpetual human and technical flux; it is virtually impossible to use as a background for drama or fiction a world that is, itself, hysterically concerned with the creation and exploitation of fiction.

Such creative problems do not perturb that other legion of sub-writers—journalists, columnists, memoirists and gossip-mongers whose occupation it is to satisfy the world's vast and methodically stimulated curiosity about the Dream Capital and to reveal the inside poop on "Stars and Starlets, Tycoons and Flesh Peddlers, Movie-makers and Moneymakers, Frauds and Geniuses, Hopefuls and

Hollywood, by Garson Kanin (Viking, 1974). Reviewed in *The New York Times.*
The Fifty-Year Decline and Fall of Hollywood, by Ezra Goodman (Simon & Schuster, 1961). Reviewed in *The Massachusetts Review.*

Has-beens, Great Lovers and Sex Symbols"—to quote the blurb on the silver cover of Garson Kanin's new book.

It is depressing to find Mr. Kanin in this company since he is himself a director and author of some distinction. I have the feeling that this is an old text rehashed for commercial purposes, for it deals with an early period of Hollywood, before television took over the town. As a precociously successful director and writer Mr. Kanin had direct and, in many cases, intimate contact with the celebrities and the situations of which he writes. Yet the result is disappointing: many of these pieces are superficial and banal. Too often they lapse into the name-dropping jargon of a show-biz columnist. "I recall a Sunday luncheon at George Cukor's in honor of an unmarried British couple recently arrived in Hollywood. The girl was to play Scarlett in *Gone With the Wind*, the man to play Maxim de Winter in *Rebecca:* Vivien Leigh and Laurence Olivier. Another of the guests was Greta Garbo." Of John Barrymore we learn only that "his acting technique was flawless," and of Carole Lombard that "technically she was a phenomenon."

Yet, in fairness, it must be reported that Mr. Kanin does occasionally come up with quite vivid and revealing memories—or, rather, mental recordings—of Hollywood's great. Though his narrative style is generally flat, he does have the ability to report dialogue with what seems like remarkable fidelity. This is due, no doubt, to a discipline he reveals when he tells us that, after a particularly hilarious meeting between Sam Goldwyn and Edgar Bergen, the ventriloquist, "we all returned to our respective offices. I have no idea what the others did, but I began to dictate an account of that extraordinary event."

This direct recording method works best when Mr. Kanin is reporting the behavior of some of the industry's most eminent and powerful tycoons—such grotesque yet awesome figures as Jack Warner, Harry Cohn, Eddie Mannix, Carl Laemmle, Darryl Zanuck and, above all,

Samuel Goldwyn, whom Kanin served for a time as apprentice, adviser and whipping-boy. ("This kid's supposed to be a smart kid and every day he says something stupid!") The figure that emerges from so many reported meetings, conversations, visions, rages and maneuvers is one for which any future biographer of Samuel Goldfish will be grateful.

In his final piece, after informing us that "American whorehouses are not, by and large, as interesting as the French, Japanese and Scandinavian varieties," Mr. Kanin describes one such establishment in the Hollywood Hills which "fascinated" him. The highest compliment I can pay to this particular reminiscence is to confess that I could not tell whether it was fact or fiction.

ANOTHER, EVEN LESS credible chronicler of Hollywood is Ezra Goodman, who claims to have covered the American movie scene for two decades as correspondent, columnist, publicist and critic—for trade papers, a Los Angeles tabloid, a New York racing-sheet and, on occasion, the Luce publications—has produced a 450-page volume for which its publishers claim that "from its fade-in on D. W. Griffith guzzling gin and grabbing at a blonde to its fade-out on a bowl of the fat, succulent chicken soup that immortalizes the name of Louis B. Mayer at the MGM commissary—here is the real story of Hollywood."

It is nothing of the kind. It is neither a history nor an organized account of Hollywood's disintegrating but still fabulous operation. It is, in fact, a trunkful of newspaperman's notes for pieces published and unpublished; anecdotes, profiles, inside dope, jokes, rumors, personal peeves and the rare enthusiasms accumulated during twenty years of pounding the Hollywood beat.

"In the course of my journalistic experience, I came to find that it was easier and more satisfying all around to write about the off-screen public achievements and hijinks of my subjects. This eliminated the touchy and mostly unrewarding area of Art, a matter that was usually of no particular interest to either reader or subject." Mr. Goodman has scrupulously adhered to this formula thoughout his book. Among the Hollywood phenomena which he describes with a wealth of bizarre and superficial detail are press agents, movie critics, directors, stars, ex-stars, stuntmen, studio cops, restaurateurs, barbers, psychoanalysts and veterinarians. Future students of Show Business may find valuable scraps and fragments here: harsh but accurate diagrams of the caste system prevailing among the five hundred men and women of Hollywood's obsolescent press corps; some *Time*-type research material on Bogart, Monroe, Novak, Cohn, Holden et al.; an alcoholic hotel-room interview with a senescent D. W. Griffith; a fair sampling of the grim Hollywood jokes uttered over the years by such celebrated local wits as Hecht, Johnson, Wilder, Mankiewicz and Goldwyn.

Who sups with the Devil must use a long spoon. Mr. Goodman's evidently was not long enough, for during his stay in the movie capital, he seems to have contracted a bad case of that most common and tedious of Hollywood's vocational diseases—a sense of inferiority and guilt. Every few pages he finds it necessary to produce his credentials of literary and artistic competence and to assure us, with pathetic eagerness, of his own ethical and esthetic superiority to the slum in which a cruel fate has forced him to labor for two decades.

Film:

Two Historians

and a Critic

❧ *An Art with a Difference*

THE NEWEST of our Theater Arts is so young that it still hasn't been properly christened. (Film, cinema, kino, movies, motion pictures—none of these terms has gained universal acceptance and not one of them can encompass the new medium's diverse forms and uses.) Yet, already the cinema can claim a Golden Age of its own. An unwelcome but irreversible mutation—the addition of sound to film in the late twenties—brought about such drastic changes in the making and showing of motion pictures that it is possible, even now, to look back and view the brilliant explosion of the Silent Film in some sort of artistic and historical perspective.

Theory of Film: The Redemption of Physical Reality, by Siegfried Krakauer (Oxford University Press). Reviewed in *The Massachusetts Review,* 1960.

Two decades, from 1910 to 1930, saw the making of most of the great silent movies, and most of the serious appraisals we possess of the art of the film are based upon theories relating to and illustrations taken from works of that period.

Siegfried Krakauer's most recent work, *Theory of Film,* is based upon the assumption that "film is essentially an extension of photography and therefore shares with this medium a marked affinity for the world of physical reality. This reality includes phenomena which would hardly be perceived were it not for the camera's ability to catch them on the wing. And, since any medium is partial to the things which it is uniquely equipped to render, the cinema is conceivably animated by the desire to picture transient material life—life at its most ephemeral."

We have long been in Dr. Krakauer's debt for his lively *Orpheus in Paris,* in which he used the life and work of the German cellist-composer Offenbach to reflect the glamorous and tragic world of mid-nineteenth century Paris. His second book, *From Caligari to Hitler,* was a fascinating if labored excursion into the German subconscious as revealed in the films of the Weimar Republic and the Third Reich. In his latest book, Dr. Krakauer is performing a further valuable service. Today, when the cinema's very existence as a theatrical medium is menaced by the world's general acceptance of television as its dominant form of dramatic communication, and as the medium itself seems to be groping for new form and substance, it is good to be reminded of film's essential nature and particular qualities.

Dr. Krakauer holds that film, "if it is an art at all, is an art with a difference," and must not be viewed or judged by the standards of the older, accepted art forms. He believes that literature, and more particularly dramatic literature, has little to do with the art of the film. "Even though the reader will presumably agree that the cinema is engrossed in the physical side of life in and about us, he may not be prepared to acknowledge the consequences of its preoccupation with externals . . . Photography tends to stress the fortuitous. It also tends to suggest endlessness. Indeed, a photograph has a character only if it precludes completeness. Its frame marks a provisional limit; its content refers to other contents outside that frame and its structure denotes something that cannot be composed—physical existence." This preoccupation with the "superficial" and "accidental" qualities of photography lead directly to the main thesis of Dr. Krakauer's book. "I submit that film and tragedy are incompatible with each other. If film is a photographic medium it must gravitate toward the expanses of outer reality—an open-ended, limitless world which bears little resemblance to the finite and ordered cosmos set by tragedy." Tragedy, as Krakauer reminds us, neglects every image that does not assist the action and retains only those that may help us to make its purpose intelligible. If tragedy acknowledges chance events, it does so by making them serve its own ends. This elimination of the accidental runs directly against the grain of the cinema, which emphasizes the *contingency* of human relationships. "The world of the cinema has no order; it is a world of movement and collision in which the camera, without any notion of its destination, presents us with interpenetrating, counter-influencing organisms." In support of his theory, Krakauer cites two great film-makers—one live, the other dead. According to Fellini, "it is immoral (in a film) to tell a story that has a conclusion. Because you cut out your audience the moment you present a solution on the screen." Eisenstein, describing his creation of what is perhaps the most famous film sequence in history, the scattering of the crowd on the Odessa steps in *Potemkin,* has stated that: "Nature, circumstance, the setting at the moment of shooting and the film material at the moment of montage can sometimes be wiser than the artist. No scene of shooting on the Odessa steps appeared in any of the montage-lists that were prepared. It was born in the instant of immediate contact."

Relentlessly, with exhaustive and sometimes exhausting elaboration, Dr. Krakauer pursues his thesis through the various forms and expressions of film art—with varying success. There are certain practical, creative aspects of filmmaking that he cannot readily absorb into his scheme of things: actors and acting, for instance. Yet, on the whole, he manages to communicate a passion for the film medium that goes far beyond its immediate function as popular entertainment. He sees in film "an art-form appropriate to the troubled and uncertain world which it serves without limitation of language or boundary." He contends that "film, our contemporary, has a definite bearing on the era into which it is born. Perhaps our condition is such that we cannot gain access to the elusive elements of life unless we assimilate the seemingly non-essential . . . Considering the modern scientist's preoccupation with physical minutiae and the contemporary decline of ideology," it is in fact inevitable that our minds, "fragmented as they are, should absorb not so much *wholes* as *small moments* of life. These small random moments, which concern things common to you and me and the rest of mankind can be said to constitute the dimensions of everyday life, this matrix of all other modes of reality. Products of habits and microscopic interaction, they form a resilient texture which changes slowly and survives wars, epidemics, earthquakes and revolutions. Films tend to explore this texture of everyday life, whose composition varies according to place, people and time. So they help us not only to appreciate our given material environment but to extend it in all directions. They virtually make the world our home. . . . It is the movies and only the movies that do justice to the materialistic interpretation of the universe which, whether we like it or not, pervades contemporary civilization."

The movie-lover, lay or professional, who has the tenacity to plow through Dr. Krakauer's book is likely to emerge better equipped to understand the problems facing the cinema in its current esthetic and economic crises.

❧*Trying the Untried*

JAY LEYDA is no stranger to theories of film. As translator and editor, he was responsible for the American editions of *Film Form* and *The Film Sense,* Sergei Eisenstein's classic analyses of the nature of film art. In *Kino* he has returned to his first love, the movies, with a clear and comprehensive report on one of the world's great filmmaking regions—Russia and the U.S.S.R.

Mr. Leyda's chronicle falls, roughly, into five acts, the first of which ends in October 1917, with the fall of the Czarist regime. Till then, Russia's film tastes had generally reflected her position as a cultural semi-colony of Western Europe. Her movie theaters (between eight hundred and a thousand of them, equipped with single projectors) were showing mainly French, Italian, Danish and American films, with a small percentage of native costume pictures based on literary and theatrical subjects. Newsreels and documentary material, once as popular in Russia as elsewhere, had been censored almost out of existence.

With the coming of war, despite ever stricter government surveillance, the native film industry, freed of foreign competition, enjoyed a period of great prosperity.

Kino: A History of the Russian and Soviet Film, by Jay Leyda (Macmillan & Company, 1960). Reviewed in *The Massachusetts Review.*

With rare exceptions (a highly styled *Picture of Dorian Gray* by Meyerhold and Protozanov's *Father Sergius*), its product was escapist and mediocre. During February 1917, the movie billboards on the Moscow streets were advertising *The Festival of Night, Then She Decided upon Revenge, The Torturing Enigma, The Bloody Exhalations of a Perverted Love, Fate's Puppet, How Madly, How Passionately She Wanted Love, Playing with Her Heart as with a Doll.* Leyda quotes two opposed but equally derogatory contemporary views of the Russian cinema. An imperial notation in the margin of a new censorship decree reads: "I consider cinematography an empty, useless and even pernicious diversion. Only an abnormal person could place this sideshow business on a level with art. It is all nonsense, and no importance should be lent to such trash." At the same time, a writer in a publication of the Left deplores "the serious and extremely harmful influence of the Kinema on the proletarian psyche ... Good in idea, this democratic theater would appear by its content to be the embodiment of bourgeois vulgarity, of commercial calculation, a slave to the taste of the spoiled upper classes, a servant of capitalists."

The second act of *Kino* begins with the Bolsheviks' seizure of power and covers the periods of revolution and reconstruction from 1917 to 1924. For the Russian film industry, the effects of the October Revolution were pervasive though not immediate. Throughout the many months of open civil war, conflict between private film industry and the state continued—with almost entirely negative results. It was not until the end of 1919 that a decree appeared announcing the transfer of the Photographic and Cinema Trade and Industry to the People's Commissariat of Education. Others, more drastic and expropriatory, were to follow, culminating in the decree of August 17, 1923, when all private film firms were liquidated and a state monopoly of film production and distribution— GOSHKINO—was declared. The poet Mayakovsky has

left vivid and exasperated accounts of early Committee
meetings, at which the word "education" was heard more
often than the word "art." The dean of Russian letters,
Maxim Gorky, came up with a scheme of his own—no less
than the "staging of the history of human culture in the
form of theatrical presentations and pictures for the cine-
matograph." But the project had to be abandoned, like
many others. For "severe and purposeful as the new Cinema Committee's attitude may have been, its movements
looked more like groping than like organization." And no
wonder, considering the shambles the fugitive filmmakers
had left behind them, the persistence of the blockade and
the grim fact that no motion picture equipment of any
kind had ever been manufactured in Russia. "Up till the
twenties, there was no Russian-made camera, no Russian-
made projector, and, above all, no Russian raw film,
either negative or positive."

Not surprisingly, the early Soviet film product was documentary rather than theatrical. Its first planned activity
called for the making of thirteen "Agitki"—single-reel
propaganda films to be shown to troops and civilians
alike. Meantime, newsreel units were touring the battle
zones, while an Agit-train was visiting towns and villages
in the hinterland. "During each period when the train was
not in motion, the traveling cinema worked with hardly a
break, with an ever-changing audience of hundreds of
children, local workers and peasants. In the evenings films
were shown on the streets near the train. . . . The following
summer an Agit-Steamboat, *Red Star*, seating eight hundred, was sent out along the Kama and Volga rivers."

An example of conditions under which Soviet filmmakers had to work in those early days of the Reconstruction is to be found in the records of a "film cooperative"
(tributary of the Moscow Art Theatre) which, in 1919,
produced the Soviets' first full-length dramatic film—
Tolstoy's *Polikushka*—at an abandoned studio in Petrovsky
Park, outside Moscow. The project was undertaken with

official approval; one form of government aid was a nationwide search for raw film. "Operating on rumors that
there were a hundred meters in a certain Kiev closet, or
two hundred meters in an Odessa warehouse, friends were
sent to acquire, somehow, every meter of decent negative
stock remaining on Russian soil." So jealously did they
husband their precious film that finally 5,400 feet were
edited and used from a total of *six thousand feet shot.* (The
average present-day feature film exposes from ten to
twenty times the footage finally used. With some directors
the ratio becomes astronomical: as much as half a million
feet have been shot for a single movie.) The physical conditions that prevailed during the making of *Polikushka*
were arduous to the point of farce: "There was no transportation between the city and the studio. The cooperative managed to acquire the services of a single sleigh,
horse and coachman, but to conserve the energies of the
hungry horse, only women were permitted its use. The
men walked there and back each day. During shooting,
tiny protected bonfires were produced from the brush-
wood combings of the park and were built inside the
stages. The freezing actors would rush toward them at the
end of a shot." The economics of the production were
equally wild. "Members of the collective received no pay
during production; they were willing to wait for equal
shares in the eventual proceeds. Non-members who
worked and acted in *Polikushka* were glad to be paid in
potatoes." (The New York subways kept running during
our Depression, and we never had to live on potatoes during the lean and thrilling days of the Federal Theatre
Project of the W.P.A., but as I read this account of collective creative enthusiasm, I found myself remembering the
selfless fervor that kept us going, night after night,
through rehearsals of the Negro *Macbeth*, in the freezing,
barren Harlem winter of 1935–36. There is no theatrical
aphrodisiac more potent or satisfying than extreme collective penury.)

By 1920, the outline of Soviet films had begun to reveal itself, assuming a shape which America played an accidental but important part in forming. Late in the previous year, "by one of the most astounding flukes in film history," a print of D. W. Griffith's *Intolerance* found its way through the blockade to Moscow, where it was viewed with excitement and admiration. "No Soviet film of importance made in the following ten years was to be completely outside Griffith's sphere of influence . . . It was in large measure from his example that the Russian filmmakers derived their characteristic staccato shots, their measured and accelerated rhythms and their skill in joining practical images together with a view of the emotional overtones of each, so the two images in conjunction convey more than the sum of their visible content."

It was in this same year that two of Russia's great filmmakers chose the cinema as their vocation; Eisenstein left the study of engineering, and Pudovkin abandoned chemistry in favor of films. Both came under the influence of Kuleshov, whose first theoretical writings on film had appeared in 1917 and who now conducted his workshop in a former private mansion in a Moscow side street. Here, amid the strange, mixed odors of "lilac, celluloid and burned electric wires," Kuleshov revealed to the young men who followed his courses that there were "inherent in a single piece of unedited film two strengths: its own, and the strength of its relation to other pieces of film." In his textbook (*Film Technique*) Pudovkin quotes Kuleshov's statement that in every art there must first be a material, and second a method of composing this material, specially adapted to this art. "Kuleshov maintained that the material in film work consists of pieces of film, and that the method of composing is their joining together in a particular, creatively conceived order. He held that film art does not begin when the artists act and the various scenes are shot—this is only the preparation of the material. Film art begins when the director begins to combine and join together the various pieces of film. By joining them in various combinations and different orders, he obtains differing realities."

Later, Eisenstein refined this theory: "Photography is a system of reproduction to fix real events and elements of actuality. These reproductions or photo-reflections may be combined in various ways; they permit any degree of distortion—either technically unavoidable or deliberately calculated."

For the new generation of Soviet filmmakers who had grown up amid the dramatic agitations of the Civil War and who were familiar with Lenin's dictum that "of all the arts, for us the cinema is the most important," the choice of subject presented no serious problem: the Revolution, its origins, its incidents and its effects furnished an inexhaustible supply of subject matter and even dictated some of the form in which it should be treated.

This happy marriage of form and subject is the theme of the third, climactic act of Leyda's story. It produced the Golden Age of the Soviet cinema. Within five years there appeared, among other celebrated films, Eisenstein's *Strike* and *Potemkin* (1925), Shub's *The Great Road*, Pudovkin's *Mechanics of the Brain* and *Mother* (1926), Room's *Bed and Sofa*, Barnet's *Moscow in October*, Pudovkin's *End of St. Petersburg* (1927), Eisenstein's *October* (1928), Vertov's *Man with a Camera*, Dovzhenko's *Earth* (1930). The first Russian sound film, Nikolai Ekk's *Road to Life* appeared in 1931. But, by then, the honeymoon was over. In what is really the core of his book, Leyda analyzes the essential problem confronting the creative filmmaker in a rapidly expanding, centrally controlled industrial society:

> Artists who had looked to use the film as a creative instrument offered themselves and their newly sensitized instruments to a fresh society whose aims they recognized as identical with their individual decisions. And so long as they had maximum encouragement from their employer-society, they

made their greatest efforts, stimulated their audiences at home and abroad to disturbingly new sensations and new ideas, created works of enduring value and served the world well. But the more intense the social engagement of the film-artist, and the greater the service he wished his films to render to society, the more inevitable his approaching conflict with the administration of the industry within which he worked. This conflict would be expressed variously, in terms of money, or form, or social function, but beneath the argument will be heard a fundamental clash between the natural need of any industrial administration for efficient, continuing uniformity and the natural need of the artist for patience and trust—for time to try the untried.

Two specific hazards now appeared to plague the new Soviet filmmakers. By the late twenties, the Stalin-Trotsky schism was already open and few artists were able entirely to evade its backwash. Eisenstein, dynamic and garrulous, suffered more than any others. Beginning with *October*, which he made on government commission to celebrate the tenth anniversary of the Revolution, the official attacks on Eisenstein and his methods had begun; they were to continue with brief respite for the rest of his days. The week of his death there appeared, in a leading Soviet weekly, a review of his last film—*Ivan, Part Two*—in which he stands accused, among other faults, of "lack of responsibility, a disdainful attitude toward the study of essential material and a careless, arbitrary treatment of historical themes."

The other, more immediate hazard arose as Soviet filmmakers found themselves, willy-nilly, included in the Five Year Plan for Soviet industry. The conflicts between the creative artists and the new centralized film administration headed by Boris Shumyatsky supply the dramatic action for the fourth act of Mr. Leyda's history. While others suffered in varying degrees, it was Eisenstein, once again, who came most sharply into conflict with the administration. In his personal loyalty and admiration for his former teacher and friend, Mr. Leyda does not spare the Soviet bureaucracy, which, "no doubt convinced that it had the best interests of Soviet cinema at heart, had projected a Soviet Hollywood to be built on the shores of the Black Sea. In this place, as isolated as Hollywood from the mainstream of national arts, Shumyatsky would purchase his right to reign supreme by turning out, from the beginning, about three hundred films a year. Anything that would interfere with this smooth flow of production must be silenced and eliminated: "anti-formalism" became a formal cloak for Shumyatsky's industrial program and furnished the suitable sacrificial victim—Sergei Eisenstein. Mr. Leyda goes so far as to suggest that Upton Sinclair's shameful disposal of Eisenstein's *Thunder Over Mexico* in Hollywood, in 1933, was actually encouraged by Shumyatsky as "a disciplinary measure."

(For anyone concerned with the making of films, all this has a terribly familiar ring. The surprise lies in discovering just how little difference there seems to be between front-office behavior in Moscow and Hollywood; between arbitary and destructive interference on behalf of the ideological doctrine of "Socialist Realism" and the inanities of a studio or network executive trying to second-guess tomorrow's public taste.)

Mr. Leyda's last act has a dying fall. Recent Russian production is covered perfunctorily—almost as a postscript to his account of the Golden Age of Soviet films and of the artists who helped to create it. For each of these, almost without exception, the War and the years that followed it were a time of frustration and death. Eisenstein died in 1948; Pudovkin in 1953; Dovzhenko in 1956. For each of them, these final years represented a period of diminishing and, in some cases, totally suspended productivity. Part of the decline may be attributed to the hardships of the invasion and to the special political pressures that preceded and followed it—but not all. Mr. Leyda, in the final paragraph of his book, restates the familiar, inescapable problem confronting filmmakers the world over: the contradictions within a medium that is both an art and an industry. "The sad, blank chapters in the careers of Stroheim and Flaherty have some motifs in common with the silences of Eisenstein and Dovzhenko. Though it is a discouraging notion to those workers and officials who give their lives to improving the physical circumstances of any film industry, it seems clear that the larger the 'Plant,' the more convenient the equipment, the more organized the distribution apparatus, the greater the danger of the film growing less individual, more uniform, and less worth everyone's effort. Throughout Soviet film history, the films were the finest when they had the individuality that any industrial administration, by its nature and purpose, was bound to distrust."

❧ A Critic with a Heart

A COLLEAGUE ONCE described Pauline Kael, not without malice, as a "critic who glows in the dark." It may be that her glow has become more incandescent with the years but she has always been an emotional movie-viewer and, for many years now, one of the industry's most readable and consistently stimulating critics.

When the Lights Go Down, by Pauline Kael (Holt, Rinehart & Winston, 1980). Reprinted from *The Chicago Tribune*.

This latest collection of her *New Yorker* reviews (1975–1979) runs to 662 pages; that so few of them are dull is a tribute to her seemingly inexhaustible enthusiasm for an art form that is still vital and fluid enough to provide an ardent critic with a wide range of subjective reactions. (I can think of no current drama critic who could turn out half as many words of such intense and interesting writing.)

Ms. Kael writes as a member of the contemporary film audience—a passionate, female member. Her erudition is impressive, as is her accumulation of personal emotional experiences collected in dark theaters during a lifetime of moviegoing. She has strong prejudices and pronounced preferences, which she is prepared to change if she has to. Thus, Robert Altman, a former favorite for whose *Nashville* she wrote a dithyrambic review after seeing a rough assembly of the film, is severely mauled in this volume for two recent pictures: *A Wedding* is "a busted bag of marbles" and *Quintet* "is like a Monty Python show played at the wrong speed."

The *New Yorker* has encouraged or at least permitted Ms. Kael to write at unusual length. Where her love or hate is particularly strong she is inclined to overwrite. Yet most of her collected reviews are absorbing—whether or not one has seen the film she is covering. There is an intensity and a sensuality about her reactions to films and actors that give the reader a vivid and positively voluptuous sense of participation. Bob Dylan's eyes, in *Renaldo and Clara,* are "heavily lined in black for a haunting, androgynous effect and you get the skin blemishes, the face hair, the sweat and bad capillaries and, when he sings, the upper lip pulling back in a snarl and the yellow teeth like a crumbling mountain range." Catherine Deneuve's cheek-muscles are "slack" but Blythe Danner's voice "is a French 75; you get the champagne through the chipped ice and cognac." Richard Chamberlain has "porcelain cheekbones and tired, empty blue eyes"; Morley "enters a scene as he enters his British Airways commercials—by pointing his gut and following it—the legs are a distance behind, holding it up." David Considine has "a close-cropped head, somnolent yet alert, the lower lip debating possible pleasure, the body lean but with the gut poking out a bit," while Travolta, in *Saturday Night Fever*, has a mouth that "may look uneducated—pulpy, swollen-lipped, slack—but this isn't stupidity, it's bewilderment. He gets so far inside the role he seems incapable of a false note." Faye Dunaway, in *The Eyes of Laura Mars*, "has a new erotic warmth. Her legs, especially the thighs, are far more important to her performance than her eyes; her flesh gives off heat," whereas Genevieve Bujold, "with her waif's face and sharp jaw, is like a little furry animal—a mink with a dirty mind." Sometimes she overdoes it, as when King Kong's movements as he climbs the World Trade Center "have the Bruckner feeling of heavy orches-tration."

This subjective intensity is applied to all aspects of filmmaking. No "auteur" nonsense here: writer, cinema-tographer, designer, composer, editor and even the makeup department are all subjected to Ms. Kael's pro-fessional scrutiny. (That great cameraman Gordon Willis is charged with lighting and photographing *Comes a Horse-man* "for an audience of bats.") But inevitably it is the director who finally faces her critical fire. Her favorites of the moment include Spielberg, Mazursky, Truffaut, Satyajit Ray, Blier, Scorsese, Bertolucci and she shows a mother's tender care for that bad boy Peckinpah, of whose recent work she writes that "his whole way of making films has become a revenge fantasy: he screws the bosses, he screws the picture, he screws himself."

Her current dislikes include the team of Simon and Ross who "have turned vaudeville into mush"; Paddy Chayefsky for his screenplay of *Network* ("a patriarchal

Jackie Susann"); *Midnight Express* ("movie Yellow Journalism"); Lina Wertmuller for everything, including *Swept Away* and *Seven Beauties* and Paul Schrader, the writer-director of *Hardcore* of whom she assures us that "for Schrader to call himself a whore would be vanity; he doesn't know how to turn a trick."

Recent films that have earned her approval are such disparate creations as *The Magic Flute, King Kong, The Battle of Chile, Encounters of the Third Kind, Adele H, 1900, The Invasion of the Body Snatchers, That Obscure Object of Desire, Saturday Night Fever* and *The Warriors,* for which she wrote one of her hyperbolic reviews that (like the ones she delivered for *Nashville* and *Last Tango in Paris*) are directly convertible into full-page advertisements in the entertainment section of *The New York Times.*

Her tastes run to strong films and one of the most revealing pieces in her book is her attack on the "gentility" of certain contemporary moviegoers "who are trying to protect themselves from their own violence and their own distress by not going to see anything that could rock the boat. . . . They're rejecting the rare films that could stir them, frighten them, elate them. And they're accepting the movies in which everything happens effortlessly and even bloody violence can be shrugged off. Within a few years everything has turned around. Violence that makes you feel afraid has replaced sex as what's offensive, exploitive, dirty; it's as though we should shove muggers and urban guerrillas under the counter. Movie sex, meanwhile, has become trivialized—made casual. It's posh, call-girl sex. Playboy sex. There's no hatred or possessiveness or even passion in it. What does it mean when someone says to you in a prissy, accusing tone that he 'doesn't like' violence? Obviously he's implying that your ability to look at it means *you* like it. He's found a cheap way to present his cultural credentials: sex is 'chic' but violence is for the animals."

I can think of no better summation of Pauline Kael's movie criticism than the final words of her own sympathetic review of a recent Indian film of which she tells us that the director's vision "comes out of so much hurt and guilt and love that the feeling pours all over the cracks and seals them up."

Facing the Fifties

"Hollywood Faces the Fifties" is the third article I wrote for Harper's *magazine about the entertainment business. It appeared during my first year as a film producer for the Metro-Goldwyn-Mayer Studio and was received in California without enthusiasm.*

❖ Hollywood
Faces the Fifties

THROUGH THE FALL and winter of 1949 the patient has been under close observation. Blood count and temperature—weekly box-office receipts and quarterly reports—have been anxiously scanned and minutely evaluated, revealing a slight but continuing decline in income and a fractional reduction in corporate profits. Dr. Gallup, one of the specialists attendant on the case, has come up with some disquieting figures on the continuing shrinkage of

Previously published in *Harper's* magazine, April 1950.

national motion picture attendance, but these are not altogether surprising or immediately alarming.

All things considered, Hollywood appears to be in good health: well enough to be turning out films of good average quality and of the greatest diversity in years; strong enough to be facing, without undue panic, the most drastic challenge in its incredible history.

How different from three years ago, when, at the peak of its unprecedented prosperity, the film industry was seized with one of those dizzying spasms of terror that occasionally catch it by the throat. Like most such panics, this one was born in the midst of plenty and fed on the richness of the organism which it attacked. From 1942 to 1946—with national employment at an all-time peak, transportation blocked, and radio converted in large part to the dissemination of war news—the movies had enjoyed a virtual monopoly of the entertainment business. Hollywood had its own "captive audience." For the studios, these were years of interminable runs and fantastic receipts, with every picture a smash and every producer a genius. For the exhibitors, here was a dream come true: an automatic attendance limited only by the hours of the day and the seating capacity of the nation's eighteen thousand movie theaters.

Since the movies were loaded with profit and blessed with official congratulations for their beneficent effect upon the nation's morale, civilian and military, it was only human of Hollywood to enjoy the wartime bonanza without giving much thought to the morrow. Lacking challenge of any sort, with much of its most creative personnel away at the war, the industry developed no new assets, human or technical. It came out of the boom richer only in lucre. When the inevitable change in the weather finally arrived, it found Hollywood off guard, soft with easy living—and terribly vulnerable.

The panic was psychological before it was economic. The first rumble of distant thunder was heard as early as

1945, when a jurisdictional strike among the studios' stagehands was permitted to rise to so high a pitch of futile bitterness that now, five years later, its echoes are not entirely silenced.

The physical effects of this disturbance were not too serious. Production did not falter and profits were unaffected, though by reducing the available supply of skilled craftsmen that strike did contribute, in some measure, to the rise in physical costs that was soon to plague the industry. The hurt was emotional. Hollywood, which wanted nothing more than to bask in the sun and enjoy its golden harvest, found itself suddenly on the front page of every newspaper in the land, the scene of labor strife and civil violence.

Some months later, still soured by the rancors of the strike, Hollywood stumbled into a deeper trap, the investigation by the Committee on Un-American Activities. In May 1947, members of the Committee appeared in the City of the Angels and held preliminary sessions in a downtown hotel. Their avowed aim was to examine the Red content of American pictures. None was found. But here, day after day, Hollywood's dirty linen was unrolled and washed before the world, while the captains of the industry stood idly by, not altogether averse to a little blood-letting among those of its more aggressive employees who had been most active in recent bargaining sessions and labor negotiations—particularly in the matter of residual rights.

Later, when the action shifted to the limelight of the full-dress Washington hearings, it became clear that in the big game for which Hollywood was so generously providing the field, the ball and the opposing players, there could be only one possible loser, the picture business. But by then it was too late. Not all the industry's frantic efforts, neither Eric Johnston's tergiversations nor the legalistic purging of the "Hollywood Ten," could erase the unfavorable national headlines, the newsreels, the recordings or the editorials. Again, as it turned out, the injury was psychological rather than material. The first to suffer was not the box office but Hollywood's morale. It is impossible to determine, at this time, how seriously the industry's creative energy has been affected by such nonsense.

Cause and effect get confused at such times. Looking back, it seems likely that Hollywood would have kept its head and its dignity somewhat better during this unfortunate period had it not, almost simultaneously, suffered several sudden and quite serious economic jolts. On August 7, 1947, the British Board of Trade announced the application of a 75 percent tax against foreign film earnings in the United Kingdom. The news was received on this side of the Atlantic with a sense of deep injury and disbelief. But when, in quick succession, one foreign government after another, following the lead of perfidious Albion, announced prohibitive restrictions against the American films for which they could no longer afford to pay, the California air rang with lamentations, mingled with howls of rage. Overnight, the producers found themselves deprived of markets upon which the industry, from its earliest days, had counted for its excess profits in good times and for its safety margin in bad.

Then, before Hollywood could catch its breath, came the bitterest blow of all. For some months, from coast to coast, family cars had been rolling again, war plants closing, sports and travel assuming their familiar place in the lives of the American people. Now, gradually, movie grosses began to level off. Though house records continued to be broken in the big cities, business in the country as a whole was becoming spotty, audiences less enthusiastically constant. Though 1947 was, by a slight margin, the industry's second biggest year, the danger signs were becoming unmistakable. During the winter of 1947-48, there reappeared on the books of an American motion-picture company that ghastly relic of the past, that almost-forgotten evil—a movie that actually lost money! And, suddenly the dream was over—the vision of goblin-gold endlessly flowing, culled without effort from ever-longer lines of ever-more-eager customers.

Hollywood, being part of Show Business, is given to manic-depressive behavior. Much of the panic of the following months was anticipatory—the fear of a bad time rather than its actual occurrence. The reality is that picture business, on the whole, has continued good. However it has been a time of change and turnover. There have been minor panics, shake-ups, retrenchments, adjustments and reorganizations in preparation for the long-delayed but inevitable government antitrust action resulting in the "separation" of production and theater operation by most of the major film companies. One major company has changed hands. Production, choked for a while by a backlog of costly films left over from the boom days, slowed down, then picked up again. The ratio of independent productions has dropped sharply, but the number of full-length features produced yearly by the major companies has not seriously varied in seven years. It remains around four hundred. (This is considerably less than the volume of the thirties before the rise in the cost of production and the boomtime prevalence of long runs.)

To meet current market conditions, a serious effort has been made to cut production costs. By the industry's own calculation, the average cost of pictures has been reduced by 33 percent. Most of this saving is directly reflected in curtailed employment. Among craft unions, according to Thomas Brady of *The New York Times,* it has fallen from 22,000 in 1946 to 13,500 in 1949. In the higher echelons, the scale of salaries has been somewhat reduced, but Hollywood will continue to be well represented in the Treasury reports of the nation's top incomes. Sundry studio economies have been effected, notably in the matter of writing costs. (The day of the $750,000 story accumulations, with twenty writers working on a single script, is over—probably forever.) "Overhead" remains high, from 35 percent to 50 percent in major studios, where the average minimum cost of a full-length feature film is still around a million dollars.

As to the foreign markets, it now appears that the fears of 1947 were, to say the least, exaggerated. Last year, according to the president of the Motion Picture Producers of America, Hollywood got more than one hundred million dollars out of foreign countries—more than in any year before the war and more than half of it still from the British Empire. Finally, with the collapse of the British film industry, in the person of that eccentric flour-miller-turned-showman, J. Arthur Rank, Hollywood finds itself today without serious commercial competition in the international movie field.

From this brief summary, it should be evident that this winter the sky over Hollywood was not uniformly dark. A stranger in town, enjoying the movie capital's Yuletide cheer and following the trade papers' jubilant reports of holiday business (HOLIDAY BIZ BOFFO; NEW YEAR IN SMASH BIZ RESPONSE) might have left with the impression that happy days were here again, the gravy boat once more ready to overflow. A more careful observer could not fail to sense a strange tension in the sunny air and a deep feeling of disquiet and anxiety—what Budd Schulberg, who has known the local climate from childhood, calls Earthquake Weather.

II

Mass Entertainment, by its nature, its form and its energy, is a fluid thing, subject to the sudden shifts of a rapidly changing world. When once a popular appetite falls away—following some strange tide of social custom, or swayed by a jolt of technological change, or just out of sheer surfeit—not all the king's horses or all the king's men, or even a giant industry's long-accumulated assets of know-how and good will can rekindle the lost enthusiasm or renew the forgotten habit. It is with understandable concern therefore that Hollywood, these days, is carefully watching the shifting trends of national taste and uneasily following the slowly falling curve of weekly movie attendance among the American people.

The Audience Research Institute sees two encouraging signs in the film industry's otherwise disturbing figures; first, the rate of decline of 1949 compared to 1948 was not so swift as that of 1948 compared to 1947; second, in comparison to 1940, U.S. movie attendance has risen faster than population, 17 as opposed to 14 percent A.R.I. believes that in another two or three months it should become clear whether or not the downward trend has been checked.

(It is worth noting that television—which presents the future's major threat to the film industry—seems so far to have had little effect on those figures; the decline has taken place as much in the areas in which television is not available as in those where it is.)

When *Life*, last summer, in one of its periodic investigations of contemporary American culture, turned its attention to the motion picture industry—to "that $2,750,000,000 cultural-commercial complex whose arbitrary but convenient name is Hollywood," the problem of the "lost audience" engaged its attention: "For the past year, more or less, the national box-office figures have been askew." It was only natural that they should decline from the enormous postwar years of 1946 and 1947. But the figures have not snapped back; the weekly magazine *Variety*, which claims to know all that is knowable about Show Business, recently headlined a front-page article "PIX BAFFLED FOR B.O. SOLUTION."

Four panels were held by *Life*, from which certain general criticisms of Hollywood emerged. These were then used as a basis for discussion at a final symposium. Its findings were well summarized by Eric Hodgins, moderator and reporter of the proceedings:

1. Hollywood is trying to comply with thousands of prohibitions and its aim is thus becoming the barren and self-defeating aim of not displeasing anybody.
2. In so doing Hollywood is neglecting its active audience and catering hardest to the habitual, passive audience which does it least good and will be the first to desert it for television.
3. The search for the "universal" picture will end in disaster if sufficiently pursued.

Around *Life*'s table were seated a number of old-timers, several representatives of Hollywood's most active talent (sometimes referred to as the "militant vanguard"), a few academics and newspapermen to needle them, one financier—no exhibitors. The debate, in the main, seemed to justify *Life*'s statement that moviemakers are "earnest and thoughtful men . . . who feel a genuine concern with serving their public as well as possible." To what extent they succeeded in clearing up the current anguish and confusion is a moot point and more than once the participants became entangled in the ambiguities that inevitably dog the steps of all those who "tread a tight-wire between the pursuit of art and the pursuit of profit."

III

There was one participant on the panel who was not at all ambiguous. Speaking as a filmmaker with a yearly income running well into six figures, his remarks were of a realistic kind. They must engage our attention here, together with the reaction they provoked, since they bear very directly upon one of the main causes of Hollywood's current concern: the basic conflict between makers of film and the controllers of film distribution.

"Who controls the movies?" asked Joseph L. Mankiewicz, himself a ranking member of the industry, credited with last year's most successful comedy, *A Letter to*

Three Wives. "Isn't it true that a real-estate operator whose chief concern should be taking gum off carpets and checking adolescent lovemaking in the balcony—isn't it true that this man is in control? Isn't it true that when he gives you 40 percent of what he takes out of the picture you have made and keeps 60 percent, he thinks he is giving you a hell of a fine deal? . . . Here is the incredible power of the real undercover man in the motion-picture industry, the exhibitor, who considers it his God-given right to make this fantastic profit, just by virtue of the fact that he owns an enormous barnlike structure with seats in it."

The points scored by Mr. Mankiewicz, with insult and injury, have been made before—particularly by independent film producers. In cold figures, out of every dollar paid by audiences to view his picture, the independent producer, if he is lucky, receives twenty cents. Of all the monies received, the theaters keep around 65 percent. Of what is left, the distributor gets about one third. Out of his take, the producer must pay for his print costs and his share of the general advertising and promotion expense, amounting to another 5 percent. When all these, plus his financing, are taken care of, he can start paying off his production! No wonder that, according to *Variety*, INDIE PROD HEADS FOR ALL-TIME LOW. Yet so rich is the market, so generous the American public in paying for its entertainment, that an astute independent, even under these adverse conditions, has a chance to come out ahead. But the mortality is high.

That outside control of moviemaking exists is generally recognized. For many years it has been the basic pattern of an industry which, according to a recent paper in the Annals of the American Academy of Political and Social Science, "is governed by self-perpetuating management groups largely responsible to banking and real-estate powers whose interests, in turn, are interwoven with a complicated network of other monopoly or semi-monopoly groupings having little to do with the movie industry directly. . . . These interlocking monopoly groupings are able, directly or indirectly, to make the important decisions for all phases of the film industry, from movie lot to ultimate consumer."

What concerns us here—as it did Mr. Mankiewicz and his fellow members of the *Life* roundtable—is the effect such control must have on production, upon the acts and thoughts of the picture-makers and thus upon the nature and quality of the movies that get made in Hollywood. Is this the force that works for standardization? Is it from this quarter that we may expect to find the main pressure for the "formula" picture? Mr. Mankiewicz thinks it is:

> Take your panel to the real-estate operators who control and exploit the greatest concentration of talent in the entertainment world and ask them "What do you want of Hollywood?" The answer, if it is honest, will be in essence, "We want four hundred items of salable merchandise every year."

If this was strongly put so were the replies received. "Only the libel laws keep me from making it more emphatic—Mr. Mankiewicz is an ass!" wrote the vice-president and general manager of a large southwestern theater circuit to the *Motion Picture Herald.* "We would not be in the 'real-estate' business long," wrote another, "if we had to rely on the likes of Mankiewicz pictures to pay our bills!" But more revealing than the personal vituperation were the impassioned letters and the earnest editorials written to refute his error.

From Hawkinsville, Georgia: "Our patrons, those people who lay down their money at the box office, say as simply and clearly as they possibly can these two simple words: 'Amuse me!' If we do, they are happy, we are happy, the distributors are happy. But, according to Mr. Mankiewicz, it ends there, because the producers are only happy when they have displayed their wonderful genius and knowledge of 'art,' or have righted some great wrong, or have broken down some psychological inhibition that is the personal property of the patron. Poor Mr. Mankiewicz!"

"What would Mr. Mankiewicz have?" asked another. "The man surely cannot be so ignorant of the prime laws of economics that he thinks the 6 percent production and distribution tail is going to wag the 94 percent exhibitor interest in the movie business." Another carries the argument even further: "What is this communism we hear so much about? Isn't it just that private property does not exist or that it receives no return and that the so-called 'creator' gets all the benefit of the so-called 'creations'? Actually hasn't Hollywood pretty much approached that ideal already? And isn't Mr. Mankiewicz only protesting that the approach is not quite close enough?"

Less abusive but equally destructive of Mr. Mankiewicz's case were the recent findings of Florence Parry, dramatic editor of the *Pittsburgh Press,* on her return from a motor-tour of the American hinterland:

> Never before had I such occasion to realize the great, important, life-saving place the movies have in the life of the people of these United States. . . . We in the densely populated, metropolitan areas of the East, are offered many diversions with which to fill our increasing "leisure." And it is easy for us to think of the movies in terms of our own tastes and needs. Nothing would work such a hardship upon the population of this country *as a whole* as to withdraw from production and general consumption the motion pictures designed to fit the capacities of the unnumbered millions who, denied the opportunity and benefits vouchsafed the favored minority, are still receiving the very kind of entertainment they most enjoy *and need.*

This is no new dispute. It is as old as the movies and it has long been one of the chronic tensions of Hollywood.

There is no picture-maker who has not, at one time or another, become embroiled in this struggle between the creator and the businessman for control of his films. Some, like Griffith and Stroheim, were finally broken by it and deprived forever of their means of production.

I am not suggesting that virtue is all on the side of the filmmakers. In a medium that has flourished so miraculously—"a business that is also an art form"—how much of the credit for this bewildering growth goes to the creators of film? How much to the performers? How much to the entrepreneurs who, by boldly exploiting their work, have developed the vast audience which, in turn, conditions their product? The truth is that they were all swept along by waves of technological advance and social and economic change over which they had no control but from which they all profited. Charlie Chaplin's genius found freer expression and fuller scope before a world audience of a hundred million moviegoers than he could ever have realized on the stages of a few hundred vaudeville houses. Conversely, how much did Chaplin's immediate and universal popularity contribute to the growth of this new public and to the miraculous rise of the industry as a whole? How much did Griffith's expansion of film with *Birth of a Nation* add to the stature and prosperity of the entire movie business? Today, how much does the general health of the industry depend upon the risky stimulus of genius? How much upon the regular satisfaction of predictable appetites? How is quality to be measured against habit? How does the thrill of novelty rate against the pleasures of repetition?

In a vain attempt to answer these and similar questions, the industry, some years ago, engaged the services of a troupe of witch doctors, pollsters, audience-experts and other self-anointed specialists in the realm of public taste. Subject matter was pre-tested, star-ratings assessed, and good money spent on Rube Goldberg devices for measur-

ing audience taste and reaction. These so-called experts'
findings were no more impressive in Show Business than
they had been in the political field, and for the same reason. To question the public's right of free choice is something neither a politician nor a showman can afford. "I
never know what the public wants and I don't think the
public does. I can only give them what I like and hope for
the best. If what I liked was consistently rejected by the
public, I would get out of the business." The words are
Carol Reed's, director of *The Fallen Idol* and *The Third
Man,* and they are an honest statement of the creative mo-
viemaker's creed.

The War strengthened the exhibitors' position. In the
sellers' market the war boom created and in the absence of
a large part of its creative personnel, the film industry
came closer to producing movies by assembly-line
methods than at any other time in its history. With the
return of its creative members and apparent decline in automatic movie attendance, that process has been reversing
itself. The recent rise in sophistication (of which Mankiewicz's films are an example) and the general, marked
improvement in the quality of Hollywood's product follow a tendency, in most studios, to have scripts once again
written by writers and not in story conferences, to have
movies made by individuals rather than by production
departments.

This does not solve the conflict raised by Mankiewicz
and his antagonists. In the development of a medium
which, by contemporary standards of growth, is no longer
young, fragmentation is inevitable. Like all maturing organisms the film business moves through stages of increasing complexity. Lost beyond recall is the happy simplicity
of Hollywood's reckless pioneer days; the question asked
here is whether we may not already have drifted past the
midpoint of the Industry's second phase—whether the

centrally controlled mechanism of the picture business is still capable of coping with the shifting and multiplying problems of filmmaking in the future.

IV

On January 1, 1950, with the "separation" of Paramount Pictures and Paramount Theaters, the long-delayed and bitterly contested "divorcement" finally went into effect. The Industry has had enough time and sufficient expensive legal resources to soften and circumvent this disruption of its affairs. Old-timers hate to see the end of a system that, with all its abuses, has been yielding golden eggs for so long. Others take a more optimistic view.

> There is a new challenge in this divorcement. The companies which have had their own theaters along with their production companies have always given the best break to the theaters. Now it's going to be different. Starting next Monday the distributors will acquire deals for their product that are a cinch to jump receipts and will take off some of the huge profits the theaters have been banking all these years.

A theater-owner is equally enthusiastic—for entirely different reasons:

> The decision means a boon for better pictures in this country. I don't say the public is going to start a revolution or go suddenly high-brow, but I do think the companies will have to make better movies because now nobody will have to buy movies they don't want. Bad movies just won't sell.

It is still too early to tell how much effect the "divorce" will have on the making and marketing of Hollywood's motion pictures. Far less, I suspect, than the great flood of television entertainment which is about to engulf us all.

Filmmakers in general have been slow to understand the nature of the threat they are facing. They cannot ignore the new medium but they choose to believe that the changes will be limited and that television and theatrical film will continue to coexist and to share the spoils. The history of the entertainment business suggests that such coexistence is improbable and that a radical shift in power lies ahead.

For the financiers and businessmen who will undoubtedly end by controlling both media, the years to come promise to be an era of unlimited expansion and astronomical profits. To the industry's creative elements such mutations offer a future filled with new opportunities accompanied by a wide range of new problems.

BOOK THREE

THE MASS MEDIA

Radio

"The Men from Mars" was the first of the seven articles I contributed to Harper's *magazine between 1946 and 1979. It was written at the suggestion of an editor whose dinner guests I had entertained with a lurid account of the national panic that followed the* Mercury's *radio broadcast of "The War of the Worlds" in the fall of 1938.*

✿*The Men from Mars (October, 1938)*

RADIO WAR TERRORIZES U.S.
New York Daily News, October 31, 1938.
Everybody was excited I felt as if I was going crazy and kept on saying what can we do what difference does it make whether we die sooner or later? We were holding each other. Everything seemed unimportant in the face of death. I was afraid to die, just kept on listening.

—A listener

> Nothing about the broadcast was the least credible.
> —Dorothy Thompson

THE SHOW CAME OFF. No doubt about that. It set out to dramatize, in terms of popular apprehension, an attempted invasion of our world by hostile forces from an alien planet Mars. It succeeded. Of the several million American citizens who, on the evening of October 30, 1938, milled about the streets, clung sobbing to one another or drove wildly in all directions to avoid asphyxiation and flaming death, approximately one half were in terror of Martians—not of Germans, Japanese or unknown enemies—but, specifically, of Martians. Later, when the excitement was over and the shadow of the gallows had lifted, some of us were inclined to take credit for more deliberate and premeditated villainy than we deserved. The truth is that at the time nobody was more surprised by the panic than we were. In fact, one of the most remarkable things about the broadcast was the altogether haphazard nature of its birth.

In October 1938, the Mercury Theatre, of which Orson Welles and I were the founding partners, had been in existence for less than a year. Our first Broadway season had been unusually successful: *Julius Caesar, The Cradle Will Rock, Shoemaker's Holiday* and *Heartbreak House* in the order of their appearance. In April, Orson, in a white beard, made the cover of *Time* magazine. In June, the Columbia Broadcasting System offered him a radio program—*The Mercury Theatre on the Air,* a series of classic dramatizations in the first person singular with Orson in the multiple function of master of ceremonies, star, narrator, writer, director and producer. He accepted. So, now, in addition to theater, a movie in progress, two plays in rehearsal and all seven of the chronicle plays of William Shakespeare in preparation, we had a national radio show.

Previously published in *Harper's* magazine, December 1948.

We opened in July with "Dracula." Among our first thirteen shows were "Treasure Island," "39 Steps," "Abraham Lincoln," "Three Short Stories" (by Saki, Sherwood Anderson and Carl Ewald), "Jane Eyre," "Julius Caesar" (with running commentary by Kaltenborn out of Plutarch), and "The Man Who Was Thursday." Our second series, starting in September, opened with Booth Tarkington's "Seventeen," "Around the World in Eighty Days" and "Oliver Twist." Our fifth show was to be "Life with Father." Our fourth was "The War of the Worlds."

No one, as I remember, was very enthusiastic about it. But it seemed good programming, coming as it did between the gloom of Dickens's London slums and the charm of Clarence Day's New York in the nineties, to throw in something of a contrasting and pseudoscientific nature. We thought of Shiel's *Purple Cloud,* Conan Doyle's *Lost World* and several others before we settled on H. G. Wells's twenty-year-old novel, which neither of us, as it turned out later, remembered at all clearly. It is just possible that neither of us had ever read it.

II

Those were the golden days of unsponsored radio. We had no advertising agency to harass us, no client to cut our withers. Partly because we were perpetually overworked and partly because that was the way we did things at the Mercury, we never seemed to get more than a single jump ahead of ourselves. Shows were created week after week under conditions of soul- and health-destroying pressure. On the whole they were good shows. And we *did* develop a system—of sorts.

It worked as follows: I was editor of the series. With Welles, I chose the shows and then prepared them. Most of the writing was done in the beginning by myself, and then, after our second theatrical season got under way, by a new recruit in the person of Howard Koch—earnest, spindly, six-foot-two—a young Westchester lawyer-turned-playwright. To write the first draft of an hour's script took him all of five days, working about fifteen hours a day. Our associate producer was Paul Stewart, a Broadway actor-turned-director. His function was to put the broadcast through its first paces and preliminary rehearsals. Every Thursday, without music and with only rudimentary sound effects, a reading of the show was recorded. From this record, played back later that night, Orson would give us his reactions and revisions. In the next thirty-six hours the script would be reshaped and rewritten, sometimes drastically. Saturday afternoon there was another rehearsal, with sound effects—with or without Welles. It was not until the last day that Orson really took over.

Sundays, at 8 P.M., we went on the air. Beginning in the early afternoon—when Bernard Herrmann, our musical director, arrived with his orchestra of twenty-seven high-grade symphony players—two simultaneous dramas were regularly unfolded in the stale, tense air of Studio Number One: the minor drama of the current show and the major drama of Orson's gargantuan struggle to get it on. Sweating, howling, disheveled and single-handed he wrestled with Chaos and Time—always conveying an effect of being alone, traduced by his collaborators, surrounded by treachery, ignorance, sloth, indifference, incompetence, and—more often than not—downright sabotage! Every Sunday it was touch and go. As the hands of the clock moved relentlessly toward air time the crisis grew more extreme, the peril more desperate. Often violence broke out. Scripts flew through the air, doors were slammed, batons smashed. Scheduled for 6 P.M., but usually nearer 7, there was a dress rehearsal, a thing of wild improvisations and irrevocable disaster. (One show was found to be twenty-one minutes overlength, another fourteen and one-half minutes short.)

After that, with only a few minutes to go, there was a

final frenzy of correction and reparation, of utter confusion and absolute horror, aggravated by the gobbling of sandwiches and the bolting of oversized milkshakes. By now it was less than a minute to air time . . .

At that instant, quite regularly week after week, with not one second to spare, this titanic buffoonery stopped. Suddenly, out of chaos, the show emerged—delicately poised, meticulously executed, precise as clockwork and smooth as satin. And above us all, like a rainbow over storm clouds, stood Orson on his podium, sonorous and heroic, a leader of men surrounded by his band of loyal followers, a giant in action, serene and radiant with the joy of a hard battle bravely fought—a great victory snatched from the jaws of disaster.

In later years, when The Men from Mars had passed into history, there was some argument among members of the Mercury Theatre as to who exactly had contributed precisely what to that particular evening's entertainment. The truth is that a number of us made a number of essential and incalculable contributions to the broadcast. (Who can accurately assess, for instance, the part played by Johnny Dietz's perfect engineering in keeping unbroken the shifting illusion of imperfect reality? How much did the original by H. G. Wells, who emphatically repudiated the show, have to do with it? Or the second assistant sound man? Or individual actors? Or Dr. Goebbels? Or Charlie McCarthy?) Orson Welles had virtually nothing to do with the writing of the script and less than usual to do with its preliminary rehearsals. Yet, first and last, it was his creation. If there had been a lynching that night, it is Welles the outraged populace would have strung up—and rightly so. Orson was the Mercury. "The War of the Worlds," like everything we did, was his show.

Actually, it was a narrow squeak. Those Men from Mars barely escaped being stillborn. Tuesday afternoon—five days before the show—Howard Koch telephoned. He was in deep distress. After three days of slaving on H. G. Wells's scientific fantasy he was ready to give up. Under no circumstances, he declared, could it be made interesting or in any way credible to modern American ears. Koch was not given to habitual alarmism. To confirm his fears, Annie, my secretary, came to the phone. She was an acid and emphatic girl from Smith College with fine blond hair, who smelled of fading spring flowers. "You can't do it!" she protested. "Those old Martians are just a lot of nonsense. It's all too silly! We're going to make fools of ourselves! Absolute fools!"

For some reason which I do not clearly remember our only possible alternative for that week was a dreary one— *Lorna Doone.* I tried to reach Welles. He was in rehearsal at the theater and wouldn't come to the phone.

The reason he wouldn't come to the phone was that he was in his thirty-sixth successive hour of dress-rehearsing *Danton's Death,* a beautiful, fragmentary play by Georg Buechner out of which Max Reinhardt, in an altered form, had made a successful mass spectacle in the twenties. Not to be outdone, Orson had glued seventeen hundred masks onto the back wall of the Mercury Theatre and ripped out the entire stage. Day after day actors fell headlong into the rat-ridden basement, leaped on and off erratically moving elevators and chanted the "Carmagnole" in chorus under the supervision of Marc Blitzstein.

Unable to reach Welles, I called Koch back. I was severe. I taxed him with defeatism. I gave him false comfort. I promised to come up and help. When I finally got there—around two in the morning—things were going better. He and Paul Stewart had decided to update the show and were beginning to have fun laying waste the state of New Jersey. Annie had stopped grinding her teeth. We worked all through the rest of the night and through the next day. On Wednesday at sunset the script was finished.

Thursday, as usual, Paul Stewart rehearsed the show, then made a record. We listened to it rather gloomily, long after midnight in Orson's room at the St. Regis, sitting on the floor because all the chairs were covered with coils of unrolled and unedited film. We agreed it was a dull show. We all felt its only chance of coming off lay in emphasizing its newscast style—its simultaneous, eyewitness quality.

All night we sat up, spicing the script with circumstantial allusions and authentic detail. Friday afternoon it went over to CBS to be passed by the network censor. Certain alterations were requested. Under protest and with a deep sense of grievance we changed the Hotel Biltmore to a nonexistent Park Plaza, Trans-America to Intercontinent, the Columbia Broadcasting Building to Broadcasting Building. Then the script went over to mimeograph and we went to bed. We had done our best and, after all, a show is just a show . . .

Saturday afternoon Paul Stewart rehearsed with sound effects but without Welles. He worked for a long time on the crowd scenes, the first sound of the Death-Ray and the roar of cannon echoing in the Watchung Hills. Also the noises of New York Harbor as the ships with the last remaining survivors put out to sea.

Around six we left the studio. Orson, phoning from the theater a few minutes later to find out how things were going, was told by one of the CBS sound men who had stayed behind to pack up his equipment that it was not one of our better shows. Confidentially, the man opined, it just didn't come off. Twenty-seven hours later, quite a few of his employers would have found themselves a good deal happier if he had turned out to be right.

III

On Sunday, October 30, at 8 P.M., E.S.T., in a studio littered with coffee cartons and sandwich paper, Orson swallowed a second container of pineapple juice, put on his earphones, raised his long white fingers and threw the cue for the Mercury theme—the Tchaikovsky Piano Concerto in B Flat Minor #1. After the music dipped, there were routine introductions, then the announcement that—this being Halloween—a dramatization of H. G. Wells's famous novel, *The War of the Worlds,* was about to be performed. Around 8:01 Orson began to speak, as follows:

WELLES

We know now that in the early years of the twentieth century this world was being watched closely by intelligences greater than man's and yet as mortal as his own. We know now that as human beings busied themselves about their various concerns they were scrutinized and studied, perhaps almost as narrowly as a man with a microscope might scrutinize the transient creatures that swarm and multiply in a drop of water. With infinite complacence people went to and fro over the earth about their little affairs, serene in the assurance of their dominion over this small spinning fragment of solar driftwood which by chance or design man has inherited out of the dark mystery of Time and Space. Yet, across an immense ethereal gulf minds that are to our minds as ours are to the beasts in the jungle, intellects vast, cool and unsympathetic regarded this earth with envious eyes and slowly and surely drew their plans against us. In the thirty-ninth year of the twentieth century came the great disillusionment.

It was near the end of October. Business was better. The war scare was over. More men were back at work. Sales were picking up. On this particular evening, October 30, the Crossley Service estimated that thirty-two million people were listening in on their radios . . .

Neatly, without perceptible transition, he was followed on the air by an anonymous announcer caught in a routine bulletin:

ANNOUNCER

. . . for the next twenty-four hours not much change in temperature. A slight atmospheric disturbance of undetermined origin is reported over Nova Scotia, causing a low-pressure area to move down rather rapidly over the northeastern states, bringing a forecast of rain, accompanied by winds of light gale force. Maximum temperature 66°; minimum 48°. This weather report comes to you from the Government Weather Bureau. . . . We now take you to the Meridian Room in the Hotel Park Plaza in downtown New York, where you will be entertained by the music of Ramon Raquello and his orchestra.

At which cue, Bernard Herrmann led the massed men of the CBS Symphony Orchestra in a thunderous and awful rendition of "La Cumparsita." The entire hoax might well have exploded there and then—but for the fact that hardly anyone was listening. They were being entertained by Edgar Bergen and Charlie McCarthy—then at the height of their success.

The Crossley census, taken about a week before the broadcast, had given *The Mercury Theatre on the Air* 3.6 percent of the listening audience as against Edgar Bergen's 34.7 percent for Maxwell House Coffee. What the Crossley Institute (that hireling of the advertising agencies) deliberately ignored was the healthy American habit of dial-twisting. On that particular evening Charlie McCarthy temporarily left the air about 8:12 P.M., E.S.T., yielding place to a new and not very popular singer. At that point, and during the following minutes, a large number of listeners started twisting their dials in search of other entertainment. Many of them turned to us—and when they did, they stayed put! For by this time the mysterious meteorite had fallen at Grovers Mill in New Jersey, the Martians had begun to show their foul leathery heads above the ground, and the New Jersey State Police were racing to the spot. Within twenty minutes people all over the United States were praying, crying, fleeing frantically to escape death from the Martians. Some remembered to rescue loved ones, others telephoned farewells or warnings, hurried to inform neighbors, sought information from newspapers or radio stations, summoned ambulances and police cars.

The reaction was strongest at points nearest the tragedy. In Newark, New Jersey, in a single block, twenty-two families rushed out of their houses with wet handkerchiefs and towels over their faces. Some began moving household furniture. Police switchboards were flooded with calls inquiring, "Shall I close my windows?" "Have the police any extra gas masks?" Police found one family waiting in the yard "with wet cloths on faces contorted with hysteria." As one woman reported later:

> I was terribly frightened. I wanted to pack and take my child in my arms, gather up my friends and get in the car and just go north as far as we could. But what I did was just sit by one window, praying, listening, and scared stiff, and my husband by the other sniffling and looking out to see if people were running . . .

In New York hundreds of people on Riverside Drive fled their homes, ready for flight. Bus terminals were crowded. A woman calling up the Dixie Bus Terminal for information said impatiently, "Hurry, please, the world is coming to an end and I have a lot to do." In the parlor churches of Harlem, evening services became "end-of-the-world" prayer meetings. Many turned to God in that moment:

> I held a crucifix in my hand and prayed while looking out of my open window for falling meteors . . . When the monsters were wading across the Hudson River and coming into New York, I wanted to run up on my roof to see what they

looked like, but I couldn't leave my radio while it was telling me of their whereabouts.

> Aunt Grace began to pray with Uncle Henry. Lily got sick to her stomach. I don't know what I did exactly but I know I prayed harder and more earnestly than ever before. Just as soon as we were convinced that this thing was real, how petty all things on this earth seemed; how soon we put our trust in God!

The panic moved upstate. One man called up the Mount Vernon Police Headquarters to find out "where the forty policemen were killed." Another took time out to philosophize:

> I thought the whole human race was going to be wiped out—that seemed more important than the fact that we were going to die. It seemed awful that everything that had been worked on for years was going to be lost forever.

In Rhode Island weeping and hysterical women swamped the switchboard of the Providence *Journal* for details of the massacre, and officials of the electric light company received a score of calls urging them to turn off all lights so that the city would be safe from the enemy. The Boston *Globe* received a call from one woman who "could see the fire." A man in Pittsburgh hurried home in the midst of the broadcast and found his wife in the bathroom, a bottle of poison in her hand, screaming, "I'd rather die this way than that." In Minneapolis a woman ran into church screaming, "New York destroyed! This is the end of the world! You might as well go home to die—I just heard it on the radio."

The Kansas City Bureau of the AP received inquiries about the "meteors" from Los Angeles, Salt Lake City, Beaumont, Texas and St. Joseph, Missouri. In San Francisco the general impression of listeners seemed to be that an overwhelming force had invaded the United States from the air, was in process of destroying New York and threatening to move westward. "My God," roared an inquirer into a telephone, "where can I volunteer my services? We've got to stop this awful thing!"

As far south as Birmingham, Alabama, people gathered in churches and prayed. On the campus of a Southeastern college,

> The girls in the sorority houses and dormitories huddled around their radios trembling and weeping in each other's arms. They separated themselves from their friends only to take their turn at the telephones to make long-distance calls to their parents, saying goodbye for what they thought might be the last time. . . .

There are hundreds of such bits of testimony, gathered from coast to coast.

IV

At least one book* and quite a pile of sociological literature has appeared on the subject of "the invasion from Mars." Many theories have been put forward to explain the "tidal wave" of panic that swept the nation. I know of two factors that largely contributed to the broadcast's extraordinarily violent effect. First, its historical timing. It came within thirty-five days of the Munich crisis. For weeks, the American people had been hanging on their radios, getting most of their news no longer from the press, but over the air. A new technique of "on-the-spot" reporting had been developed and eagerly accepted by an anxious and news-hungry world. *The Mercury Theatre on the Air,* by faithfully copying every detail of the new technique— including its imperfections—found an already enervated

---

* *The Invasion from Mars,* by Hadley Cantril, Princeton University Press, from which many of the above quotations were taken.

audience ready to accept its wildest fantasies. The second factor was the show's sheer technical brilliance. To this day it is impossible to sit in a room and hear the scratched, worn, off-the-air recording of the broadcast, without feeling in the back of your neck some slight draft left over from that great wind of terror that swept the nation. Even with the element of credibility totally removed it remains a surprisingly frightening show.

Radio drama was taken seriously in the thirties—before the quiz and the giveaway became the lords of the air. In the work of such directors as Reis, Corwin, Fickett, Welles, Robson, Spier, and Oboler there was an eager, excited drive to get the most out of this new, all too rapidly freezing medium. But what happened that Sunday, up on the twentieth floor of the CBS building, was something quite special. Beginning around two, when the show started to take shape under Orson's hands, a strange fever seemed to invade the studio—part childish mischief, part professional zeal.

First to feel it were the actors. I remember Frank Readick (who played the part of Carl Phillips, the network's special reporter) going down to the record library and digging up the Morrison recording of the explosion of the Hindenburg at Lakehurst the previous year. This is a classic reportage—one of those wonderful, unpredictable accidents of eyewitness description. The broadcaster is casually describing a routine landing of the giant gasbag. Suddenly he sees something. A flash of flame! An instant later the whole thing explodes. It takes him time—a full second—to react at all. Then seconds more of sputtering ejaculations before he can make the adjustment between brain and tongue. He starts to describe the terrible things he sees—the writhing human figures twisting and squirming as they fall from the white burning wreckage. He stops, fumbles, vomits, then quickly continues. Readick played the record to himself, over and over. Then, re-creating the emotion in his own terms, he described the

Martian meteorite as he saw it lying inert and harmless in a field at Grovers Mill, lit up by the headlights of a hundred cars—the coppery cylinder suddenly opening, revealing the leather tentacles and the terrible pale-eyed faces of the Martians within. As they begin to emerge he freezes, unable to translate his vision into words; he fumbles, retches—and then, after a second, continues to report.

A few moments later Carl Phillips lay dead, tumbling over the microphone in his fall—one of the first victims of the Martian Ray. There followed a moment of absolute silence—an eternity of waiting. Then, without warning, the network's emergency fill-in was heard: somewhere in a quiet studio a piano, close on mike, playing "Clair de Lune," soft and sweet as honey, for many seconds, while the fate of the universe hung in the balance. Finally it was interrupted by the manly reassuring voice of Brigadier General Montgomery Smith, Commander of the New Jersey State Militia, speaking from Trenton and placing "the counties of Mercer and Middlesex as far west as Princeton and east to Jamesburg" under martial law. Following the Goebbels technique—tension, release, then renewed tension—our next item was an eyewitness account of the fatal battle of the Watchung Hills; and then, once again, that lone piano was heard—now a symbol of terror, shattering the dead air with its ominous tinkle. As it played, its effect became increasingly sinister, a thin band of suspense stretched almost beyond endurance.

That piano was the neatest trick of the show—a fine specimen of the theatrical "retard," boldly conceived and exploited to the full. It was one of the many devices with which Welles succeeded in compelling, not merely the attention, but also the belief of his invisible audience. "The War of the Worlds" was a magic act, one of the world's greatest, and Orson was just the man to bring it off.

For Welles is at heart a magician whose particular talent lies not so much in his creative imagination (which is

considerable) as in his proven ability to stretch the familiar elements of theatrical effect far beyond their normal
point of tension. For this reason his productions require
more elaborate preparation and more perfect execution
than most. Like all complicated magic tricks they remain,
until the last moment, in a state of precarious balance.
When they come off, they give, by virtue of their unusually high intensity, an impression of great brilliance
and power; when they fail—when something in their balance goes wrong or the original structure proves to have
been unsound—they provoke among their audience a particularly violent reaction of unease and revulsion. Welles's
flops are louder than other men's. The Mars broadcast
was one of his unqualified successes.

Among the columnists and public figures who discussed
the affair during the next few days (some praising us for
the public service we had rendered, some condemning us
as sinister scoundrels) the most general reaction was one of
amazement at the "incredible stupidity" and "gullibility"
of the American public, who had accepted as real, in this
hour's broadcast, incidents which in actual fact would
have taken days or even weeks to occur. "Nothing about
the broadcast," wrote Dorothy Thompson with her usual
aplomb, "was in the least credible." She was wrong. The
first few minutes of our broadcast were, in point of fact,
strictly realistic in time and perfectly credible, though
somewhat boring, in content. Herein lay the great tensile
strength of the show; it was the structural device that
made the whole illusion possible. And it could have been
carried off in no other medium than radio.

Our actual broadcasting time, from the first mention of
the meteorites to the fall of New York City, was less than
forty minutes. During that time men traveled long distances, large bodies of troops were mobilized, cabinet
meetings were held, savage battles fought on land and in
the air. And millions of people accepted it—emotionally if
not logically.

There is nothing so very strange about that. Most of us do the same thing, to some degree, most days of our lives—every time we look at a movie or listen to a broadcast. Not even the realistic theater observes the literal unities; motion pictures and, particularly, radio (where neither place nor time exists save in the imagination of the listener) have no difficulty in getting their audiences to accept the telescoped reality of dramatic time. Our special hazard lay in the fact that we purported to be not a play but reality. In order to take advantage of the accepted convention, we had to slide swiftly and imperceptibly out of the "real" time of a news report into the "dramatic" time of a fictional broadcast. Once that was achieved without losing the audience's attention or arousing their skepticism—if they could be sufficiently absorbed and bewitched not to notice the transition—then, we felt, there was no extreme of fantasy through which they would not follow us. If, that night, the American public proved "gullible," it was because enormous pains and a great deal of thought were being spent on making it so.

In the script, "The War of the Worlds" started extremely slowly—dull meteorological and astronomical bulletins alternating with musical interludes. These were followed by a colorless scientific interview and still another stretch of dance music. These first few minutes of routine broadcasting "within the existing standards of judgment of the listener" were intended to lull (or maybe bore) the audience into a false security and to furnish a solid base of realistic time from which to accelerate later. Orson, in making over the show, extended this slow movement far beyond our original conception. "La Cumparsita," rendered by "Ramon Raquelo from the Meridian Room of the Hotel Park Plaza in downtown New York," had been thought of by the scriptwriter as running only a few seconds; "Bobby Millette playing 'Stardust' from the Hotel Martinet in Brooklyn," even less. At rehearsal Orson stretched both these numbers to what seemed to us, in the control room, an almost unbearable length. We objected. The interview in the Princeton Observatory—the clockwork ticking monotonously overhead, the woolly-minded professor mumbling vague replies to the reporters' uninformed questions—this too he dragged out to a point of tedium. Over our protests, lines were restored that had been cut at earlier rehearsals. We cried that there would not be a listener left on the air. Defiantly, Welles stretched them out even longer.

He was right. His sense of tempo, that night, was infallible. When the flashed news of the cylinder's landing finally came—almost fifteen minutes after the beginning of a fairly dull show—he was able suddenly to spiral his action to a speed as wild and reckless as its base was solid. The appearance of the Martians, their first treacherous act, the death of Carl Phillips, the arrival of the militia, the battle of the Watchung Hills, the destruction of New Jersey—all these were telescoped into a space of twelve minutes without overstretching the listeners' emotional credulity. The broadcast, by then, had its own reality, the reality of emotionally felt time and space.

V

At the height of the crisis, around 8:31 P.M., the "voice of the Secretary of the Interior" was heard on the air with an exhortation to the American people. His words, as you read them now, ten years later, have a Voltairean ring. They were admirably spoken with emotion in a voice more than faintly reminiscent of the President's, by a young actor named Kenneth Delmar (who later grew rich and famous as "Senator Claghorn").

THE SECRETARY

Citizens of the nation: I shall not try to conceal the gravity of the situation that confronts the country, nor the concern of your Government in protecting the lives and property of its people. However, I

wish to impress upon you—private citizens and
public officials, all of you—the urgent need of calm
and resourceful action. Fortunately, this formidable enemy is still confined to a comparatively small
area, and we may place our faith in the military
forces to keep them there. In the meantime, placing
our trust in God, we must continue the performance of our duties, each and every one of us, so
that we may confront this destructive adversary
with a nation united, courageous and consecrated
to the preservation of human supremacy on this
earth. I thank you.

Toward the end of this speech (*circa* 8:32 P.M. E.S.T.),
Davidson Taylor, supervisor of the broadcast for the Columbia Broadcasting System, received a phone call in the
control room, creased his lips, and hurriedly left the studio. By the time he returned a few moments later—pale as
death—clouds of heavy smoke were rising above Newark,
New Jersey, and the Martians, tall as skyscrapers, were
astride the Pulaski Highway preparatory to wading the
Hudson River. To us in the studio the show seemed to be
progressing splendidly—how splendidly Davidson Taylor
had just learned outside. For several minutes now, a
kind of madness had seemed to be sweeping the continent—somehow connected with our show. The CBS
switchboards had been swamped into uselessness but from
outside sources vague rumors were coming in of deaths
and suicides and panic injuries.

Taylor had been instructed to interrupt the show immediately with an explanatory station-announcement. We
refused to obey. By now the Martians were across the
Hudson and gas was blanketing the city. The end was
near. We were less than a minute from the Station Break.
The covering organ was allowed to swirl out under the
slackening fingers of its failing organist and Ray Collins,
superb as "the last announcer," choked heroically to
death on the roof of the Broadcasting Building. The boats

were all whistling for a while as the last of the refugees perished in New York Harbor. Finally, as they died away, an amateur shortwave operator was heard, from heaven knows where, weakly reaching out for human companionship across the empty world:

> 2X2L calling CQ
> 2X2L calling CQ
> 2X2L calling CQ
> Isn't there anyone on the air?
> Isn't there anyone?

Five seconds of absolute silence. Then, shattering the reality of World's End—the announcer's voice was heard, suave and bright:

> ANNOUNCER
> You are listening to the CBS presentation of Orson Welles and the *Mercury Theatre on the Air* in an original dramatization of *The War of the Worlds,* by H. G. Wells. The performance will continue after a brief intermission.

The second part of the show was well written and sensitively played—but nobody listened. It recounted the adventures of a lone survivor, with interesting observations on the nature of human society; it described the eventual death of the Martian invaders, slain—"after all man's defenses had failed, by the humblest thing that God in his wisdom had put upon this earth"—by bacteriological action; it told of the rebuilding of a brave new world. Finally, after a stirring musical finale, Welles, in his own person, delivered a charming informal little speech about Halloween, which it happened to be.

I remember, during the playing of the final theme, answering the phone in the control room and listening to a shrill voice through the receiver announcing itself as belonging to the mayor of some Midwestern city, one of the big ones. He is screaming for Welles. Choking with fury, he describes mobs in the streets of his city, women and children huddled in the churches, violence and looting. If, as he now learns, the whole thing is nothing but a crummy joke—then he, personally, is coming up to New York to punch Orson Welles in the nose!

I hang up quickly. We are off the air by now and the studio door bursts open. The building is suddenly full of people and dark blue uniforms. Orson and I are seized and hustled out of the studio, downstairs, into a back office. Here we sit incommunicado while network employees are busily collecting, destoying, or locking up all scripts and records of the broadcast. Then the press is let loose upon us, ravening for horror. How many deaths have *we* heard of? (Implying they know of thousands.) What do *we* know of the fatal stampede in a Jersey hall? (Implying it is one of many.) How many traffic deaths? (The ditches must be choked with corpses.) The suicides? (Have you heard about the one on Riverside Drive?) It is all quite vague in my memory and quite terrible!

Hours later, instead of arresting us, they let us out a back way. We scurry down to the Mercury Theatre like hunted animals to their hole. It is surprising to see life going on as usual in the midnight streets, cars stopping for traffic, people walking. In our theater, when we finally get there, the company is still rehearsing—falling downstairs and singing the "Carmagnole." Welles goes up on stage, where photographers, lying in wait, catch him with his eyes raised up to heaven, his arms outstretched in an attitude of crucifixion. Thus he appears on the front page of a tabloid that morning over the caption, "I Didn't Know What I Was Doing!" *The New York Times* quotes him as saying, "I don't think we will choose anything like this again."

We were on the front page for two days. Having had to bow to radio as a news source during the Munich crisis, the press was now only too eager to expose the perilous irresponsibilities of the new medium. Orson was their

whipping boy. They quizzed and badgered him. Con-
demnatory editorials were delivered by our press-clipping
bureau in bushel baskets. There was talk, for a while, of
criminal action.

Then gradually, after about two weeks, the excitement
subsided. By then it had been discovered that the casualties were not as numerous or as serious as had at first been
supposed. One young woman had fallen and broken her
arm running downstairs. The Federal Communications
Commission held some hearings and passed some regulations. The Columbia Broadcasting System made a public
apology. With that the official aspects of the incident were
closed.

As to the Mercury—our new play, *Danton's Death*, finally opened after five postponements. Not even our fantastic publicity was able to offset its generally unfavorable
notices. On the other hand, that same week, figuring that
if we could sell the Martians we could also sell tomatoes,
Campbell Soups signed up our radio series at a lavish figure.

Of the suits that were brought against us—amounting
to over three quarters of a million dollars for damages, injuries, miscarriages and distresses of various kinds—none
was substantiated or legally pursued. We did settle one
claim, however—against the advice of our lawyers. It was
the particularly affecting case of a man in Massachusetts,
who wrote: "When the Martians came I thought the best
thing to do was to leave town. So I took three dollars
twenty-five cents I'd saved and got going. After I'd gone
sixty miles I knew it was a play. Now I don't have money
left for the shoes I was saving up for. Will you please have
someone send me a pair of black shoes size 9B!"

We did.

The Press

In the fall of 1948 I received a surprising offer from Joseph Barnes, who had been my superior at the Overseas Branch of the Office of War Information and with whom I had worked on the creation of the Voice of America during World War II. He had recently resigned from the New York Herald Tribune, *where he had long been Foreign Editor, to become co-publisher of a short-lived New York afternoon paper—*The Star. *What he proposed to me was a weekend column of around one thousand words dealing with the Performing Arts in any way that I pleased. Its title—"Show Business"—was Joe's choice.*

I wrote thirteen Star *columns in all, on which I labored all week before submitting them tremulously each Thursday afternoon to my editor—the charming but formidable Leon Edel. The day my thirteenth column appeared* The Star *folded, but much of my later thinking and writing about the Mass Media and their place in our society had its origins in that column.*

❧*The New York Star*

(*October 3, 1948*)

American Show Business is of a nervous disposition. Lately it has been exhibiting clear symptoms of manic-depressive behavior; after a long spell of uncontrolled optimism it is suffering, at the moment, from an attack of acute melancholia.

Motion picture attendance is off almost thirty percent from last year, which in turn was down from the year before that; Broadway this summer was back to its prewar doldrums; Radio, heavy with the infant Television in its womb, has spent uneasy dog days among crime, quiz and give-away shows; book publishers are once again filling the eastern air with their howling.

All this can be explained, to be sure. It is an inevitable hangover after the war-boom and the inescapable consequence of continued inflation. Meat and milk and children's shoes come before fun. Spiraling commodity prices are squeezing entertainment right out of the family budget. With such plausible arguments Show Business rationalizes its dwindling grosses and tries to appease its anxieties. But, as Arthur Hopkins realistically remarked to his gloomy box-office man one rainy night, gazing across his own deserted lobby to the long line at the ticket-window of the rival Music Box Theatre across the street: "It's raining there too!"

Theater tickets are too high for the average purse? So are automobiles—yet they can't make enough of them. Movie prices are up? So are admissions to the Yankee Stadium—yet baseball attendance hasn't fallen. It has been greater than last summer's, which in turn was greater than the year before that.

May I suggest that the trouble with Show Business is not exclusively economic, but that it also represents a clear manifestation of the law of diminishing returns? Is it just possible that the stimuli and satisfactions shrewdly devised by the agencies of organized entertainment have, finally, through long usage, grown pale and stale and lost their potency? Is it remotely conceivable that a continent which seemed slavishly dependent for its thrills on the commercialized titillations of its Mass Media, has become gradually apathetic, then positively bored—to the point of abstention?

Show Business has always been subject to public caprice and the hazards of fashion. Contrary to general Hollywood belief, there is no law on the statute books compelling citizens to attend movies twice a week. Hooper ratings notwithstanding, there are other ways of spending an afternoon or even an evening than listening to the radio.

Radio, Theater, Movies and Publications—none of these exists in a euphoric world of its own. Together, they are the mirrors of our national life; they reflect our aspirations, our tastes and our fears. Show Business remains healthy just so long as it fulfills an essential function. It must satisfy some dominant appetite, illustrate some currently compelling myth, assuage some prevalent anxiety. For the nervous society in which we live, still mourning the loss of our long-time leader and overshadowed, as we are, by the ever-present threat of a new and horribly destructive war, this is a tall order—one which leaders in many fields besides entertainment are finding it difficult to fill.

It is symptomatic that we find ourselves, today, in the midst of the least inspiring presidential campaigns of many years—one in which both major parties are equally deficient in the inspiration and excitement of significant ideologies or the stimulus of intense personal loyalties.

Our most tired movies are not more dreary, our most stereotyped broadcasts are not more flat than the main themes and figures of our national political life.

Because we are a vital and resourceful people with rich reserves of energy in our social and spiritual life, I have no doubt that, under our apparent apathy and confusion, fresh aspirations are forming and new appetites are being born which will presently find their cultural expression. These, together with the technical details attending their birth and the circumstances affecting their popular growth will be, henceforth, the main concern of this column. I shall promote my favorite projects, deal with personal bugbears and put forward occasional hopes. And I shall not worry too deeply over sins of preconception and personal prejudice . . .

(*October 10, 1948*)

The condemnation of Socrates, Jesus' appearance before Pilate, the trial of Joan of Arc, the treason proceedings against the Earl of Essex, the hanging of Major André and the successive stages of the Dreyfus case—all these significant juridical events are known to mankind through the accounts of disciples or witnesses and the subsequent chronicles of historians.

We of the mid-twentieth century are more favored. The major sessions of the House Un-American Activities Committee are being recorded and broadcast for our infomation and entertainment on wire, tape, film, radio and televison apparatus.

No pale reconstruction here—no *oratorio obliqua* dependent on the accuracy of the reporter, the biased memory of the participants or the prejudices of the historian. This is the genuine thing: the informers' charges, the suspects' denials, the personal confrontations, the real and simulated rages of the committee and its victims, even the crowd's reactions—all these are recorded and reproduced for us at the very instant of their happening. As drama it is great stuff; it is also valuable evidence, available to the entire world, of one of the least elevating aspects of our democratic society.

The sociological consequences of man's newfound ability to record events at the moment of their occurrence and to communicate them simultaneously to audiences unlimited by numbers or distance, go far beyond the scope of this column. What concerns us here is the technical accomplishment and its possible effect on the future of the entertainment business. (The Roman Catholic Church, ever alert and informed, has taken to broadcasting certain of its religious services from St. Patrick's Cathedral, including that of Holy Communion. But, with its usual vigilance, it has made it clear to members of its remote electronic audience that they are observing, *not participating* in that ceremony.)

Drama is the "imitation of an action," and the satisfaction we derive from it is "man's universal pleasure felt in things imitated." Aristotle's famous definition has remained descriptive of all forms of dramatic entertainment through the ages—until today. Now suddenly, overnight, man has discovered that he need no longer be satisfied with "imitation." By simply turning a dial or flicking a switch, he may now sate his appetite for information or excitement with a direct, simultaneous contemplation of the action itself. The jump is terrific. What will be its consequences?

Drama is the essential expression of an age—the articulate residue of man's social and spiritual experience. Under these new technical conditions what form is it likely to take? What, henceforth, will be the ratio of "reality" to "imitation"? Of News to Entertainment? What will the public demand? What will the commercial needs of the media dictate?

We have one interesting precedent. One hundred years ago, photography (a recently discovered instrument capable of fixing and reproducing the visual "reality " of life) was generally expected to replace and supersede the "imitation"—painting.

In fact it did exactly the opposite. Photography coincided with a renaissance of easel-painting such as Europe had not witnessed in two hundred years. And it had one clear esthetic effect—literal "imitation" went out of fashion; photography did it better. In its place appeared widely varying expressions of personally interpreted reality—the visual equivalents of poetry—from Monet to Van Gogh, through Cézanne and Picasso to today's surrealist and abstract art.

For the entertainment business the parallel is clear. The invention of electrical transmission—with the easily available thrills of real action directly and simultaneously observed—will, one hopes, furnish the irresistible competition that will liberate the living theater, once and for all, from the constrictions of imitative realism in which it has enmeshed itself. As an alternative to annihilation the theater has only one place to go—back to the rich fields of poetic imagination which it has so long and so woefully neglected.

(November 7, 1948)

With the final results of the campaign and the election of Harry Truman, the American people have just staged a more dramatic finale than their impresarios had designed for them. Right through election eve the campaign seemed to be winding up as it had begun—as a dull show.

A group from Columbia University made a detailed study, a few years back, of when and how the American voter makes up his mind when voting in a presidential election. As specimens for their investigation, they selected the population of a medium-sized county in a Midwestern state. The election was that of 1940 but their findings were general enough to apply to any campaign or locality. They confirm the commonly accepted belief that, under normal conditions, the new President has been elected by or before May, to which they add: "The more interested people were in the election the sooner they decided how to vote. The same decisions which impelled them to choose a candidate early in the game also served to make them concerned about this election. The campaign managers were thus continuously faced with the task of propagandizing not only a steadily shrinking segment of the electorate but also a segment whose interest in the election steadily shrank. By the end of the campaign the managers were exerting their greatest efforts to catch the few votes of the least interested persons."

In estimating the effects of the voters' exposure to the sundry media of political propaganda (Radio being judged on the whole more potent than the Press) the investigators were forced to the conclusion that "the people who did most of the reading about and listening to the campaign were the most impervious to any ideas which might have led them to change their vote. Insofar as campaign propaganda was intended to change votes, it was most likely to reach the people least likely to change."

People, in short, read what they want to see; they listen to what they want to hear; become excited only by what they are already predisposed to get excited about.

With this continuously in mind, I listened on election eve to the concluding broadcasts of the 1948 presidential campaign. Here was my opportunity to assay, as objectively as possible, the quality of the human values conveyed and the validity of the ideas expressed by the three leading contenders.

THE REPUBLICANS

At 9:00 P.M., E.S.T., with a triumphant crash, the "Dewey Bandwagon" hit the air—"an hour of entertainment and good fellowship." A galaxy of top-flight professional talent (of a fairly advanced average age), augmented by bands and assorted choruses, put on a show that was fast, self-confident, buoyant, slick, high-powered—and hollow as a drum.

> Zip-a-dee doodah, zip-a-dee day!
> Plenty of sunshine headin' my way!

was its theme. Leo Carillo spoke in dialect, Jeanette MacDonald sang; "Dagwood," Frank Morgan and others performed. Adolphe Menjou got in a quick plug for his book. The comic peak of the show was reached with Abbott and Costello's old, old baseball routine; the depths of bathos were plumbed when Miss Irene Dunne, Mr. Ray Milland and Believe-It-or-Not Ripley presented a brief dramatic sketch concerning Dan Kelso, an ex-convict who died a-voting.

In impact and energy the broadcast was reminiscent of the Roosevelt roundups of the past three election eves—is it flagrant prejudice on my part that caused me to find its content so dismally inferior? If I had not already mentally committed my vote elsewhere, would I have been more tickled by ZaSu Pitts as a babysitter? More affected by the heroism of Dan Kelso? More deeply stirred by the candidate's well-modulated eulogy of our country's natural beauties and resources—backed by a mass-choir rendition of "America the Beautiful"?

THE PROGRESSIVES

At 10:00 P.M. E.S.T., profiting from its juxtaposition with the glittering powerhouse immediately preceding it, came the Progressive Party broadcast. I doubt if it won Mr. Wallace many votes, for it was essentially a show of protest with the sharp edge of a minority party making its final, defiant statement in a hopeless fight. But, judged as Radio, it showed the only true quality of the evening. Using the personal-witness, dramatized-document technique, it avoided most of its customary faults—the clichés and the sentimentalities. It was direct and simple: a scientist, an ex-soldier, a foreign correspondent, a famous author, the wife of a murdered Negro. They spoke with quiet sincerity and I found myself moved by what they had to say. It was not until the candidate himself started speaking that a note of evangelical anxiety made its appearance and, with it, certain stereotypes of word and thought of which, till then, the show had been free.

THE DEMOCRATS

At 10:30 P.M. E.S.T., Senator Alben Barkley opened the Democratic show. Again the juxtaposition was striking. Suddenly the room was filled with orotundities; political platitudes rolled in the mouth and boomed in the ear. Mr. Truman followed him, speaking from his home in Missouri. He sounded lonely but he spoke convincingly and sincerely . . . and quite briefly. When he was through, an unusual thing happened. Apparently no timings had been made; the networks and the Democratic National Committee seemed to be caught unaware. For several minutes the world's most elaborate and expensive system of communication was occupied by standby pianists sending out nineteenth-century Polish nocturnes over the night air.

AFTER-THOUGHTS

Once again the pollsters have disgraced themselves with their dangerous and fallacious forecasts of the election results. Everyone is mad at them. With loud halloos, victors and vanquished join in the pursuit of the fleeing medicine men. I can only hope that in the exhilaration of tarring and feathering the rascals for their phony tips, we shall neither forgive them for the very real mischief they have done nor underestimate the menace their operations hold for us in the future.

On the realistic premise that there is no better time to hit a man than when he is down, I urge the men and women of my profession to take advantage of the pollsters' current political discomfiture to flush these self-appointed experts out of a field in which their operations have become increasingly bold and baneful—Show Business.

The Theater, with its modest financial turnover, has so far been spared the interference of "audience researchers." Radio has been their special domain—and no wonder, for it is a mixed-up, double-duty business. It is financed by industry, using entertainment as an instrument of distribution. Radio advertisers' billings amount to many millions of dollars a year; yet, lacking the ultimate test of the box office, the final impact of Radio on the nation's audience is almost impossible to gauge either qualitatively or quantitatively. In this misty world of big money and doubt and hope, it is not surprising that the public opinion experts have assumed, over the years, an enormous importance; in their elaborately presented statistics the advertisers have found some measure of reassurance—some feeling that maybe, after all, they are getting their money's worth.

It is not until you reach Hollywood that you discover the full extent of the pollsters' presumption. Where the most seasoned showmen and experienced artists tread with diffidence and nightly prayers, audience research has recently moved in with reckless aplomb and costly paraphernalia to interpret, estimate and predict the public taste. Encouraged by insecure executives and financiers who have found in this new pseudoscientific jargon a useful weapon in the never-ending battle between the front office and the people who make the pictures, audience research has gradually extended the sphere of its gimmicks from merchandising to production—and way beyond. Consistently and inevitably they have worked toward the stereotyped and the mediocre.

Here, suddenly, we are given an opportunity to put an end to this nonsense. Before little dials are clamped to readers' wrists and registers to listeners' ears and scales to spectators' eyes—ARTISTS AND SHOWMEN OF THE WORLD, UNITE! The pollsters have no place in our affairs. Without respite, they must be harassed, pursued, ridiculed and utterly destroyed. Now is our chance! We may never have such another. Now, while they are floundering in the water, their fingers nervously groping for the gunnels—before they can collect themselves and climb back into the boat, all together now . . . One . . . Two . . . Three . . . WHAM!

Television

The Seven Lively Arts *was a national television series of which I was executive producer. When we left the air on the afternoon of Sunday, February 16, 1958, we had broadcast ten shows that included drama, music, animation, dance, documentary material and what may well have been one of the great jazz concerts of all time. We received an Emmy for our pains but, in the Industry, we were best remembered for the unmitigated catastrophe of our opening show—"The Changing Ways of Love."*

❧ Trouble in the Intellectual Ghetto (1958)

WHAT *TIME* DESCRIBED as "the liveliest artistic success and costliest financial flop of the 1957–58 television season" was conceived in the Oak Room of the Plaza Hotel during a luncheon I had there with Louis Cowan.

He and I had worked together on the Voice of America, where he was our contact with the Pentagon on the shows we were broadcasting to our armed forces all over the world. We had remained friends ever since. In private life Cowan had been a public relations expert specializing in religious groups; he had gone on to become a successful producer of radio shows, including *The Quiz Kids,* which he created and owned and which he later transferred to television together with a number of other nationally rated quiz shows. As a result, he had recently been offered and had accepted the presidency of CBS Television, to whose vast annual profits his programs had substantially contributed.

Like many of his kind Cowan combined a sincere yearning for "better things" with a shrewd, irresistible appetite for money and I listened with wandering attention while he outlined his plans for the network which included a new show—*The Seven Lively Arts*—that was to be broadcast on Sunday afternoons in the middle of what had come to be known as the "intellectual ghetto" of television.

With dessert he came to the point: since he knew me to be "ass-deep in culture," (sic) I might be the very man the network was looking for to develop and produce this prestigious project. I rose to the bait and within a few days I had met with Hubbell Robinson, head of production for CBS and with the "chairman," William S. Paley, whom I had not encountered in eighteen years, since the excitement of the Men from Mars. Two weeks later I signed a two-year contract with CBS-TV, at a higher salary than I had ever earned before, as executive producer of *The Seven Lively Arts.*

The more I looked into it the more evident it became that this was a project about which everyone was enthusiastic but no one had any clear or defined ideas—beyond the feeling that it should be original, entertaining, instructive, prestigious and, of course, successful.

With so much lead-time (it was not due to go on the air until November of 1957) my initial approach to our problems was leisurely and discursive. Throughout that winter and spring, dozens of ideas and projects were discussed, considered, accepted or rejected: they comprised "live" drama, film, documentary, animation, music, dance or all of them combined. To develop a series of shows out of such infinite possibilities three teams were chosen for their diverse talents and for their experience in various forms of television: under my supervision, it became their collective assignment to convert these sundry notions into a viable television program.

The first of these units was under Robert Herridge—a young TV writer and director, with the head of a gladiator and a rising reputation in serious "live" television drama. To balance him (on Ed Murrow's recommendation) I engaged "Shad" Northshield, a man dedicated to the creative recording of documentary material, whom I named head of our film unit. Finally, from California, I summoned Jud Kinberg (who had been my associate producer on eight films at MGM) and invited him to join my production unit on *The Seven Lively Arts.*

Around these three units there began to form an organization which I hoped would be capable of preparing and broadcasting twenty-six original, hour-long television shows for the most hazardous and highly publicized series of the 1957–58 television season. By early summer we had seven shows approved and in development. But my own efforts, then and in the months to come, were concentrated on the preparation of what was to be our first, all-important broadcast. It was called "The Changing Ways of Love" and it was intended as a blockbuster.

Actually it was Hubbell Robinson's idea of a flashy opener which I had accepted with some reservation: it was a risky one with which to open a series that was already suspect and controversial and had not yet found a commercial sponsor.

The idea was to review and illustrate the changing social, sexual and sentimental behavior patterns of American men and women over the past thirty years—as revealed and exploited through popular examples of theater, film, music, radio and finally television. Later in the series we would present more sober cultural material.

Using the overwhelming mass of research that Kinberg and his staff had accumulated over the summer, "The Changing Ways of Love" was to be divided into three parts:

1. The Jazz Age of the Booming '20s;
2. The years of the Great Depression;
3. World War II and its aftermath.

Each section would contain a dramatized love scene by a well-known author typical of the sexual-emotional confrontations of the time and each would have its own historian-narrator whose reports would be introduced and coordinated by our own Master of Ceremonies who would thus assume a position of great importance and would help to set the tone and character of the entire show. To discover a suitable M.C. for this and subsequent programs occupied much of our time and thought, as we sought to find a figure who would give an impression of authority, erudition and charm.

Finally he was found. 1957 was the year in which the quiz shows reached the peak of their popularity. The most successful of these pseudointellectual programs was *Twenty-One,* from which a young scholar named Charles Van Doren had emerged to win the hearts of the entire nation. He had everything in his favor—youth, looks, distinction and brains: he was even sexy in a scholarly way. By midsummer (after two epic struggles in which he defeated a sophisticated jockey and a well-informed but unlikable professor) his winnings exceeded $100,000 and he had made the cover of *Time.*

At that point Hubbell decided that Charles Van Doren would make the perfect master of ceremonies for *The Seven Lively Arts* and contracts were being signed when, suddenly, the sky darkened. An insidious rumor began to circulate concerning skulduggery on the quiz shows; it was suggested and then confirmed that favored candidates had been given advance notice of subjects and questions. At the first suggestion that young Mr. Van Doren's encyclopedic knowledge might not be entirely his own, the world turned against him; national enthusiasm changed to fury, admiration to contempt. He was hauled before a grand jury, exposed and stripped of his ill-gotten gains, including his contract with CBS on which the ink was not yet dry.

We had little time left to find a substitute. Clifton Fadiman of the *New Yorker*, who had once been a leading candidate, was no longer available and things were beginning to look grim when the network had a second inspiration—John Crosby! Such was Hubbell's excitement at discovering that he was available that he engaged him before I had a chance to meet him.

We have no equivalent today of John Crosby. He belonged to the Golden Age of Television: as critic and columnist for the *Herald Tribune* syndicate, he had, within a few years, established a unique, national reputation for literate, independent and fearless reviewing that made him the darling of the middle-brows and the terror of networks and advertisers. His highly publicized and ethically dubious appointment as Master of Ceremonies for *The Seven Lively Arts* received a predictably mixed reception in the press and in the trades but generated a lot of publicity as we met to discuss the nature of his functions on the show.

He was to act as general consultant on the series (most of which was already prepared and written); he was to write and edit his own material and to speak it in person on the air. It was in this final capacity that he came to play a dramatic part in the future of the series.

John Crosby's charisma was essentially literary. In person he was mild-mannered and myopic. And, though this was by no means abnormal or shameful in an intellectual,

I felt that very thick glasses would not add to his popular image as our brilliant M.C. I suggested that he visit an oculist and get a prescription for the new contact lenses that had recently come into general use. He agreed and the most expensive optician in the city was put to work on two pairs of contact lenses with the assurance that they would be available long before the start of rehearsals.

With that detail satisfactorily disposed of I was able to turn my attention to other more urgent matters of production. By mid-October we were able to announce the lineup of our first three broadcasts, and the elements of our opening show seemed to be falling into place.

"The Changing Ways of Love" was an elaborate contraption—half film and half "live"—complete with animations, humor, songs, dancing girls, stills, soundtracks, dramatic sketches, and social commentary. At our first reading Crosby appeared without his glasses and, though he complained mildly about his new lenses, they enabled him to read his text without difficulty. During the next few days, as we ran through the show, he seemed to be at ease and to have no problem following his cue cards.

On Saturday, November 2, halfway through our final on-camera rehearsal and twenty-four hours before air time, Crosby asked to speak with me in private and informed me that his lenses were driving him mad—to the point where he had decided to appear without them. I said if that's how he felt, he should go back to wearing his glasses. He said he wasn't going to do that either. He assured me that he had a prodigious memory and was entirely confident of his ability to M.C. the show without either glasses or lenses. I objected but he was adamant.

The atmosphere in the studio was tense that Sunday but not more so than at most premieres of a major TV show. I was tired and nervous; Kinberg, as usual, was wallowing in anxiety and despair. Yet, our dress rehearsal at noon had gone surprisingly well for such an elaborate show. Crosby was a bit stiff, but he sounded intelligent and sincere and he seemed quite capable of deciphering and/or memorizing his cue cards. At 3:55 P.M. we retired into the control room and sat staring at the studio's electric clock as its second-hand moved toward air time. We had piles of telegrams of good wishes from both coasts.

A few seconds after 4:00 we went on the air. We opened with a lovingly and carefully selected gallery of the "love-goddesses" of the twenties—Swanson, Pickford, Naldi, Bow, the Talmadge sisters, Harlow, Garbo. "This is the face of love," Crosby declared as the montage ended and he himself made his first appearance in a close shot that filled the screen. He informed the nation that his name was John Crosby and that this was the opening program in a new series called *The Seven Lively Arts.* He explained that our first show was about Love—

> Because love is not only an art in itself but is the constant theme that runs through all the other arts. Love, theoretically, is eternal. Its objectives and techniques shouldn't change much whether you are in a penthouse or a haystack. They shouldn't, but they have. How? Let's go back to the twenties and find out. For this leg in the journey we have with us tonight—

The world never found out what we had. For, at that moment, Crosby's voice stopped in midsentence and a look of abject panic came over his face. For a second or two we waited, confident that he would recover himself and go on. Instead, the face on the monitor froze; the mouth went slack, then hung open like that of a dead man. The only thing that remained alive in his sweating face were the eyes, desperately attempting to focus on the boob card the assistant was waving in front of him, Then, as he gave up, the eyes, too, glazed into a rigid stare of utter despair.

In the control room we sat helpless and numb with horror. No one moved. Even our technical director's hands seemed frozen to the controls. (The next day, running the kinescope of the show, we clocked the time during which millions of Americans stared at the silent death mask of John Crosby. It added up to eighteen and a half seconds. It seemed like six months. And it made TV history.) Finally, like members of Sleeping Beauty's court, we returned to life. Orders flashed over the intercom. Our dancing girls, warming up in a neighboring studio, were herded onto the set and into the "Black Bottom." Sid Perelman, the narrator-historian of our first act, pacing nervously back-stage behind a flat as he prepared for his entrance, was grabbed and hustled before a camera which caught him in a state of bewildered alarm as Crosby's voice, partially restored, reading from a cue card that the assistant was holding directly under his nose, introduced him as "S. J. Perelman, the celebrated humorist and Academy Award winner for the screenplay of *Around the World in Eighty Days*—himself a survivor of the reckless twenties." Whereupon Perelman, his glasses flashing and his voice supercharged with forced gaiety, heroically launched his jocular commentary into a void of bewilderment and despair.

Slowly the blood began to flow back into our bodies. We were still alive but we were ruined and we knew it. Such an occurrence on major network television was unprecedented and unforgivable. After such a disgrace there was only one way to go—to disappear and never come back! But, for the moment, we had no choice; we had to go on with the show and it was agony. As face after glamorous face appeared on the monitor, they all seemed to be smiling at our humiliation. The frantic dances of the twenties were dances of death; Rudy Vallee (whose voice Perelman introduced as "the velvety, nasal woodnotes of our first radio troubadour") was crooning our funeral dirge. It was not until we were deep into the erotic melancholy of Scott Fitzgerald's *Winter Dreams* that the show finally moved back into focus.

"It was a wonderful world while it lasted," observed Perelman as the lovers went off into the dark to the strains of a Cole Porter melody and the sudden sharp clicking of the ticker-tape announced to the world that the great Crash of 1929 was upon us—and that the first act of "The Changing Ways of Love" was finally and mercifully over!

During the station break I ran down into the studio to restore morale and to check on Crosby's condition. He seemed to have recovered some of his composure—or maybe he was still in shock. He looked pale but determined as he prepared for the second act—the years of the Great Depression—of which he was himself the narrator and which contained, among other things, a scene from Clifford Odets's *Awake and Sing.* Our third act, whose presiding deities were Hayworth, Grable, Lamour, Sinatra and Elvis Presley, dealt with the sexual revolution brought about by World War II and was efficiently narrated by that relentless investigator, Mike Wallace.

Our reviews were about as expected.

ROMANCE AT RANDOM
A CONFUSED, INERT PICTURE OF LOVE

reported *The New York Times,* while *Variety* pronounced it "a lively if not entirely inspired hour."

Predictably, the critics' principal victim was John Crosby, whose colleagues from coast to coast made no attempt to conceal their delight over his discomfiture. They found in his "cathode baptism" comforting evidence that "critics can be human" and "should be read and not seen." They reported gleefully that "he was better at roasting than hosting" and "tense as a terrified titmouse." Others were more personal: "Crosby grunted as if in constant pain and close-ups did him few favors, for they presented his face with a seemingly endless mouth which, when speaking, seemed to be pulled apart vertically by unseen strings."

One of the blessings of a television series is that it leaves you no time to brood over your failures. Within hours we were in rehearsal with our second show—"The World of Nick Adams." This was a loose assembly of five early stories by Ernest Hemingway, produced by Robert Herridge and directed "live" with simplicity and feeling by Robert Mulligan. (On neither this nor the next show did Crosby have much to say on camera.) Our third, produced by Shad Northshield, investigated the behavior of "those men and women, black and white, who dedicate their fanatical energy to bringing people to God." It started with footage from the Deep South, where, in a broken-down barn, a black preacher, Cat-Iron Carradino, whipped his ragged congregation into a rising fever of frenzied devotion. This was followed by scenes of immersion, some "healing" rituals and brief visits to Billy Sunday and Aimee Semple McPherson. The last third of the broadcast was devoted to that most successful of all modern evangelists, Billy Graham.

> After scoring last week with "The World of Nick Adams," *The Seven Lively Arts* established itself as one of the season's brightest new corners with *The Revivalists.*

reported *Time.*

But, in the harsh world of national network television, a series is judged by the success of its premiere. Since ours had been a disaster, we found ourselves more than once, in the months to come, replaced by football games and other more popular network events. And, around CBS and the industry in general, I felt myself treated with nervous commiseration as the leprous creator of the season's biggest turkey.

We continued to turn out shows, including a "filmed

essay" by E. B. White and two programs produced in collaboration with the choreographers George Balanchine and Agnes de Mille. Then, before the end of the year, we delivered a blockbuster:

> *The Seven Lively Arts* came into its own yesterday with a brilliant and exciting program on Jazz. The spontaneity and artistry of modern music were presented with more authenticity, understanding and appreciation than television has ever managed before.

Historically the show was notable for being one of the last public appearances of the great Billie Holiday "who did 'Fine and Mellow' in a haunting voice that was worth the hour by itself." Among other jazz giants scattered around the soundstage that afternoon were Count Basie, Lionel Hampton, Teddy Wilson, Thelonious Monk, Pee-Wee Russell, Coleman Hawkins, Jimmy Giuffre and Roy Eldridge.

The Seven Lively Arts died prematurely but with honor. For our final show we presented what I have always considered one of the most dramatic and moving broadcasts I have ever been associated with. "The Blast in Centralia Number Five" was the true story, reported in *Harper's* magazine by John Bartlow Martin, of an Illinois mine disaster that cost 120 lives. It was a tragedy that everyone knew was coming and that no one—neither management nor the union nor the U.S. Bureau of Mines—made one single move to prevent. Its dramatization, which combined documentary reality and personal drama, was directed by George Roy Hill and performed by Maureen Stapleton and Jason Robards. The tributes it evoked were emotional and nationwide: "A truly great example of television at its finest." "A tragic, memorable documentary." "A searing indictment of government red tape, of big business, of union inertia and of a politically appointed bureaucracy." *Variety,* not given to exaggeration, called it "a masterpiece."

It was ironic that these tributes were also our obituaries. This, our final show, was broadcast on the afternoon of Sunday, February 16, 1958, when we left the air after eleven shows instead of the originally scheduled twenty-six. We still had not found a sponsor.

There is a happy ending to this story. Some months later, when I received my invitation to the annual awards of the National Television Academy, I declined. I was still sore from the beating I had taken and resentful over what I considered the network's betrayal. The next day I received an account of what happened from Hubbell Robinson.

Unlike Hollywood's Oscars, the Emmys were distributed at a dinner, with the nominees and the audience seated at tables. Hubbell and his wife, Vivienne Segal, the singer, were at the official CBS table. Bored to tears as the long evening wore on, she announced finally that she was off to the little girls' room. There she ran into a friend and it was some time before she returned. When she did, she became aware of a strange object in the middle of the table that had not been there when she left. It was a brass statue about one foot tall—a species of angel with a hollow globe over its head.

"What the hell is that?" she asked.

It was the National Academy of Television Arts and Sciences' award for the best new show of the year—and it had been won by *The Seven Lively Arts!*

❖*Wooden Indian*

*This piece is adapted from a foreword I wrote for the unpub-
lished memoirs that Hubbell Robinson's death in 1974 kept
him from completing.*

THE CHANGEOVER from radio to television was complicated in this country by the fact that both of these golden
geese were owned by the same commercial interests,
whose managers had a hard time deciding which offered
the best immediate opportunities for exploitation and
profit. One of the men who participated in the transition
and who played an important part in the development of
both media was Hubbell Robinson, for many years vice
president in charge of production and programming for
the Columbia Broadcasting System.

For anyone who wants to understand the mechanism
through which mass entertainment was developed in this
country, there is much new and authoritative information
in his still unpublished memoirs. They are plain and direct; they contain no single reference to "public interest,
conscience or necessity" and they are written as though
Doctor McLuhan had never existed. Rather, they represent a breezy, personal, hard-boiled inside account of
what it was like for a young American with brains, some
education, vast ambition, energy and nerves of iron to operate successfully in the highly competitive and rapidly
expanding field of the Mass Media during the forties, fifties and sixties.

The society Hubbell Robinson describes is familiar but
frightening. Balanced uneasily between the towering mass
of Big Business and the sordid fantasies of Show Biz, its
members finally recognize only one standard of judg-

ment—the audience-counts supplied by Nielsen and other national polling and rating systems. From that demographic verdict there is no appeal. Hubbell himself neither in his life nor in his book ever seriously questioned its rightness. This does not mean that in his thirty years of activity, first on radio and then in television, he never cherished creative aspirations or hopes for better, more original and more stimulating shows on the air. It *does* mean that as executive vice president in charge of production for the country's leading network, he fully accepted the ratings (as one follows the rules of the game one is playing) and functioned pragmatically and quite contentedly within their limitations. It was this acceptance, no doubt, that helped him to achieve that apparently imperturbable composure which earned him the admiring professional nickname of "The Wooden Indian." It also made him the best production executive I encountered in the business and the most satisfying to work with—by far.

Playhouse 90, Hubbell's personal and most prestigious television creation, was solidly established by the time I came to it as a producer in 1958. But *The Seven Lively Arts,* also his invention, was a fancy and risky show from the start. It eventually won the Emmy as the best new program of the year, but by network standards it was an unmitigated disaster for which, as the executive producer, I should, by normal network tactics, have received the entire blame. Some of my colleagues were, in fact, inclined to stare through me when we met in the corridors of the CBS building. Not Hubbell. No word or look of reproach ever passed between us: despite the show's consistently abysmal ratings he continued to treat me with friendly respect and to express his regret, almost his apologies, for our joint failure to marshal an audience. (I am sure that many of those who worked with him in that savage and hazardous business could tell the same story.)

All this occurred at a time—the mid-fifties—when

Hubbell could afford to be magnanimous. He was at the peak of his career with a power that was greater and lasted longer than that of any other program executive in the business. This power (as Hubbell makes it quite clear in his book) was dependent on the continuing personal favor of that Olympian figure, the chairman of the board of the Columbia Broadcasting System—W. S. Paley. "If W.S.P.'s vote was for you, nothing else counted. If it went against you, well, nothing counted either." When that favor was finally withdrawn (for reasons that are not entirely clear) Hubbell's position at CBS became untenable. He continued his executive career elsewhere but his imperial days were over.

I watched Hubbell in the darkest days of his later, unhappy association with the Music Corporation of America. Now he was no longer the all-powerful chief executive of the country's most successful network; he was the well-paid hireling of a rapacious and ruthless production machine—pushed around, frustrated and humiliated at every turn. The Wooden Indian remained outwardly intact. But, at night, in the privacy of his Bel Air home, Hubbell had his own special way of seeking release from the awful pressures of the day.

His secret hobby had long been the American Civil War. The walls of his New York office and later his house in Bel Air were covered with books, prints and photos of its major battles. Now, on several evenings on which I visited him (after the martinis, the wine and the after-dinner highballs) he would disappear for a moment, then reappear with a battle-stained military cap on his head. With a bayonet in one hand and a glass in the other, uttering bloodcurdling yells as he leaped over and around the scattered furniture of his living room, he would reenact with fierce passion and total accuracy some of the more dramatic actions of the Civil War. When I drove away around midnight he was hardly aware of my going. Be-

hind me, in his lighted house, I could hear the diminishing
sound of those great victories of long ago with which he
was trying to compensate for his own present defeats.

Our next collaboration took place soon after his brief,
abortive return to CBS when we were preparing an
American historical series to be known as *The Great Adven-
ture*. It was a brief, disagreeable experience as we both, in
rapid succession, fell victims to the maneuvers of James
Aubrey (the "Smiling Cobra"), Paley's current favorite.
Later still Hubbell and I produced a musical special for
ABC based on a story by John Collier with music and
lyrics by Stephen Sondheim. We also appeared together
on a panel promoted by the Ford Foundation that was
considering the future of television drama in this country.
A few days before he died Hubbell called me one morning, his voice weak and rasping from the lung cancer that
was destroying him, to ask how I would like to appear as
Nero Wolfe in a new series he was developing.

The importance of Hubbell's book lies not so much in
his personal reminiscences as in the events that are vividly
described in this frank, subjective account of life on the
networks during the Golden Age of U.S. radio and television. For specific, dramatic examples of the hideous ordeal
by which a major TV show is begotten, conceived and finally delivered, I recommend his accounts of the birth of
such famous shows as *Lucy, Climax, The Red Skelton Show*
and *Playhouse 90;* also, for sheer unmitigated horror, the
nightmarish thirty-six hours preceding the first Judy Gar-
land Special. Here you will find the wonders and squalors
of Show Business magnified by the complicated, arbitrary
and often conflicting pressures of the Mass Media, advertising agencies and network operation.

Names crowd these pages—the names of famous shows
and illustrious performers. These are not "dropped": they
form an integral part of Hubbell's story and of the history
of radio and television in America. Many of them belong
there because Hubbell put them on the air as stars—se-

lected them, nurtured them and fought to make them the celebrities they became. How this was done—the sordid and occasionally creative machinery through which so many hundreds of thousands of hours were ground out month after month for our national entertainment—is described here quite simply and honestly, together with the tactics and crises, the threats and wooings, the power-plays, the bluffs, the ass-lickings, the perpetual anxieties, the wild hopes, the flashing victories and the ignominious defeats that make up the vast and extravagant operation in which Hubbell himself, for so many years, played such an essential part.

Hubbell died at the age of sixty-seven. After a crowded and successful life, The Wooden Indian is at rest. He earned it. He was shrewd, tough, resourceful and, in my experience, consistently and surprisingly fair and considerate.

❧ Kingsfield's Folly: The Life and Death of <u>The Paper Chase</u>

My seventh and last piece for Harper's *was written in anger some months after* The Paper Chase *had been dropped by CBS from prime network time. It was rejected in its original form on the grounds that it was too long, too personal, and too self-serving. It appeared in its present revised shape in December 1979.*

My favorite among all our proposed new shows was The Paper Chase, *a top-quality adaptation from the motion picture, starring John Houseman in his Academy-Award-winning role. . . . This was clearly an outstanding program in every way, serious and yet witty, pertinent to our times, heartwarming, mature, believable.*

    —William S. Paley, Chairman, CBS

The Paper Chase *is dead. What might have been the most intellectually stimulating dramatic series presented on television during the 1970s has been buried by CBS. . . . In a typical case of corporate duplicity, it turned out that while CBS was bragging itself into a frenzy of publicity over the series, it was doing everything possible to torpedo it.*

    —Garry Deeb, Chicago Tribune

PROFESSOR KINGSFIELD entered my life in the fall of 1972 and changed it completely. He appeared without warning, disrupted the academic calm into which I had withdrawn and threw me back, before I knew what had happened, into the whirlpool of Show Business.

The main agent of this transformation was a young man named James Bridges, a native of Paris, Arkansas, whom I first met in Los Angeles in the early sixties. Barely out of his teens, he had written a play about low life in Venice, California, that had been performed in one of the many small theaters that were springing up at the time all over Hollywood. I found his play original and interesting and asked to meet him. He was eager to learn more about the theater and asked if he could join the Professional Theater Group of the University of California, of which I was Artistic Director. Starting as a coffee-bearer and third assistant stage manager, he soon became one of the most

Previously published in *Harper's* magazine, December 1979.

valuable members of our organization and a close personal friend.

When I moved to New York some years later and set about creating the Drama Division of the Juilliard School, Jim Bridges and I continued to communicate regularly—mostly through late-night phone calls. After writing eighteen TV shows for Alfred Hitchcock, he had finally achieved his dream of writing and directing films of his own.

During the summer of 1972 he called one evening to report that he had just signed a contract to write the screenplay and direct a film about Harvard Law School based on a first novel by John Osborn. Two months later he called again: he was all set to go—except for one thing: he was still lacking an actor to play Professor Kingsfield, a distinguished and formidable curmudgeon in his late sixties and a senior professor of contract law. (The part was to have been played by James Mason who had been delayed in Spain on a film. All other casting attempts had failed for one reason or another.) What Bridges was asking me was whether I would consider playing the part.

Concealing my surprise, I told him (though I had never for one moment thought of myself as an actor) that I'd be delighted. But I warned him that if he made such a lunatic suggestion to his employers, he stood an excellent chance of being thrown off the picture.

Two weeks later I flew to Toronto to make a film test. Bridges and I agreed that if it stank we would quietly burn it; if it turned out well we would show it to the studio. Fifteen months after that I was once more on a plane—this time on my way to appear at the Chandler Pavillion for the presentation of the Academy Awards. According to Nick the Greek I had a slight edge in the betting for the Best Supporting Actor of 1973.

In accepting my Oscar I gave thanks to my fellow actors, to Gordon Willis, whose dramatic cinematography had made me look more impressive than I was, and to my director, James Bridges, "for his courage in entrusting such a wonderful role to an obscure and aging schoolmaster."

For the next four years I continued to run the Drama Division of the Juilliard School and to perform variations of Professor Kingsfield in films and television. I became head of the CIA in *Three Days of the Condor* and the suave, ruthless executive of a futuristic global corporation in *Rollerball.* I was flown to Stockholm to film a commercial for Volvo automobiles and to Hamburg to play Winston Churchill in a television film about the Potsdam Conference.

In all that time no one seemed to have thought of recycling *The Paper Chase* for television. For a few weeks in the winter of 1976, Twentieth Century-Fox, which had made the film, considered it as the possible basis for a thirty-minute situation comedy. Since neither Bridges nor I nor the author were willing to consider it in that form, the idea was abandoned. Instead, we came up with our own plan for an hour-long dramatic series. NBC, the first network approached, gave Fox an order for a sample script, which Jim Bridges wrote between pictures—based on a legendary Harvard Law School incident suggested by Osborn. NBC delayed, then lost interest in the project; CBS picked it up and ordered a pilot in which I was engaged to repeat my role of Professor Kingsfield and to hold myself available for six months while the network decided if it wished to proceed with the show as a series.

In October we filmed the pilot—mostly on the Fox lot in Century City. In the film, Kingsfield's classroom had been a meticulous reproduction of Harvard's Langdon Hall: for television it was somewhat reduced, and we used the campus of the University of Southern California for our exteriors; for our dormitory we used an abandoned wing of the Queen of the Angels Hospital in downtown Los Angeles. Our film was edited, scored, recorded and sent over to CBS for approval—one of the 150 pilots ordered annually by the networks, each at a cost of between $300,000 and $400,000 for an hour, $200,000 to $300,000 for a half-hour show. The first reaction to *The Paper Chase* pilot was one of qualified approval.

In the weeks that followed—as more and more people got to see it—word spread that it was one of the best dramatic pilots of the season. It was also reported that the two CBS executives in charge of programming were dead set against it. (An experienced and cynical friend explained to me that this was the kind of show that network executives most feared and detested: too "good" for popular appeal and not "bad" enough to dump in a hurry, it would hang like an albatross around their necks, a dead weight and an encumbrance in their race for "ratings.") There was further confusion when word came from an authoritative source that William Paley, the powerful chairman of CBS, had fallen in love with the pilot.

Four months later we learned to our delight that *The Paper Chase* was included in the CBS program schedule for the fall. We didn't learn until the next day, when the new schedules were formally announced in the press, that *The Paper Chase* would be aired on Tuesdays at 8:00 P.M.—opposite ABC's *Happy Days* and *Laverne and Shirley*—in what was known throughout the industry as "The Death-Slot" or "Murderers' Row."

To appreciate the dimness of our future in "Murderers' Row" the reader must be informed that, for two years, ABC's *Happy Days* and *Laverne and Shirley* had completely dominated the airwaves between the hours of eight and nine on Tuesday evenings. The average Nielsen ratings of these two successive half-hour sitcoms had been between 25 and 35 with a "share" of between 40 and 50 percent of the nation's viewing audience. In other words, while those two shows were on the air, less than one half of America's total viewing public was left available for all other stations—including those of CBS, NBC, Public Television, ethnic and other local and independent broadcasters.

Financially these figures are of overwhelming importance. Commercials aired during prime time (between 8:00 and 11:00 P.M.) cost the advertiser as much as $200,-000 for sixty seconds—with seven minutes of every hour devoted to advertising. Rates are computed on a cost-per-thousand basis determined by estimating how many million persons are watching a particular show at a particular time. Such estimates are known as "ratings," and their main supplier is the A. C. Nielsen Company, which delivers to its clients overnight computations of audiences in major cities followed, the next day, by a more complete and detailed national survey. These figures are awaited with frantic impatience by networks, producers, and advertisers alike, for they form the basis of American commercial broadcasting.

A highly rated show does more than triumph during its own airing; it pulls up the network's entire weekly rating and enables it to command a higher across-the-board price for airtime. By contrast, a low-rated show (no matter how high its quality or how much it is critically admired) pulls down the network's standing and reduces the price it can command from advertisers on the basis of a guaranteed number of viewers.

Each point in the Nielsen index represents 750,000 households, which, in turn, represent roughly 1.5 million people. (A comedy show, or one that is known to appeal to children, is credited with 2.2 viewers per set; news and "heavy" shows, which are supposedly avoided by children, rate 1.7.) Thus a spread of a dozen points in the Nielsen rating means a difference of between 15 and 20 million potential clients for the advertiser. This spread is directly reflected in the earnings of the networks: a loss in rating can affect a network's profits to the tune of fifty to a hundred million dollars a year—not to mention loss of ex-

ecutive prestige and the long-term damage suffered by the
defection of "affiliated" television stations that tend to
gravitate to a more highly rated rival network. How are
these all-important figures arrived at? What is the system
that all parties concerned (including the press) seem willing and eager to accept?

The Nielsen index is arrived at through a mechanism
that is awesome in its simplicity. It is based on the reading
of 1,200 boxes "installed in homes in various parts of the
country." Each of these homes is selected *at random* (much
is made of this) from one of the population units into
which the United States has been divided. Thus these
1,200 daily samplings are supposed to represent a total of
74 million households from which are extrapolated the
tastes and viewing habits of the entire nation. To question
their accuracy is to attack the entire structure of commercial television; it is a subversive attempt to rock the boat
and to kill the goose that lays the golden eggs. How golden
these eggs are may be judged from the recent balance
sheets of all three of the networks.

The first ratings for *The Paper Chase* were predictably
low. For our opening show, which was aired on a Friday
with considerable promotional fanfare, we received a national rating of 13 with a 27 percent share of viewers. The
following Tuesday, on our first appearance in our regular
8:00 P.M. death-slot against *Happy Days* and *Laverne and
Shirley*, we were down to 11.3 with a share of 19 percent.
There we remained with minor fluctuations for the next
three months, as compared with *Laverne and Shirley*'s average rating of more than 20 with a 40 to 45 percent share.
In other words, *The Paper Chase* was being watched in
some 8.5 million households, *Happy Days* and *Laverne and
Shirley* in about 15 million.

These figures should have surprised no one, yet a deep
gloom enveloped the studio when it was realized that we
were being watched by less than 15 million people as
against ABC's 30 million. This depression was only

slightly relieved by our great reviews, by far the best received by a new dramatic series in this or any other recent season. Two dozen of these raves were reprinted in the full-page advertisements that CBS took out in a number of the nation's leading newspapers.

While this lavish praise had no perceptible effect on the show's ratings, it did succeed in making us all feel a little less unhappy. For, as the time approached for the ordering of the second half of the series, it seemed inconceivable that CBS would yank us off the air immediately after so much boasting. Early in December the network authorized Fox to go on producing *The Paper Chase* until further notice. They never formally exercised their option for a second set of twelve shows, but we continued to produce shows from week to week until the end of the season.

So strong was the normal television pattern (of low ratings automatically followed by cancellation and banishment) that our survival was treated as hot news in every television column in the country.

"PAPER CHASE STAYS," reported *The New York Times;* we became "the show that Nielsen couldn't kill"; we were described as "eluding the Nielsen axe" and "breaking the law of TV." None of this had the slightest effect on our ratings.

In late January CBS suddenly moved us out of the "graveyard." Tuesday remained our evening but we were switched from 8:00 to 10:00 P.M., where we were no longer up against *Happy Days* and *Laverne and Shirley* but opposite *Starsky and Hutch* on ABC and movies on NBC. Unfortunately the move was made following several "preemptions" (cancellations to make room for athletic or other "hot" programs), with virtually no announcement or notice, so that many of the regular viewers we had managed to collect at 8:00 P.M. thought we were off the air.

For our first two 10:00 P.M. shows our Nielsen showed little change. Then in our third and fourth weeks there was a perceptible rise—particularly in our big-city ratings. It is idle to surmise what might have happened if we had been allowed to remain in that spot; early in March, following two more preemptions, we found ourselves back in "Murderers' Row" with ratings that were back to what they had been before. And there we remained, with frequent preemptions, for the rest of the season. When the new season's programs were announced in mid-April it surprised no one that *The Paper Chase* was not included in the CBS lineup. To protests from the press and in reply to the half-million letters it received from disappointed viewers, the network explained that *"The Paper Chase* simply did not generate sufficient interest to make it a viable program."

Driving along the Pacific Coast Highway, on my way home from the party that constituted the wake of *The Paper Chase,* I held a small interview with myself. I was eager to discover, now that we were all washed up, how I really felt about this project that had occupied more than a year of my working life.

Q. You seem angry. Are you?

A. Yes, I am.

Q. Who're you mad at?

A. I'm not sure.

Q. CBS?

A. Why should I be mad at CBS? For paying me half a million dollars to appear in a show I really loved? For letting me play a role I found consistently exhilarating and satisfying?

Q. You've been saying such awful things about them—

A. Of course I have. And I'll go right on. To defend his creation an artist may use any weapon at his disposal—including blackmail.

Q. But you—

A. As a matter of fact, I've had a long and fertile association with CBS, going back more than forty years. It's the only network that has consistently employed me to do unusual, occasionally lunatic and mostly fascinating things. It also happens to be the only network that would touch *The Paper Chase* in the first place. No—I'm not mad at CBS.

Q. How about their program executives? The ones who never favored *The Paper Chase?* Do you hate *them?*

A. Not really. They had their assignment from their chairman, which is to put CBS back into the first place in the ratings which it occupied for so many years. You don't become Number One with a show like *Paper Chase*.

Q. Whom *do* you blame, then? The A. C. Nielsen Company?

A. Blame? For what? They're running a business, supplying a service that is highly appreciated by advertisers and networks alike. The fact that I detest what they do and question the way they do it is beside the point.

Q. You mistrust their findings?

A. I didn't say that—though I do, in fact, harbor a deep dislike and mistrust of all those who mess around in the delicate and mysterious area of public opinion. My personal allergy to ratings goes far back—to an evening in November 1938, when I participated with Orson Welles in a broadcast known as "The Men from Mars." That week our ratings indicated a figure of 3.6 for the *Mercury Theatre on the Air,* whereas our competition, Edgar Bergen and his dummy, Charlie McCarthy, representing Chase and Sanborn coffee, had a whopping 34.7—almost ten times as great as ours. Yet history records that it was *we* and *not* the dummy who panicked the nation!

Q. So then, finally, whom *are* you mad at? Or don't you know?

I have devoted much thought to this question over the past few months and I believe I have found the answer.

While it is true that I am not "mad" at anyone, I *am* deeply disturbed and view with rising abhorrence and apprehension a force that is increasingly impinging on our lives, corrupting our culture and undermining our sense of values. I refer to the growing influence of numbers in our society, as they are manipulated and exploited in statistics, polls, ratings and other computerized phenomena. More and more of our decisions and choices are being conditioned and determined by numbers—to the point where these figures are acquiring an attraction and a power of their own, almost independent of the subject to which they are related. So strong have these compulsions become that we seem, at times, to be losing our capacity for free will: more and more of our movements are made in response to emotions that are, themselves, provoked and stimulated by numbers.

Americans have always loved a winner. Today winning, in most fields, is equated with numbers, which in turn, in this anxious, inflationary society of ours, are automatically equated with dollars. In this wild game of huge figures, the American public is coming to resemble those passive bewildered visitors who stand around the tables in Las Vegas and get their vicarious thrills from watching the big gamblers do their stuff—with the difference that, unlike blackjack or roulette, those numbers directly affect every aspect of the lives of every one of us.

Throughout theatrical history "counting the house" has been a normal and necessary habit, with the size of the audience determined by the dimensions of the theater. Today, with the advent of the electronic media, there is almost no limit to the audience that can be reached by Show Business. This has created a state of mind in which the size of the audience—the sheer magnitude of the numbers involved—has become more significant and exciting than the show itself.

It is natural that television, the world's dominating medium of mass communication, should be intensely concerned with numbers—especially when those numbers are directly translatable into profits. What is more difficult to understand is the attitude of the press, for whom the A. C. Nielsen Company has become a source of news only slightly less important than the Associated Press. The same newspapers that in their critical and editorial columns inveigh against the nefarious influence of ratings on the quality of television furnish their readers with daily headlines on the latest results in the numbers race. Thus we learn, not from a trade paper but from a headline in *The New York Times,* that "ABC TOPS RATINGS—CBS IS CLOSE." The following week the *Los Angeles Times* revealed the earthshaking news, "COMEDY RERUNS AT TOP OF WEEK'S NIELSENS," soon followed by the staggering information that "50TH ALL-STAR GAME TOPS WEEK IN NIELSEN GAME." When our nation's President finally made his long-awaited "energy" speech, what he said was deemed of less importance than the fact that he received a 63 percent share.

The virus has spread to the other arts. The astronomical costs and "record-breaking" grosses of a successful film are followed with rising excitement by far more patrons than will ever go near the theaters when the film finally reaches their neighborhood. In museums, too, the main excitement these days seems to be generated by numbers: the highly publicized attendance figures of the recent Monet, Rothko and Tutankhamen shows have thrilled far more vicarious art-lovers than will ever visit the buildings that housed those exhibitions. Even in the prestigious publishing business, a highly promoted and publicized best-seller acquires an aura that often bears no relation to the contents or quality of the book. And if the book sections of the country's leading newspapers bring us epic accounts, every Sunday, of six- and seven-figure paperback purchases and movie sales, it is because news editors know that this mention of millions is an aphrodisiac few Americans resist. It is the numbers that bring on the orgasm.

Where have these ruminations led us? What have they to do with *The Paper Chase?* They are a sobering reminder that in this overwhelming swirl of numbers the life and death of a television series is a very minor (though not totally insignificant) event. In the months that have passed since our cancellation, much of my righteous indignation has evaporated. And most of my personal malice. As I sit here, looking out over the ocean, in this house that was paid for with money earned in the Mass Media, I reflect that I, too, for all my high-falutin' talk, have long been a habitual and active player in this big-time numbers game.

Its rules have changed substantially since I started to play many years ago. Increasingly tied to its "ratings," network broadcasting is richer but less free and imaginative than it was. Gone are the days when CBS, in the name of public service, would carry a "sustaining" show that advertisers were too timid to sponsor. Gone, too, for better or for worse, are the giant motion picture studios where it was possible, once in a while, to sneak a *Julius Caesar* or a *Lust for Life* past the front office into the studio program. Today, with the hot breath of inflation on their necks, the dream of a "blockbuster"—with grosses of fifty or seventy or even one hundred million dollars—dominates and stultifies most filmmakers' thinking.

The future mutations of the Mass Media remain uncertain, though it seems probable that we shall be moving in the direction of yet more technological variety, more numerous outlets and ever greater numbers. For the resolute and imaginative there will be new, uncharted, independent roads to creative and material satisfaction. For those who prefer to remain within the Establishment and to play the big-time for ever-rising stakes, the opportunities will, without doubt, be as great as ever. But whatever forms the new structure of show business assumes, is it too much to hope for a day, in the not-too-distant future, when it will no longer be said of a television show of high quality, viewed each week by an audience of more than 12 million people, that it "has not generated sufficient interest to make it a viable program" for the American viewers?

UPDATE

Since this piece was written, there have been many changes in the network situation and the Nielsen ratings. Needless to say, today's figures are substantially different and generally higher but the structure remains roughly the same, futher complicated by the growth of the cable systems.

BOOK FOUR

TWO SPEECHES

These two speeches were delivered more than twenty years apart on opposite sides of the continent. The first is my opening address as Regents' Lecturer at the University of California, Los Angeles, in the winter of 1963. The second is my commencement address to the graduating class of 1985 at the College of Arts and Engineering of The Johns Hopkins University in Baltimore.

They reflect my reactions, at two very different stages of my own development, to some of the technical and cultural changes that have taken place in the Western world during my lifetime.

Entertainers
and the Entertained (1963)

IT IS WITH PLEASURE and alarm that I make my first appearance before you as Regents' Lecturer in the Department of Theater and Film and that I invite you this evening to join me on a brief and necessarily superficial excursion through that turbulent and fascinating region variously known as Theater, Show Business, Mass Communication, the Media, or more simply and generally—Entertainment.

I am inviting you to join me in a double capacity: first, as future colleagues about to engage in an occupation which, at different times and in different societies, has been revered and persecuted—one which today, more than ever before in the history of man, plays an essential, if not always a constructive part in reflecting and influencing the feeling and thinking of our rapidly changing world. I greet you as future *Entertainers*.

I greet you also as individual units of the nine-figure statistical aggregate which, in America, in the sixth decade of the twentieth century, watches television for several hours a day, consumes vast numbers of periodicals of all sorts and a small number of books, visits movie theaters in ever-diminishing numbers and attends theatrical performances in almost no numbers at all. I address you as fellow-members of the Mass Audience of *The Entertained.*

In both these capacities—as the Entertainers and the Entertained—you and I live in an exciting but confusing age; we form part of the largest, richest and, we like to believe, the freest democracy in the history of civilization; the freest to choose not only its political, social and economic systems and leaders, but also the nature of its amusements and the objects of its material, spiritual and esthetic stimulations and satisfactions.

In these respects ours differs from any society that the world has ever known. Our anxiety to be entertained is enormous and insatiable; so are our resources for entertainment. We enjoy unprecedented economic and technical advantages that allow us to pursue our quest for diversion through the full range of time and space. If such a variety of choice is unique in the annals of the human race, so are our opportunities for indulging it. Never have so many people had so much time on their hands, most of them with pay, as today in the United States of America.

Until now, in the Western world, leisure was the exclusive possession of a privileged class, which took upon itself the task of playing on behalf of the whole overworked society. For all the injustices which this entailed, it can be argued that this inequality in the distribution of leisure gave the minority that enjoyed it a certain responsibility for the quality of its amusements.

Today our machines have turned leisure into an almost universal and obligatory state, one which many of us are finding enervating and even painful. To live free of the burden of grinding toil is the oldest of man's dreams. Yet no sooner has he rid himself of the cursed necessity of earning his living by the sweat of his brow, than he is confronted by a huge and alarming vacuum which—if he is not to go mad—must be quickly and entirely filled. With this new and abundant leisure come certain inescapable demands not to squander unimaginatively the resources that industrialization has opened for us. Many of us—consciously seldom, but unconsciously often—find this challenge so disturbing that we flee back to artificially strenuous work or even to war in order to escape the perplexities of choice presented by abundant leisure.

This is a problem which you, as members of the Mass Audience, will be sharing with hundreds of millions of your fellow citizens the world over. Its solution is a challenge in which those of you who are students and apprentices of the Theater Arts will sooner or later become personally and actively involved.

As an occupation Entertainment, in its various current phases, offers obvious attractions. It may give you a chance to express yourselves and, while still quite young and without too much effort, to earn more money a year than is earned by the President of the United States. Socially and professionally you may enjoy the feeling that you belong to that energetic, knowledgeable and influential elite known as "opinion-makers."

But artistically and morally the entertainment business as it exists today may give you a rough time. The more clearly you see the problems ahead of you, the better you will understand the hazards and temptations that are inherent in your mercurial occupation, and the better your chance if not of success then at least of satisfaction and purpose in your work. Once you are caught up in the whirlpool of activity and power and glamour, sober judgment becomes more difficult. It may take a personal disaster or some squalid and irrelevant scandal like "quiz" or "payola," or even some new political witch hunt to restore you, belatedly, to your senses.

In order to understand the true nature of our mass communication system and to define its place and function in our society, it is necessary to go back into the past. A Canadian scholar, a man of wonderful ideas but forbidding style, Harold A. Innis, has left us some provocative studies on this subject under the general title *The Bias of Communication*. It was Dr. Innis's theory that control of the means of communication has always represented the main force of history, affecting the military destinies no less than the political and religious organizations of entire civilizations. He felt with Hume that "as force is always on the side of the governed, the governors have nothing to support them but opinion. It is therefore on opinion that government is founded and this maxim extends to the most despotic and military governments as well as the most free and the most popular."

Dr. Innis believed that in human affairs language has generally proved tougher than force. He held that the history of the Western world has been, in large measure, the adaptation of force to language. Dr. Innis traces man's instruments of communication from the clay and stylus of the Mesopotamia Valley through the development of machine-made paper, the application of power to the printing press and the invention of the telegraph. Out of that combination, late in the nineteenth century, the multimillion circulation newspaper was created. Here, for the first time, was true Mass Communication—*through the medium of the Printed Word*.

It was one of Innis's theories that civilizations where oral and vernacular communication prevail, such as classical Athens or the England of Elizabeth, tend to be superior in spiritual and political vitality to those in which a rigid written or codified tradition of learning have facilitated monopolistic control and a deliberate freezing of the means of communication—as for instance, in Egypt or medieval Europe. For this reason he was deeply concerned with the consequences of what he regarded as the monopolistic control, in our modern world, of press and newsprint. "The large-scale mechanization of knowledge is characterized by imperfect competition and the creation of monopolies in communication that prevent understanding and foster appeals to force."

Innis lived long enough to witness the development of film and the beginnings of radio, but not their metamorphosis into television. He was not able to include the electronic screen and its effects in his theories of human communication.*

Indeed, it is well to remember that, as recently as the First World War, anyone attempting to project into the future man's changing modes and methods of communication would have been justified in predicting quite confidently that the printed word (its symbols transmitted and reproduced by ever more potent and far-reaching technical means,) must inevitably and quite soon displace the spoken word as the dominant means of human communication.

Yet, in our lifetime, precisely the opposite has taken place. Within half a century a series of electronic miracles has enabled man to transmit simultaneously, over infinite distances, first the human voice and then his combined voice and image. Within one generation the printed word and its symbols have been reduced to a secondary role in mass communication. If any illustration of this were needed, consider the current political scene and, more particularly, the so-called "Great Debates" that have taken place between our presidential candidates over the nation's three combined networks. On four occasions the Messrs. Nixon and Kennedy have been seen and heard, examined and appraised simultaneously by an estimated seventy million of their countrymen. You may have read, on the morning after their first debate, the Hearst papers' last-ditch statement on behalf of the lost cause of the printed word. "The press," said a Hearst editorial, "can still offer service beyond the means of TV. In the permanency of print, newspaper readers have the opportunity to compare and study the views of the candidates and return

---

* This was done with great style by his disciple and fellow Canadian, Marshall McLuhan, whose catch-phrase, "The medium is the message," did not come till years later.

to them as often as they wish." The irony there, of course, is that because the debates *were* tailored for TV (tailored and organized and set up and cut up into a snappy format of opening and closing statements and questions and answers calculated not to tire or tax the attention or the intelligence of the most casual and simpleminded spectator), these so-called Great Debates contained very little that anyone would really wish or need to "return to." In this respect they invite obvious and odious comparison with the Lincoln-Douglas debates, which were seen and heard in their day, as part of a Midwestern congressional campaign, by crowds that never exceeded a few thousand. The impact of those eloquent debates was felt almost entirely *in print,* as they were reported and appeared in the nation's newspapers.

Comparisons aside, it is evident that we *are* paying a price for our electronic miracles. As one critic of the medium has expressed it: "Superficiality becomes essential to the various demands of a larger number of people and is developed as an art by those compelled to meet those demands." These demands include the titillations of incessant excitement and the satisfaction of trivial curiosity. After the first of the Great Debates, the general complaint was not so much that the candidates had been cagey and evasive but that, as entertainers, they had let us down by failing to put on an exciting show for the American public. They tried to do better in the following rounds—without much success.

For better or for worse, it is a fact that mass communication in our day is no longer conducted in the static symbols of print but through the spoken word uttered by living figures and electronically reproduced and transmitted. Does this mean that ours is becoming a civilization with what Dr. Innis would call an "oral tradition" with all the "mobility" and cultural energy that that implies? Not necessarily. The "oral" civilizations which he admired were in one respect, at least, the opposite of our own. The

Athens of Pericles and the England of Elizabeth were small, compact societies whose members were in a position to communicate directly and constantly with each other. They both found their most intense and eloquent form of communication *in the theater*—during periods of high dramatic achievement which were as brief as they were brilliant. (A mere thirty years separate Marlowe's first play, *Doctor Faustus*, from Shakespeare's retirement and the subsequent corruption and dissolution of Elizabethan theater.)

What is true of time is true also of space and numbers. The tragedies of Aeschylus, Sophocles and Euripides were performed before a few thousand citizens assembled on festive occasions. The most successful of Shakespeare's plays were seen in his lifetime by a mere fragment of the population before being totally submerged and lost for more than half a century. It is here that effects of our recent inventions and the changes they have brought about in our attitude toward entertainment are most striking and significant. A recent televised performance of *Romeo and Juliet* by the Old Vic Company was considered a disheartening failure by sponsors and network when ratings tests indicated it had been seen by only a *few million* people.

This brings up a problem that some of you will certainly be facing before long and which constantly confronts those of us who work in one or more of our new world's dramatic media. It is the problem of that world's current obsession with *numbers.*

Each of the twentieth century's new performing arts has its own characteristics, determined by its technical nature and conditioned by the audience for which it is intended. Artistically there should be no relation—direct or inverse—between size and merit, quality and quantity. Yet, practically, for those of you who are intending to work in these new forms and who hope to express yourselves through the arts of your time, this relation of excellence to

numbers and quantity presents an inescapable problem
that will confront you at every turn and affect every
choice you make—as actor, writer, technician, director or
producer.

Some of these choices are practical and economic. It is
generally true that the larger your audience, the more
money you are likely to earn. It is also true that you cannot mobilize the exciting resources of modern technology
without incurring its problems and its consequences—the
need to satisfy the vast new audience that the latest inventions permit you to reach. Even if you do not allow
money to play a determining part in your decisions, this
dilemma persists as one of the inescapable problems of
modern life.

When, after infinite travail, you have created something
that satisfies you, is it more desirable or rewarding to expose it to twenty million people than to a few hundred?
To what extent should numbers be equated with success?
Or with artistic fulfillment? If you have something dramatic and original to communicate, will its impact be
sharper and deeper and more effective if it is observed by
a small but understanding and sensitive audience than if
it is viewed in twenty million homes as part of the evening's bouillabaisse of news-comment, stranglings, kid-
nappings, gunshots, deep-sea diving and the prerecorded
cackle of situation comedies?

My questions are, of course, rhetorical. Your choices are
rarely so absolute or dramatic; often they can only be
judged in retrospect. Let me illustrate this with an example from my own personal experience

Shakespeare's tragedy of *Julius Caesar* has played an important and recurrent part in my life—beginning with
Orson Welles's brilliant modern-dress version with which
we opened our first Mercury Theatre season in the fall of
1937. It was a wonderfully effective production which
soon became one of that season's smash hits and presently
landed Welles on the cover of *Time*. Our theater, the Mer-

cury, held around 650 and because we played *Caesar* in repertory (with *Shoemaker's Holiday, The Cradle Will Rock* and *Heartbreak House*), it never played more than three or four times a week and was seen, that winter, by approximately twenty thousand people. Yet its impact and its influence were enormous and lasting: all over the country and in subsequent theatrical chronicles it is remembered as a unique and unforgettable theatrical experience.

The following year, by popular request, we repeated *Caesar* as a radio drama on our *Mercury Theatre on the Air* program. To conform to our fifty-seven-minute format and because we were now working in a purely aural medium, substantial cuts and narrative adaptations had to be made. What went out on the air was not Shakespeare's tragedy, but an impressive and moving radio drama, heard by several million grateful listeners from coast to coast, many of whom had never before experienced a Shakespearean performance.

Fifteen years later (following Olivier's success with *Henry V* and *Hamlet* and to reward me for a couple of profitable movies I had made for the company) I was invited to produce a Shakespearean film for Metro-Goldwyn-Mayer. I chose *Julius Caesar*. It had brought me luck before and, with its violent, political plot and its absence of soliloquies, it seemed particularly well suited to the medium of film. Joseph Mankiewicz was my director and our illustrious cast included James Mason, John Gielgud, Louis Calhern, Greer Garson, Deborah Kerr and, last but not least, Marlon Brando. Neither Mankiewicz nor I deluded ourselves into thinking that we were filming Shakespeare's play. In translating a masterpiece, with as little loss of quality and intention as possible from one period to another and from one medium to another, we were making what we hoped would be an effective motion picture, based on Shakespeare's tragedy and adapting his situations and dialogue to the idiom of film.

The movie's critical and financial success made us

proud and happy. It was seen the world over, in movie theaters and schools and, later, on television, by many millions of people—probably fifty times more people than had heard it on radio and several thousand times as many people as had seen it in our original Mercury production!

The question remains—which of these *Julius Caesars* had the greatest effect? The most influence? Culturally? Emotionally? Artistically?

I am inclined to believe (though I have no way of knowing it) that its dramatic impact was finally greater and more intense and lasting on those few who saw it in its pure, theatrical form, in the concentrated atmosphere of that small, cramped playhouse—and who participated in the miraculous communion that is generated by the direct emotional communication of living actors and their participating audience—than among the many millions who watched and heard it in its effective but diluted and adapted electronic forms.

Not everyone would agree with this judgment. We are members of a democracy—and proud of it. Can we exempt art from the general rule by which we live—the rule that says the opinions and tastes of the majority are right and must be obeyed? If so, what happens to the minority among the customers of the Mass Media? Are their tastes to be altogether ignored and neglected?

Dr. Frank Stanton, for many years president of the country's leading network and a frequent spokesman for the industry, leaves us in no doubt as to where he stands:

> The Mass Media believe in the broad dissemination of as much as can be comprehended by as many as possible. A Mass Medium survives when it maintains a satisfactory batting average on affirmative responses and it goes down when negative responses are too numerous or too frequent.

Dr. Stanton is a sophisticated executive from whom you would never hear such a crude opinion as that expressed

by a rival network president who likened his responsibility
to the public to that of "the plumber who lays the pipe: it
is not our function to dictate what goes through the pipe";
or that of the advertising executives who recently declared:

> Our business is to move goods. That is all. We
> are not here to elevate taste, to inform, to enlighten,
> to stimulate. Our business is to move goods. Period.

Dr. Stanton would like the network he heads to enjoy—
in addition to its splendid annual profits—the esteem and
gratitude of the society whose "public interest, conve-
nience and necessity" he sincerely believes it is serving.

I'm afraid I have in my day furnished Dr. Stanton with
at least two examples of what he would regard as "negative response." For some years, first in radio and then in
television, I was employed by his company to produce
high-class and expensive programs. (I was once hired—
according to one of his lieutenants—because "I was ass-
deep in culture.") One of these programs, *The Seven Lively
Arts,* is still mentioned nostalgically in television circles; it
won the industry's highest awards for the best new television show of the year 1957. Yet it was hustled off the air
after ten shows, presumably because it failed to maintain
"a satisfactory batting average or affirmative response"; in
other words it never found a sponsor and its Arbitron and
Nielsen ratings did not justify its cost as a sustaining network show.

Three years later, the network's most admired dramatic
series, *Playhouse 90* (of which I was one of the producers for
two years), joined the other full-length TV dramas of
radio's "Golden Age" in limbo and was replaced by *The
Beverly Hillbillies.* I'm sure Dr. Stanton lamented its passing even more than he had lamented the quick demise of
The Seven Lively Arts. But if the "negative responses are too
numerous or too frequent," what choice does a commercial network have? If your rating compares unfavorably

with that of *Gunsmoke, Bachelor at Large, Have Gun Will Travel, Rawhide, 77 Sunset Strip, Bonanza, Aquanauts* or *Adventures in Paradise* then, by Dr. Stanton's version of democratic procedure, your time has come. When you gotta go, you gotta go!

The fallacy—the deliberate fallacy of invoking democracy to justify commercial opportunism—is that it equates majority with unanimity and totally ignores the tastes, rights and opinions of the minorities—not necessarily ethnic—to which *you*, or some of you, surely belong.

How vast does a public have to be before it can claim service from the Mass Media? Or, stated in another form: It is claimed that so-called "quality" programs are appreciated by relatively small audiences—presumably the Highbrow. Nevertheless, even if the audience is relatively small, it still consists of several million viewers. Does it not seem that such an audience should have a right to *its* share of the airwaves?

No satisfactory answer has been given by the networks to this vexed question. None can be, so long as the Mass Media are run by Mass Marketing Methods, according to which "the greater the mass, the greater the service," and, needless to say, the greater the profits. As long as a network regards it as its mission to "get into most of the houses and stay there, pleasing most of the people most of the time and hardly ever displeasing any of them," the problem of creating entertainment capable of satisfying the tastes and needs of diverse kinds of audiences will not be faced.

Here, of course, we find ourselves at the heart of the problems besetting the Mass Media—problems that affect you directly and urgently in both your capacities, that of future entertainers and entertained. For this reason I shall return to it.

But first I would like to confront you with another no less disturbing problem. If I may, once again, quote the late Dr. Innis: "Constant changes in technology, particularly as they affect communications, become a crucial factor in determining cultural values. They increase the difficulties of recognizing balance, let alone achieving it." One of the most obvious characteristics of the Mass Media during their brief and turbulent history has been their bewildering rate of technical change. From the day of their invention, they have been in a state of rapid and continuous flux.

As I was preparing this lecture, I came across the transcript of a talk I gave at an International Design Conference held in Aspen five years ago, where I tried to identify and differentiate between the world's two dominant means of communication:

> Between TV and Motion Pictures, for all their constant overlapping functions, there *are* certain deep and basic differences—esthetic, operational and historical. TV was born full-grown as a Mass Medium with the accumulated resources of the world's great communications systems behind it. Technically and functionally it was an elaboration of Radio, which in turn was conceived and originally utilized as an extension of the telegraph. In a most literal sense, therefore, Television is a medium of direct and immediate communication. Herein lies its special power—in its ability to bring into millions of homes the excitement of an unpredictable action, recorded, transmitted and witnessed by the viewer at the instant of its occurrence. Add to this the thrill to be derived from the feeling that your emotions as a spectator are shared, simultaneously, with many millions of other persons who are viewing and hearing the same event under conditions similar and from a perspective identical to your own.

(Looking back five years later, I find that I was at least fifty percent mistaken. While TV remains simultaneous in its transmission and in its handling of reportorial and informational material, the overwhelming bulk of the stuff that you see on your TV set today is prerecorded and edited, either on tape or on film. For better or worse, TV *drama* has virtually abandoned live or simultaneous transmission. The average TV series—each segment shot on film over a period of several days—has a quality and a texture in no way different from those of an old-time C-grade movie.)

In comparing the two media I made another point:

> Film has a very different and far humbler origin than TV. "Movies" started as a cheap sideshow, with no audience beyond what could be snatched from the vaudeville houses, the shooting galleries, the novelty seekers and the illiterate. Created by gadgeteers and exploited by small-business men, the cinema was never thought of as anything but a show, created and marketed primarily as theatrical entertainment. Indoors and outdoors, whether the audience consists of several thousands at Radio City or half a dozen at a private 16-mm home viewing—in each case, for the duration of its running, a temporary and palpable community is formed among the members of the audience which is physically assembled to view the film.

Here again time has proved me wrong. The volume of motion-picture film being shown in the theaters and drive-ins of the United States today is negligible as compared with the amount of film that is being transmitted over television. I have before me this week's shooting schedule of the world's largest motion-picture studio, Metro-Goldwyn-Mayer in Culver City. There are thirteen television crews shooting in that studio today—against one single, solitary motion picture that is being shot, not on the Culver City lot, but on location in Europe.

The production of American films for theatrical release is less than half what it was fifteen years ago and continues to shrink. How are the filmmakers faring in these changing circumstances? What has happened to the men, your predecessors, who devoted years of apprenticeship and the first half of their professional lives to studying and acquiring the technical and artistic skills necessary to fit them for creative work in motion pictures? Where are they today? Many of them—actors, technicians, directors, writers, editors, cameramen, producers, etc., those who are not too old and stiff to make the jump, have gone over to TV where, under strict network and agency supervision, they are turning out segments of series which, with few exceptions, represent the kind of hackwork they thought they had left behind them.

Am I unduly gloomy and critical? Suffer for yourselves through all but two or three of the current crop of American movies; through all but one or two hours a week of what is shown on your TV set at home. Never has the nation's entertainment been so consistently unimaginative, so inanely repetitive, so utterly lacking in quality and so horribly, catatonically dull. And never, may I add, has it made so much money.

Historically, Theater has rarely been characterized by the originality of its plots. According to Leo Rosten, "There are only a limited number of dramatic plots, stories or themes and a limited number of ways of communicating this limited body of material. Audiences develop a cumulative awareness of resemblances. Even the deepest departures from routines can become familiar and routine." But the current crisis in entertainment goes far beyond that. Much of the present staleness is deliberate. Repetition has been found to be commercially profitable. One successful suspense-series automatically breeds half a dozen others. One Philip Marlowe begets a whole troupe of private eyes—from here to Hawaii. Produce one deep-sea diver with a rating and within a year your living room will be filled with bubbles and octopuses. One wonders how long this cynical tedium can last without loss of audience and, ultimately, of revenue. But the end does not appear to be in sight.

There is one ray of light in this darkness: it lies in the hope that these doldrums represent a calm before the storm—a storm of violent and far-reaching technical changes throughout the Mass Media. I like to think that the managers of the two great rival industries (Movies and Television) are husbanding their resources and energies for the revolution to come. Call it Telemeter, Photovision, Skyatron, or more crudely, Pay TV, it seems fairly certain that some sort of merger of the Mass Media is imminent—a shotgun marriage perhaps, but a union nevertheless. There is every reason to believe that, before long, some form of home-viewing will supplement, though certainly not entirely displace, the current advertiser-subsidized network monopoly and that it will offer audiences a wider and freer choice of entertainment. One also hopes that it will offer broadcasters the possibility of a commercially viable operation with a smaller audience than that currently required by the networks. Exactly how this will work technically and commercially or which system will be employed nobody knows. The networks are mum on the subject. Like the movie-studio heads in the early days of TV, they deny any knowledge of or interest in the forthcoming change. At the same time, they are busy as beavers, lobbying and maneuvering to prevent or delay its coming. Among the more farsighted moviemakers, for obvious reasons, it is believed that direct access to the nation's sixty million home screens will result in a huge new crop of feature pictures followed by the closing of all but a fraction of the nation's unprofitable movie theaters. Time will tell how this will work out. Either way, it can only result in a future increase in the aggregate volume of mass entertainment. And more jobs for us!

Yet for those who are creatively involved, such changes in the Mass Media present serious and sometimes painful problems. For the makers of motion pictures, this total transfer of their product from theater to home screen will represent the third major technical revolution in the industry's brief history. Thirty-three years ago, sound was ruthlessly and permanently imposed upon the silent image despite the impassioned protest of almost every creator and critic in the world. Ten years ago, in a desperate attempt to counter the growing competition of television, the giant vermiform screen was introduced and imposed for reasons of business and exploitation. The particularly repulsive form of wide screen adopted by the movie industry—Cinemascope—was introduced solely as a novelty and because it could be adapted to the projectors and theater screens currently in use quickly and cheaply. The fact that Cinemascope with its long, narrow, eccentric screen was a betrayal of almost everything that was characteristic and good in the art of the motion picture cut no ice at all. The filmmakers were forced by their executives to accept this technical monstrosity. Some resisted for a while and then surrendered. Finally, with their characteristic adaptability, they made some reasonably good films in Cinemascope; in a few cases, the eccentric shape was actually used by directors and cameramen to artistic advantage.

This infinite capacity for adaptation is one of the amazing and wonderful things about the Theater Arts and those who practice them. The stone amphitheatre on the hillside, the converted inn-yards and tennis courts, the platform and sawhorses in the public square, even the central staging recently set up in vacant shopfronts and warehouses—each of these was imposed upon actor, author and director by social and economic circumstances beyond their control. Each was accepted and utilized to produce unique and sometimes inspired theatrical entertainment.

For two generations now, the Mass Media have been treating the Theater as a poor relation, with condescension and envy. While openly despising the "legitimate theater" for its poverty and minuscule size, they have never hesitated to snitch its ideas and hijack its talent. Year after year, they have continued to raid and plagiarize it, till today in its shrunken and pitiful form, the American commercial theater is so subordinated and dependent on the Mass Media as to be virtually indistinguishable from them.

According to the dean of New York's theater critics,

> The Theater is no longer an art but an unsuccessful form of high-pressure huckstering. The whole business is conducted in an atmosphere of crisis, strain and emergency. Crisis is the normal state of affairs on Broadway. The plight of the theater today is not merely economic, it is much more serious than that, for the fun has gone out of it. It is a wonder that anybody stays in it. The present is intolerable; the future very gloomy indeed.

Since Brooks Atkinson wrote this jeremiad in *The New York Times* more than ten years ago, things have changed—mostly for the worse. The Theater continues to be saddled with costs and wage scales that can be absorbed by the Mass Media with their national audiences of many millions but which make no sense at all when applied to a play that is presented in a theater of a thousand seats or less.

It is true that the stage is still the only place in the entire entertainment world that is free of direct censorship, executive interference and the icy squeeze of group pressure. But when it costs between a hundred and a hundred-fifty thousand dollars to take up the curtain on a one-set drama, which must then run for six months before over a quarter of a million persons if it is not to be regarded as a disaster; when you find yourself forced to buy advertisements for your play that are just as large and expensive as those for a ten-million-dollar film—then you are working under pressures that are perilously similar to those of the Mass Media. When you must count on movie companies to finance your productions and on TV to support your actors, so that they can afford to come and work for you in their spare time—then you are hardly in a position to boast of your independence. No art is an island. Whether you like it or not, you must resign yourselves to the fact that our theater, as presently constituted, is related and geared to the Mass Media. This is not necessarily fatal. There are indications that certain quite large sections of the American public are beginning to hunger for more living theater than Broadway is giving them. Perhaps, at long last, all those thousands of college students from all those hundreds of drama courses offered in all those dozens of liberal arts colleges all over the country are finally justifying the money their parents spent on them and helping to give some guidance and leadership to the theater-hungry the country over. There are clear indications that this is so. The rise of the small, so-called "off-Broadway" experimental theater—in New York and other American cities; the moves for decentralization and for organized financial and audience support of the nonprofit, so-called "regional" theaters that are springing up all over the country; the success and proliferation of Shakespearean and other summer festivals in various places; the dream of repertory that is about to be realized in the plans for Lincoln Square in New York and the Tyrone Guthrie Theater in Minneapolis, to mention only two; the modest success, right on this campus, of your own Professional Theater Group of the Extension Division of U.C.L.A.—all these are encouraging signs. They represent a small but seminal stirring in the cultural life of our time.

And now, from these vague hopes, let us return to a consideration of that mass culture in which, as artists and audience, as educated and thinking human beings, each one of you is called upon to play a significant and inevitable part.

Earlier I quoted Dr. Stanton in defense of his network.

Here is an additional statement of his which appeared in a special issue of *Daedalus* (the Journal of the American Academy of Arts and Sciences), devoted to culture and the Mass Media: "Democratic procedures, to some extent even democratic values, necessarily involve quantitative considerations about which intellectuals are always uneasy . . . Indeed some sort of hostility on the part of intellectuals toward the Mass Media is inevitable, because the intellectuals as a minority are not really reconciled to the basic patterns of democratic life."

I have already questioned Dr. Stanton's interpretation of the democratic process. But I can sympathize with his desire to protect himself and his network from the blasts being loosed against the Mass Media in highbrow quarters.

The fact is that mass communication *does* seriously bother the intelligentsia, behind whose attitude lies the following basic inescapable question: Is it possible to extend a high civilization to lower classes without debasing its standards and diluting its quality to the vanishing point? Is not any civilization bound to decay as soon as it begins to penetrate the masses?

The nature of this penetration is examined by the intelligentsia with a critical intensity that places in doubt the values of our entire civilization—not merely the operation of its current instruments of communication. In the opinion of one social historian, "The total effect of mass culture is to distract people from lives which are so boring that they generate obsession with escape. Yet, because mass culture creates addiction to prefabricated experience, most people are deprived of the remaining possibilities of autonomous growth and enrichment and their lives become even more boring and unfulfilled."

"Why should cheapness of expression and response be profitable?" asks another critic, I. A. Richards. "If our civilization is a 'mass civilization,' without discernible respect for quality and seriousness, by what means has it become so? With the increase of population, the problem presented by the gulf between what is preferred by the majority and what is accepted as excellent by the most qualified opinion has become infinitely more serious and appears likely to become threatening in the near future."

According to T. S. Eliot: "You cannot, in any scheme for the reformation of society, aim directly at a condition in which the arts will flourish; these activities are probably by-products for which we cannot deliberately arrange the conditions. On the other hand, their decay may always be taken as a symptom of some social ailment to be investigated." Mr. Eliot's investigation leads him to describe the "steady influence which operates silently in any mass society organized for profit for the depression of standards and culture. The increasing organization of advertisement and propaganda—or the influencing of masses of men by any means except their intelligence—is all against them. The economic system is against them; the choice of ideals and confusion of thought in our large-scale mass education is against them; and against them also is the disappearance of any class of people who recognize public and private responsibility of patronage for the best that is made and written."

I hope, as you listen, you are recalling Dr. Stanton's democratic yardstick of the "batting average of affirmative responses," and General Sarnoff's simile of the plumber and the hollow pipe. May I also quote one of the Mass Media's most successful writers, Paddy Chayevsky, who recently declared, "I have never, never written down for television, but I have never aimed very high." And let me further quote Hedda Hopper's syndicated column in which she quotes the vice-president of one of the nation's leading TV-producing companies on the subject of Fred Astaire: "A perfectionist who works fifteen hours on a dance number which runs four minutes on the air—Who can afford it?"

And now, back to the intellectuals. Dwight MacDon-

ald, critic and journalist, carries the assault against the
Mass Media one step further:

> The collective monstrosity—"The masses," "The
> Public"—is taken as a human norm by the techni-
> cians of Mass Cult. They at once degrade the pub-
> lic by treating it as an object, to be handled with
> the lack of ceremony of medical students dissecting
> a corpse, and at the same time flatter it and pander
> to its taste and ideas by taking them as the criteria
> of reality. . . . Mass Cult is fabricated by techni-
> cians and hired by businessmen. . . . It offers its cus-
> tomers neither an emotional nor an esthetic
> catharsis, for these demand effort. The production
> line grinds out a uniform product whose humble
> aim is not even entertainment, for this too implies
> life and hence effort, but merely distraction. It may
> be stimulating or narcotic, but it must be easy to
> assimilate. It asks nothing of the audience . . . and
> it gives nothing.

Randall Jarrell, poet and critic, assails The Medium
"as a mixture of rhetoric and reality that gives people
what we know they want in the form they like . . . the
watcher is halfway between two worlds paying full attention to neither; it is half life and half art and competes
with both life and art. It spoils its audience for both, spoils
both for its audience."

On the other hand, let me assure you that life in the
world of entertainment can be exciting and rewarding.
Take *my* word for it! For twenty-seven years I have rushed
around the highways and byways of Show Business,
laughing and scratching all the way! I have produced
eighteen feature movies, a number of propaganda films
and two dozen full-dress television dramas; I have worked
as a writer, editor and producer on dozens of radio shows
and I have been responsible for many thousands of propaganda broadcasts for the Voice of America. In the course

of these activities, I have earned just about as much as I would have in any other business. I have had my share of success and failure. I have done a number of shows which pleased me and some of which I am deeply ashamed. But, overall, my life as an Entertainer has been a ball!

Many years from now, when future generations come to judge our civilization, it is not unlikely that ours will be recorded in history as a period of high technical energy and cultural sterility. Your generation may well see the first man on the moon, but no single example of great dramatic writing. If that is so—and I suspect that it may be—it is still not a cause for despair or cynicism. "Don't despise mediocrity," wrote Vincent van Gogh shortly before his death, "for it takes much work and great pains to achieve even that."

Your generation may not carry the marks of genius; and you personally may not have been born into an artistically creative era. But you *do* control instruments of fantastic power that give you unique and special opportunities and responsibilities for guiding and influencing the tastes, the thoughts and feelings of mankind. I do not presume to predict the future. I can only express the hope on your behalf that in your eagerness to succeed you do not allow the excitement or power or greed with which you are surrounded to corrupt you. Let no one be justified in saying to you one day what Ruskin said to the Birmingham industrialists of his time: "When you retire into private life you may, as one subject of consolation for your declining years, reflect that your life has been successful in retarding the arts, tarnishing the virtues and confusing the manners of your country."

Commencement '85

As I LOOK DOWN on this vast sea of caps and gowns—each with the tassel properly placed in its correct position—I find it superfluous to remind you of the solemnity of the occasion. Rather I would like to spend a few moments talking about the society you are about to enter and to explain in what respects I believe your graduation to be different from that of your predecessors.

Two years ago I had the great privilege of being on a panel with Dr. Jonas Salk, the creator and popularizer of the vaccine that saved the world from the nightmare of polio, who now heads an institute that concerns itself with the future of mankind. We had met to consider the effects of technological change upon our arts and culture, and Dr. Salk was our principal speaker.

During his address Dr. Salk turned to the blackboard behind him and started to plot a long, rising curve intended to illustrate man's accelerating rate of progress during his time on earth. When he approached the top of his steeply rising curve, he stopped suddenly, turned, put away his chalk and explained that he found it impossible to continue his curve any further into the future.

In less than a century, he pointed out, life on earth has changed far more drastically and completely than in all the previous hundreds of thousands of years of man's his-

torical presence on this globe. The scientific and technological changes that have taken place in our lifetime have
been so vast, so violent, so far beyond anything that was
ever imagined before, and so unpredictable as to their
final effects, that the future can no longer, as heretofore,
be considered a continuation of the past. As a result, an
intelligent projection of the curve of man's progress has
become impossible. Man's new capacities for creation and
destruction are so radical and so unpredictable in their
scope that an entirely new range of human values must be
developed to deal with them. If man is to survive he may
have to revise his morality, his ethics, and most of the personal, social, cultural and spiritual attitudes with which
he has lived until now. If he is to avoid destruction he will
have to follow up his new technological capacities with
equivalent changes in his behavior and in his thinking: ag-
gression, acquisitiveness, competition, sectarian and national loyalty, all of which have been generally esteemed
human virtues, have suddenly become too dangerous to
live with in this new universe that we have created: they
will have to be modified and adjusted to man's new terrifying capacity to destroy himself.

My view is less cosmic than his. My own personal expertise is in the limited field of entertainment. Yet here
too the past fifty years have witnessed changes, mostly of a
technical nature, that have transformed its entire structure. We tend to take these changes for granted. Familiar-
ity has tempered our wonder at the miracles that have
been taking place all around us. We accept these incredible mutations without pausing to realize what they have
already done to our lives or to reflect on what they are
likely to do to our ways of living in the years ahead.

Your present concern, as graduating students, is no
doubt less with the ultimate fate of the human race than
with the state of the world that awaits you when you leave
these sheltered academic precincts and meet the challenges that await you on the outside. Like Galileo you

know that the earth moves: you must face the truth that it does not necessarily improve. Our forefathers believed that it did—today we know better. Our grim experiences during recent decades have dispelled that illusion. We know now that it follows its own particular motion and that it is directly affected by the social, economic, spiritual, historical and, above all, the scientific and technological changes to which we ourselves expose it.

In our time, as Dr. Salk pointed out, those forces have asserted themselves with unusual rapidity and violence. We have, for instance, in my own lifetime, eliminated or totally modified man's concepts of space and time. And though these changes may seem on the surface to be mainly technological, they do in fact permeate and change the entire social, cultural and spiritual structure of the human race. In that sense your generation does face problems unlike any that have gone before: it confronts a future that is more problematic and unpredictable than that faced by any generation in human history.

To give you a few concrete examples: my colleagues in the entertainment business, and particularly the young who are graduating today from theater departments all over the country do not know and dare not surmise what form the living theater (which we believe to be the highest expression of human culture) may assume two hundred years from now; we fervently hope it will survive in a form not dissimilar to the one we know and love and that it will continue to play its seminal part in the cultural life of generations to come—but we're not at all sure. The same is true of the other performing arts. Will opera or symphonic music, as we know them, survive or will some other form of vocal and musical communication take their place? For dancers—whether they practice classical ballet or the less formal movements of what we rather curiously continue to call the "Modern Dance"—what does the future hold? What are the coming mutations in musical instruments and the social and artistic uses to which they will be put? The same is true in the visual arts: what is the future of sculpture and easel-painting and its social and decorative uses? What will be the architect's and the engineer's main function in generations to come? Office buildings? Homes? The planning of cities and their environments? Space-stations? This is true in one form or another of most of the professions and occupations you may be considering. No other generation, I repeat, has had so many choices or faced uncertainties of this particular intensity.

Are these idle rhetorical questions? I don't think so. You are, in a sense, the guinea pigs of the future. Some of the answers to my questions may, in fact, be determined by the thoughts and actions of *your* generation the world over. We are living—and shall more and more be living, I hope—in a world that will be increasingly and, finally, totally interdependent. Technology knows no national boundaries. Through our electronic miracles we have made human communication instantaneous and universal. "Ask not for whom the bell tolls; it tolls for thee" is today physically as well as spiritually true. We hear and see that bell via satellite at the moment of its tolling, no matter where in the world it may be situated.

But what of human nature in the midst of all this electronic hubbub? Under such pressures is *it* changing too? And how? These are the questions raised by Dr. Salk which I, for one, have no intention or ability to answer. But I would like to suggest to you a few thoughts related to the world's attitudes toward human culture in our time and in generations to come.

I recently spent a few days in central France. As an adoptive citizen of the New World, I found it deeply moving to enter once again the churches and public buildings that had been created seven or eight hundred years ago, and to tread on stones that had been worn by human steps for the better part of one thousand years. But what impressed me above all in those beautiful and durable monuments was the quality of the human spirit that had erected those wildly audacious and delicate structures in an era that we know as the Dark Ages—a harsh and somber time in history when human existence was precarious and dominated by two major terrors, the fear of hunger and the fear of sudden death. What made possible those gloriously soaring cathedrals, what inspired and animated and paid for them was their makers' unqualified devotion to one particular concept of Christianity—the myth of the Trinity to which was added the dominant figure of the Virgin Mary. Together these supplied the men and women of the society with the symbols, the images and the creative fervor through which they raised themselves from the hardships and brutalities of their daily struggle for survival to such a high level of social and artistic accomplishment.

Today our monuments are no longer cathedrals built to the glory of God and intended to last throughout eternity. The tall towers of our office buildings are financed and erected usually for one generation, on the premise that they will be obsolete, unprofitable and replaceable within half a century. If we *have* a religion and a myth—beyond our preoccupation with money and power—it is difficult to find its symbols in the television sets that have become our contemporary shrines.

In fact, we Americans *do* have a myth, a very powerful one, that has played a dominant part not only in our own history but in that of the entire modern world. It is our own particular concept of *democracy*—expressed in terms that were revolutionary and wholly original when they were first formulated in our Declaration of Independence more than two centuries ago. It has underlain every aspect of our brief history and it continues to condition much of our collective and individual thinking and feeling today.

Like all such human concepts (including Christianity) democracy has, of course, meant different things at different times to different people. It meant one thing to the

Pilgrim Fathers, another to Thomas Jefferson, another to Lincoln, another to Eugene Debs, another to Franklin Delano Roosevelt, another to Ronald Reagan and his advisers, and yet another to today's network executive who devises his programs with both eyes fixed on the audience ratings supplied by the self-styled experts who believe that they too are interpreting democracy. And right here, in this corruption of democracy, we run into one of the most serious and disturbing problems facing our society today. Democracy is a delicate and finely balanced instrument. When it is functioning properly it represents far more than a mechanical tallying of numbers. Yet in our present technologically controlled and organized world, we are in grave danger of becoming just that—a society entirely dominated and ruled by numbers so vast that they can no longer be counted in men's heads but must be extracted from the electronic bowels of giant computers.

More and more our choices and our judgments and even our values and decisions in life are being conditioned and formed by numbers—to the point where these numbers have acquired an attraction and a power of their own, often almost independent of the subject to which they happen to relate. So strong has this compulsion become that we seem, at times, to be losing our capacity for free will; all too often we find ourselves acting in response to emotions that are, themselves, provoked and stimulated by numbers.

This is true today of almost any profession you may be considering. Nowhere, however, is this rule of figures more prevalent and more dangerous than in my field—the performing arts—where quality and quantity are increasingly confused and a work of art is judged by the size of its audience rather than by the intensity or the nature of the emotions it provokes. Throughout the history of the performing arts "counting the house" has been a normal and salutary habit. But with the advent of the electronic media, the "house" is no longer limited by the architectural dimensions of the building in which a performance is taking place. Today, in the Mass Media, there is virtually no limit to the audience which now ranges over tens of thousands of miles and runs into hundreds of millions of people. This has created a state of mind in which the size of that audience—the sheer magnitude of the numbers involved—becomes more significant and more exciting than the performance itself. And this is true not only of Show Business but of most of the activities through and for which our world seems to be run.

Americans have always loved a winner. Today, being Number One, in most fields of human endeavor, is equated with numbers which, in turn, in this anxious, material and generally inflationary society of ours, are automatically equated with dollars. Quantity is regularly identified with quality, though they are, in fact, utterly unrelated. Indeed, in this wild game of huge figures the American public is coming to resemble those passive, bemused visitors who stand around the tables in Las Vegas, getting their vicarious thrills from watching the big gamblers do their stuff. I need not point out how gravely this attitude endangers the intelligent, moral functioning of our lives and how it runs directly counter to the disciplines you have been absorbing here and the attitudes toward your future activities that, I believe, you have been acquiring during your four years at this institution. The truth is that, for all man's miraculous technical progress the quality of life on this globe still depends, finally, on the personal energy, courage, honesty and imagination of those individuals of whom a democracy—no matter how swollen its numbers and how vast its collective power—is finally made up. Today, more than ever, it has become the obligation of the individual to resist this tyranny of numbers and to make his life's work central to his own personality, which inevitably includes his taste and his moral sense.

Let me return finally to the arts to illustrate this point.

There is a well-known musical legend about the great French musician César Franck. He was a respected composer and teacher but it was a critical day for him when one of the great Paris orchestras performed the premiere of a new symphony on which he had been laboring for years. The work had a mixed reception: part of the audience was shocked by its novelty and, following the custom of European audiences, loudly hissed and booed the work at its conclusion. When Franck reached home that night his anxious family asked him the obvious questions: "How did it go?" "Was it a success?" "Did they like it?" "Did they applaud?" To which Franck is said to have replied, "It sounded exactly the way I hoped it would."

That is the most any creative person who has studied his or her craft and been true to his or her intellectual or professional ideals finally has any right to hope for.

Acknowledgment

My thanks to *Harper's* magazine, *The New York Times,* the *Nation, The Washington Post,* the *Chicago Tribune,* the *Los Angeles Times, New Letters* and *Vogue* for permission to reprint material that first appeared in their columns. And, once again, my special thanks to Diana Fleishman, without whose industry and devotion this book could not have been assembled.

Index